愛、自由與療癒

~ 巴赫醫師的人生哲學 ~

═══════════════

Free Thyself
Ye Suffer From Yourself
Heal Thyself

艾德華・巴赫 醫師 / 著
Dr. Edward Bach

魏愛娟、黃韋睿 / 翻譯
李穎哲 / 審定

愛、自由與療癒
巴赫醫師的人生哲學

作者：艾德華・巴赫 （Dr. Edward Bach）
翻譯：魏愛娟、黃韋睿
審定：李穎哲
校搞：洪翠娟、王建軍
編輯總籌、封面設計：林鈺傑

發行人：林鈺傑
出版發行：巴赫實業有限公司
通訊地址：台灣 10647 台北市羅斯福路三段 271 號 6 樓
總經銷處：IFEC 國際花精研究推廣中心
電話：(02)2369-7366　　　　　　　傳真：(02)2363-3420
網址：www.ifecentre.com　　　　　電郵：flower@ifecentre.com

2008 年 12 月 20 日 初版一刷
2012 年 8 月 20 日 初版二刷
排版印刷：葛瑞特印刷事業有限公司
定價：新台幣 700 元（精裝）

本書如有缺頁、破損、裝訂錯誤，請至「IFEC 國際花精研究推廣中心」更換

要獲得自由，必先給予自由

— 艾德華·巴赫 醫師

"To Gain Freedom, Give Freedom"

— Dr. Edward Bach

【鄭重聲明】

　　花精療法的創始人艾德華・巴赫（Edward Bach）醫師，生於 1886 年 9 月 24 日，卒於 1936 年 11 月 27 日，他最知名的著作包括《十二個療癒者與其他花精》（The Twelve Healers & Other Remedies）和《自我療癒》（Heal Thyself）；此外，有些學者將他其它的著作、演講稿和手稿集結成書，如 ˋCollected Writings Of Edward Bach ˊ 是由英國的 Julian Barnard 先生收集出版。

　　本書的翻譯原稿，已經獲得 Julian Barnard 先生的同意，是採用 ˋCollected Writings Of Edward Bach ˊ（1987 Bach Educational Programme, Hereford）中的部分內容，而且這些內容，都是當年巴赫醫師著作的原始版本。Julian Barnard 表示，依據大英法律規定，巴赫醫師已經過世七十多年，其著作的版權已經過了保護期，因此所有的人都可以運用和翻譯他的著作，不需取得其他人的同意。

　　坊間或許已經有許多巴赫醫師的原著或翻譯版本，但本中心為了讓巴赫醫師的哲學理念能夠更清楚明確的呈現，特別將他的原始著作再做一次翻譯，並且舉行讀書會加以深入地研究和探討，希望能夠將我們的研究心得與大家分享。在讀書會期間，我們發現巴赫醫師的醫學理念和哲學思想意義深遠，越是深入地探討，越發現其中的奧秘，真不是三言兩語就可以一一說明完畢。此書除了譯文之外，還加入了原文，希望讀者在無法了解翻譯的內容時，可以從原文去領悟；此外，我們還將

鄭重聲明

讀書會的淺見紀錄，加在每一個章節的後面，倘若當中對巴赫醫師的理念體會有所偏頗，也請大家多多指教。

　　此書能夠順利出版，特別感謝魏愛娟小姐和黃韋睿先生的鼎力相助，他們在百忙之餘還能夠抽空來幫忙翻譯的工作，雖然他們都不是專業的翻譯人員，但因為對巴赫花精療法的深入研究，而能夠將巴赫醫師原著的內涵，正確而深入地呈現給讀者。此外，還要特別感謝參加讀書會的學員，由於你們的參與，讓我們有更多的動力和決心來出版此書，也因此讓此書的內容更生動、更有活力。

【前言】如何運用此書？

此書分作三個部分，主要翻譯自巴赫醫師的原始著作和演講稿，分別是：

Part I　–《自我療癒》（Heal Thyself）、

Part II　–《人因自己受苦》（Ye Suffer From Yourself）、

Part III –《讓自己自由》（Free Thyself）

內文以中英文對照的方式呈現，目的是要讓大家在閱讀中文翻譯而無法領略其中道理時，可以透過英文原文，更深入地體會巴赫醫師的人生哲學。

此外，每一部分內容，還穿插著 IFEC 國際花精研究推廣中心讀書會的重點摘要和討論稿；為了和原文作明顯的區別，此書特地將這些摘要和討論內容放在灰色框欄中。為了力求對巴赫醫師哲學思想一致性的了解，我們建議讀者在第一次閱讀此書時，可以先跳過灰色框欄內的文字，直接閱讀巴赫醫師全部著作，之後可以寫下自己對內容的體會，而在往後的閱讀時間裏，再參照讀書會學員的心得。

【目錄】

接受改變和了解改變的意義

朱力安・巴納德

　　知道巴赫花精及使用巴赫花精的人當中，每一千人或許只有十個人曾經讀過巴赫醫師所寫關於健康方面的主題，甚至更少。巴赫醫師的理念並未隨著花精產品的發展而散佈開來；在這種情況下，為了抗衡和平衡巴赫花精如此商業性的發展現況，我們在 1986 年出版了 ˋCollected Writings Of Edward Bach ˊ。該書涵蓋所有巴赫醫師遺留下來的文稿；這些文章很值得我們閱讀，因為可以從中了解巴赫醫師發展花精的過程，以及花精療法背後所蘊含的觀念和哲學思想。這本書包含了他的信函、隨筆以及演講出版集，而其中的 ˋHeal Thyself ˊ、ˋFree Thyself ˊ 以及 ˋYe Suffer from Yourselves ˊ 三本代表性著作，是巴赫醫師思想觀念的精華所在；也因為這些思想種子的萌芽，才引導他發現 38 種花精－也就是「巴赫花精」。

　　我們接觸巴赫花精的途徑都不一樣，每個人都有自己的故事，而我，則是因為 ˋThe Twelve Healers & Other Remedies ˊ 這本書。不論是我無意間發現了這本書，還是這本書找上了我，它已經改變了我的人生，而這就是巴赫醫師的文字所擁有的力量－給生命帶來改變！甚至有些人認為這些文字所表達的思想觀念能夠改變世界，希望果真是如此，因為現今這個世界比任何時候都還需要鼓舞和洞見。巴赫醫師的理念以及巴赫花精改變了許多人的生命，但對於巴赫醫師的哲學理念，千萬不要只是概略翻閱而已，請仔細研讀，因為這是整個巴赫花精系統的立論基礎，是值得互相分享的偉大傳統智慧；巴赫醫師所描述的，是更有意義的生命歷程，讓我們得以瞭解疾病的起因和真正的療癒，而不只是呆板的物理分析而已。

　　巴赫醫師的著作其最重要的主題是「接受改變和瞭解改變的意義」。「改變」是一切事物的核心－改變、瞭解，然後瞭解改變的意義，簡單來說就是「我們是如何生病的？如何痊癒的？」。在 ˋFree Thyself ˊ 中，巴赫醫師先探討一般對疾病的解釋，他寫道：「長久以來，我們都將之歸咎於病菌…」，並且進一步指出一個截然不同的病因－不和諧與不快樂。巴赫醫師認為，不和諧與不快樂源自於人偏離了他自身的生命目標和天命，因為偏離了讓我們真正快樂的目標，所以才會生病；而真正的快樂來自於遵行我們此生應走的道路，也就是變成我們此生應該成為的人。我們都具有維持內在平和的能力，也因此我們可以去調和存在於現況中的衝突與困境。

　　這聽起來或許像是個深奧難懂的哲理，也因此某些人只是單純地使用花精，而不管書上寫些什麼，這很能令人理解，因為每個人都喜歡簡單的選擇；但如果能夠持續研讀巴赫醫師的理念，獲益還會更多！我們就更能夠讓生命本身成為我們的導師，從生命中學習；這也就是巴赫醫師所費力解釋的－人因自己受苦。在我們的生命當中，我們就是問題的本身，不是因為其他的原因或邪惡的力量而造成這些問題；所以我們自己擁有決定的力量，我們擁有決定的自由，因而能「讓自己自由」。

　　如果從唯物主義（純科學考量）的角度去看，或許比較難做到「接受」這件事，包括「如何解釋受苦的現象？」、「我們的缺點該歸咎於自己嗎？」，不如讓我們以信念去面對，而不是用絕對的態度去探討；

讓我們試著去瞭解，而不是一味地去控制與支配。生病其實並不意謂著失敗，而是代表有學習的機會；所以可以這麼說，為什麼疾病會存在，它是要帶給我們學習、了解和改變的機會。如果我們已經很完美了，就不會有疾病出現；然而，我們離完美的境界還有一段距離，所以需要不斷改變，這就是進化：

自學得教訓及錯誤根除的那一刻起，就再也不需要修正了，
因為我們必須記住，苦難的本身是慈善的，會在我們走錯路時
給予指引，並加速進化的過程，以達到那榮耀的完美境地。

或許某些人不認同這個道理，但這就是巴赫醫師想要傳達的。

　而這本巴赫醫師著作的中文譯本，所要介紹的是一些需要時間參透的理念，然而這對於東方人來說並不完全陌生的，因為巴赫醫師部分的理念，其實源自於東方哲學，其精髓是：「我為自己的生命負責」。一味顧影自憐、責怪他人，或變得易怒、沮喪和害怕都是沒有用的，這些並不會帶來成長。每個人都必須努力克服生命中的難題；我們生來就是為了要學習知識以及學習同理心的，並且以積極的態度去面對人類意識的提升，正如**巴赫醫師所說：「宇宙是神的體現；宇宙的誕生即神的再生；宇宙的終止即是神最極致的發展。」**問題不在於我們臆測了什麼，或者否認上帝的存在，而是人類意識的進化；這和所有進化都一樣，是從一種狀態轉換至另一種狀態的程序。

　　巴赫醫師更提到同胞與同胞之間，應該要無私地互相傳遞這美好的
領會，沒有任何秘密。我們必須迫切認清人類之間的情誼，是根基於知識
的分享、互相關懷以及捨棄所有的權力控制。巴赫醫師以他的著作無私
地分享了他的知識，並且將所有關於花精 (地球上強大的療癒者－療癒的
藥草) 的發現都分享出來，展現了他對人類同胞的關懷。而他清楚地敘述
了發現花精的過程，以及花精如何能夠幫助人們，再再展現出他已經捨棄
了所有的權力控制，沒有隱藏任何秘密！請仔細閱讀巴赫醫師的著作吧！
然後你就可以變得更堅強、更覺醒、更有力量；還有，別忘了巴赫醫師
最重要的一句箴言：「要獲得自由，就必須先給予自由」。

【推薦者簡介】朱力安・馬納德（Julian Barnard），英國植物學家，也是研究
巴赫花精的專家之一，出版多本有關巴赫花精書籍集結及巴赫醫師的著作出版
`Collected Writings of Edward Bach´，並曾在全世界超過 20 個國家進行演說。
1988 創立 Healing Herbs 公司，是依據巴赫醫師原始與傳統的方式來負責製作巴赫
花精。目前致力推廣巴赫醫師的理念與思想。

【推薦序一】

Accept and Understand Change

Julian Barnard

For every 1,000 people who know of and use the flower remedies discovered by Dr Edward Bach perhaps ten people, or even fewer than that, have read what he wrote on the subject of health. The Bach flower remedy product has been developed at the expense of understanding his ideas. And so, in 1986, to counter and rebalance the commercial development of Bach flower remedies, we published the Collected Writings of Edward Bach. This contained all the available texts written by Bach. It makes fascinating reading since we see there the development of his ideas and the philosophy behind his discoveries. This book contained letters, essays and published editions of the lectures he gave. It also contained the seminal texts: Heal Thyself, Free Thyself and Ye Suffer from Yourselves. These three represent the distillation of his ideas, ideas which were the germ and seed which led to his discovery of the 38 flower essences – the Bach flower remedies.

We each come to flower essences in different ways – each of us has a unique story. For me it was a book: The Twelve Healers & Other Remedies. I do not know if I found the book or it found me. But that event changed my life. And this is what Bach' s writings can do: change lives. Some people believe that ideas can change the world. Let us hope that is so. Because we need inspiration and vision; now more than ever. Of course, the ideas of Dr Bach have changed the lives of many of us. His ideas and the flower remedies he discovered. But we can go deeper and deeper into the subject. Do not be satisfied with a quick glance at the philosophy which underpins the Bach flower remedies. Study it with care. What Bach writes about is a part of Great Tradition of wisdom, wisdom which we can all share. He describes a more meaningful process of life, not merely mechanical, where we can come to understand 'the real cause and cure of disease'.

The real subject of Bach's writings is the need to accept and understand change. It is change which is at the heart of the whole thing – change and understanding, understanding change. In short this means 'how do we become sick, how do we get well?' In Free Thyself Bach discusses the usual explanations of illness: 'we have so long blamed the germ…' and points rather to a different cause of illness. To disharmony and unhappiness. Disharmony and unhappiness he says, are caused by a disassociation between the individual person and their real purpose and destiny in life. We get sick when we become diverted from the purpose of being happy. And happiness derives from following the true path for our being: becoming what we entered life to become. We need to reconcile the conflict and difficulty of our current situation with the potential we have to be at peace.

This may sound like abstruse philosophy, too difficult to understand. And that is why some people reach more readily for the brown bottle than the book. We want the easier path. But if we persevere in our study then the benefits are greater. We allow life to become the tutor; we learn from life. And this is what Bach is at such pains to explain: we suffer from ourselves. In my life, I am the problem. It is not some other agency, some malignant force which decides what happens to me. I decide, I am free to decide: hence Free Thyself.

Apply a very materialistic (scientific) measure to this and perhaps it becomes more difficult to accept. How do we explain suffering? Am I to blame for my failings? But let us deal with principles rather than absolutes, understanding rather than rules. It is not that every sick person has failed, rather that a sick person has a greater opportunity to learn. Almost, by definition, that is why there is disease and illness in the world. It provides for us an opportunity to learn, to understand and to change. If what we were doing were perfect there would be no need for change. But since we are less than perfect, change we must. That is evolution:

> *From the moment the lesson is understood and the error eliminated there is no longer need for the correction, because we must remember that suffering is in itself beneficent, in that it points out to us when we are taking wrong paths and hastens our evolution to its glorious perfection.*

Now this may not sit comfortably for some of us. But it is what Bach had to say.

So this book, a new translation into Chinese of Bach' s writings, is introducing some difficult and demanding ideas. But they are not foreign to the Chinese mind. They come, at least in part, from the East.

The essential message is this: I am responsible for my life. It is no use feeling sorry for myself, blaming others, becoming irritable, discouraged or afraid. No progress will be made. Each one of us must struggle to overcome individual life difficulties – (man is born to gain knowledge and understanding) – and to play an active part in the evolution of human consciousness.

The Universe, says Bach, *is God rendered objective, at its birth its birth it is God reborn, at its close it is God more highly evolved.* It matters not what we imagine or deny God to be. This is the evolution of human consciousness. An evolution as sure as any development from one state to another.

Bach spoke of the responsibility held by a brother (sister) to pass this understanding to younger siblings. No secrets. No mystery. There is an urgent need to recognise the common fellowship of all humanity. This must be based upon a sharing of knowledge, the care for all our fellows and the renunciation of all power. He unfailingly shared his knowledge – his writings bear witness. His care for his fellows is demonstrated in his desire to share his discoveries of the Healing Herbs – the powerful healers of the plant kingdom. His renunciation of power? He told everybody what he was doing and how they might help themselves. He never created a secret. Read what he wrote and you can be stronger, clearer and more powerful. But please, remember Bach' s best epigram: to gain freedom, give freedom.

【推薦序二】

療癒必然來自於內在

李穎哲

　　巴赫醫師一向強調「自我療癒」，又說：「真正的療癒必然來自於內在，藉由認知並糾正自身的錯誤，重新獲得內心的寧靜。」─《人因自己受苦》（Ye Suffer From Yourself）從前我無法深入體會巴赫醫師的觀點，總覺得每個人與生俱來自我療癒的能力，只要透過花精協助，就能啟動自己的療癒系統；也因此近幾年在花精方面的研究和努力，特別著重於替病患找出最有效的花精處方，來解除他們身體的病痛，而將病人的健康責任都扛在自己身上。

　　剛開始運用花精療法的時候，發現花精對於情緒的調整以及身體病症的緩解，其效果確實令人驚訝不已。但經過幾年來的臨床觀察卻又發現，花精的療效僅能達到某種程度，有些人只要停止使用花精，病症很容易又回到原點；有些人則開始對花精產生排斥，不想繼續使用；有些人則是舊病復發，甚至比以前更加嚴重；另外有些人則在處理到深層問題時無法面對，而逃離的無影無蹤，或表現出強烈的情緒反彈。

　　這時我的內心又出現了許多疑問：為什麼巴赫醫師使用花精的功效那麼好？他是否也遇到上述的情況和困難呢？問題到底出在哪裡？我回過頭去研究巴赫醫師的原著，希望從中獲得答案。在閱讀過以下內容之後才恍然大悟，原來巴赫醫師早已有所指示：「病患必須準備好面對疾病的真相，瞭解疾病完全肇因於病患自身的錯誤，就像罪惡的代價即是死亡；即使病患能從醫生那裡獲得指引和協助，仍必須親自改正錯誤，才能過著更美好有益的生活。」《人因自己受苦》。原來身為醫師的我，一直認為自己擁有強大的療癒能力，必須為整個療癒過程負起責任，因而忘記了

療癒能力其實存在於每個人內心；任何治療師都只能扮演協助者的旁觀角色，因為疾病其實是自己創造出來的。

　　上天透過疾病讓每個人都有學習功課的機會，並從中培養自己所欠缺的美德，因此人人都得負起自我療癒的責任。倘若治療師一直在替病患開立花精處方，不僅讓人產生依賴，他們也無法體會戰勝疾病的法則。巴赫醫師說：「自從哈尼曼過世後，各種非自我療癒的技巧蘊育而生，而這些都只是唯物方式；這種靠他人力量取得的療方，缺乏病患自身的省思與自救，只能抒解症狀而已，但卻傷害了內在靈魂本質，病患無法習得自己所欠缺的部分，因而讓錯誤延續。」又說：「真正的健康無法用金錢買到，就如同教育不是繳了學費就能獲得知識的，而是要自己有意願去學習。」《人因自己受苦》

　　因此，花精療法不僅僅是一種治療（Cure），而是一種真正的療癒（Healing）方式，而花精也已經超越了藥物的物質形態和價值，它可以幫助我們去聆聽內在的聲音，明白心理情緒的意義，瞭解自身行為背後的訊息，並且從疾病或健康當中去看見生命的完整，而完全地接納自己和愛自己。所以當病患內心還沒準備好去面對問題的時候，花精只能暫時調理心理情緒，或者暫時緩解生理病症；唯有病患找出自己真正的錯誤，準備好面對問題，並且痛下決心克服自己的缺點，依循靈魂的指示而走上自我療癒之路，那麼，此刻使用花精來協助自己，才能夠發揮它真正的療癒力量。

愛、自由與療癒

　　有鑑於此，我們在 IFEC 國際花精研究推廣中心的花精教育課程，
特別重視巴赫醫師醫學理念和哲學思想的教授，而不是一味地傳授開立
花精處方的技巧，以及花精複方的套用。由於巴赫醫師的英文原著所蘊涵
的道理相當深厚，所以特地請魏愛娟小姐和黃韋睿先生加以翻譯，讓大家
能夠深入了解花精療法的內涵。或許剛開始接觸花精療法時會覺得這門
學問相當簡單，但越是簡單純粹的道理其意義卻是越深越遠；每一次當我
治療個案遇到疑惑，或自己的人生經歷遇到瓶頸時，都會從巴赫醫師的
著作中尋求解答，通常也會有令人相當振奮的領悟和收穫。但願此書的
出版，能夠讓更多人與花精世界獲得共鳴，一窺花精療法的美麗殿堂，
找到真正自我的生命價值。

【推薦者簡介】李穎哲醫師，在臺灣具有中、西醫雙執照的中醫師，自 2001 年開始
研究巴赫花精並運用在臨床實踐上已超過 10 年，並任 IFEC 國際花精研究推廣中心
專任講師進行教育教學工作。目前致力推廣巴赫醫師的理念與思想。著有《巴赫醫師
的人生科書》、《巴赫花精的心靈療癒法》等書。

Part Ⅰ   **自我療癒**

Heal Thyself

【譯者序】

從尋求治療到自我療癒

魏愛娟

　　我原本只是個病患，因為身心極度失序，在不想求助主流醫學的情結下，找到了巴赫醫師的花精療法。於是，我開始踏上自我療癒之路；這條路找來不易。從小到大，內心似乎有一個聲音在向我召喚，因而一直以來都特別「鐵齒」！

　　我的父親是中醫師、大姊是中醫師兼另類療法師、堂哥是中醫師⋯這樣的背景，讓我從小就離西醫遠遠的。小時候，就算生病，除非不得已，也不上醫院診所。從小例行性的感冒、發燒、出疹、水痘⋯甚至跌打損傷，都是由父親診治。看西醫，實屬情非得已。上了中學後，到外地讀書，才開始有機會至醫院接受醫治。在那個年代，中醫尚未被主流醫療體系所接納，仍被視為民俗療法，但在台北要找一個合宜的中醫師看病，也很不容易。

　　結婚生子後，不改一貫的鐵齒，孩子生病，尤其是老大，剛開始還會去看新生兒門診，有一次老大感冒哮喘，診所醫師一急，拿起氣喘噴劑往兒子嘴裡就是一噴！此後，兒子每次感冒必定哮喘，而且不易壓下來！幾次後，我內在的聲音又出現了，當時剛好接觸到肯園的精油，於是買了精油回來，一次一次地在孩子發燒、哮喘時用精油按摩，古老的日本民間療法加上來自母親那一輩的民間療法，徹夜陪伴。最後，兒子不再因感冒而哮喘，這也更堅定了我的想法：西藥的療法對於疾病的根除，是無解的！

　　兩年前，甲狀腺機能亢進再度復發，且一發不可收拾！身體的代謝功能完全失調，每天水瀉不止，體重遽降！不得已的情況下，求助於西醫。服用了近兩個月的西藥後，有一天我再也按耐不住了，不想再用西藥治療，於是約了見面的肯園芳療師，詢問是否認識不錯的中醫師？那一天，她帶了花精來給我試，這是我第一次貼敷花精。如果說我是一個敏感度很差的人，或許也不太正確，不過當時的我，真的沒有很明顯的感受！只有在服用了她為我調製的花精處方水後，第一次感覺到自己的情緒波動，當時非常地震撼！

　　之後，我開始去看李醫師的門診；不久之後，開始花精初階課程，閱讀花精療法書籍；然後，參加花精的進階課程，開始閱讀巴赫醫師的《自我療癒》；又不久之後，主持《自我療癒》的讀書會，並開始《自我療癒》的翻譯工作；就在這一連串過程下，我已經不知不覺地走在自我療癒的道路！我真實地體驗到了療癒的四個過程：身體症狀的緩解─情緒的舒緩─反抗期─內在心靈美德的提升。

　　在療癒的過程中，最明顯的改變是從參加花精課程開始，周遭的人全部見證了我的改變，不論是生理的還是心理的。而更進一步的，內心靈性層次的提升與反抗期，可以說同時交互產生，而這個階段最重大的改變，則是從開始翻譯《自我療癒》與主持讀書會開始。

愛、自由與療癒

　　之前雖然閱讀過《自我療癒》的翻譯本，但卻沒能讀懂！直到自己翻譯，加上要主持讀書會，不得不逐字逐句地徹底了解。這才發現，巴赫醫師真是個得道者啊！字裡行間，透露出他對人類的那份無私大愛，還有他殷切地想把這美好的訊息傳播給大家的心情。口氣中充滿了急切與苦口婆心，同樣的道理，從第一章講到最後一章，講的都是相同的一件事：聽從內在靈魂的指引，找出內在的錯誤，培養相對的美德以真正根除疾病！說了再說，用各種方式來說，好像很囉嗦，卻滿滿都是他無私的愛！

　　誠如 Julian Barnard 在其著作 ˋThe Pattern of Life Forceˊ 的序言中所說的一般：「人類文明與智慧的來源都來自同一口井，艾德華・巴赫的花精療法並不代表那一口井，卻是引領我們走向那口井的道路。」我們所有人的努力，同樣是為了要到達那口井而做的一點點付出。感謝引領我進入這條道路的所有人，更感謝我的靈魂，對我「不離不棄」。

　　這個版本的翻譯，不一定是最正確與最好的翻譯，卻是我個人自我療癒的過程，是為了讓更多人也能接受到這個無私大愛所付出的一點點力量。因為，巴赫醫師說：「我們愈是進步，我們就愈能成為周圍人們的恩賜。」就讓我們大家，帶著滿心的歡愉，一起踏上自我療癒的旅程吧！

【譯者簡介】魏愛娟小姐，現任職國立臺北藝術大學學務長室助教，畢業於國立藝術學院音樂學系，大學主修中提琴、同校碩士班主修音樂學。

【導讀】

單純、統一、和諧

魏愛娟

人類一直以來所追求的不過就是這個；然而，在愈來愈進步的物質生活中，人的思想卻愈來愈不單純，整個地球似乎籠罩在一股複雜糾結而鬱鬱的情緒氛圍中，大氣層的日益混濁，尤如人心的日益淆雜。尋找一個單純而無害（不破壞宇宙的一致性）的可能也是愈加地困難。上天透過各種方法為人類指點迷津，但愈是文明，卻愈是盲目。彩虹，原是上帝與人的信約。然而，在觀看彩虹時，人類幾乎忘了上帝派祂的兒子，為人類的原罪上十字架，為人類承擔苦難。耶穌說，我必將再來。他來過了，但很少很少人看見。因為，祂透過花朵、彩虹以及像是巴赫醫師的手，傳遞祂對人類無私的大愛。花一直都能給我們撫慰，當我們看著花朵時，卻讀不到它的訊息，因為我們眼中盡是自私自利！

佛陀的教導，同樣是那麼地單純而和諧，祂說，生命在一呼一吸之間。祂捻花微笑，不多說，而宇宙和諧的訊息就在那花朵中。不會是巧合，而是道，是「一以貫之」的。「一」是最單純的，「一」是最統一的，「一」是包含宇宙無盡藏的，「一」更是和諧的。「一」為有，「零」為無；「一」與零造就了我們肉眼所見、肉身所體的萬象現象界。「一」與「零」所構成的數位世界不是偶然，是必然，數位世界在「一」與「零」中是個無遠弗屆的天地。過去所認為不可思議的、肉眼不可見的，如今在人類智慧中，一一呈現。

所以，不是看不到的就不存在，而是一個大有的存在。任何物體極大之後皆要歸於零，最大的力量來自於無形。當人類發現了宇宙，人類也

發現黑洞，黑洞是一切有的開端，黑洞是不可測量的，在人類有限的理解是無盡頭的。巴赫醫師的理念是如此地單純而無私；透過對巴赫醫師其語言的了解，我們可以理解宇宙是萬有的，就從我們自身這個小宇宙的探索開始。當我們求得我們內在的完美和諧與平衡，我們當能與宇宙的中心連結，而成為一體。這就是單純、統一、和諧。

自我療癒

Heal Thyself

....

— 解說疾病產生的真正原因及治癒的方法 —
僅將此書獻給所有承受著苦痛或磨難的人們

An Explanation of the real Cause and Cure of Disease
This book is dedicated to all who suffer or who are in distress

1931 CW Daniels 出版

第 1 章
Chapter One

> 疾病　表面上看起來是那麼地殘酷
> 本身卻是仁慈的　是為我們好的
> 它能引導我們找出自身根本的錯誤
> 是我們解除自身錯誤而更臻良善的主要依據
> 苦難是一個矯正法門
> 它為我們指出人生中尚未實踐的功課
> 除非我們真正學得了這門功課
> 否則苦難將永遠無法消除

本書的宗旨並非暗示治療技術的不必要，也絕對無此意圖；僅衷心希望它能指引受苦的人們，從內在找到疾病的真正根源，以幫助他們達到自我療癒。此外，更希望激勵心繫人類福祉的醫事人員及神職人員，能加倍努力尋求眾生離苦得樂之法，好讓戰勝疾病的那一天早日到來。

It is not the object of this book to suggest that the art of healing is unnecessary, far be from it any such intention; but it is humbly hoped that it will be a guide to those who suffer to seek within themselves the real origin of their maladies, so that they may assist themselves in their own healing. Moreover, it is hoped that it may stimulate those, both in the medical profession and in religious orders, who have the welfare of humanity at heart, to redouble their efforts in seeking the relief of human suffering, and so hasten that day when the victory over disease will be complete.

現代醫學之所以失敗，是因為它只針對疾病的結果處理而非從起因探求。長久以來，疾病真正的本質被唯物主義所蒙蔽，疾病得以伺機展開破壞，就是因為沒從源頭加以擊潰。這種情況猶如在一場戰事中，敵軍從周圍建立起強大的要塞，並四處發動游擊戰；人們卻對這些強大的駐軍視若無睹，只滿足於修補因殘殺者突擊所造成的受損房舍及掩埋亡者的作法之中，使得掠奪者得以入侵。所以，大體而言，我們現今醫藥體系的情況就像是這樣，只不過在做些修補損害及埋葬被殘殺者的事罷了，完全沒考慮要建立起堅固的防禦系統。

The main reason for the failure of modern medical science is that it is dealing with results and not causes. For many centuries the real nature of disease has been masked by materialism, and thus disease itself has been given every opportunity of extending its ravages, since it has not been attacked at its origin. The situation is like to an enemy strongly fortified in the hills, continually waging guerrilla warfare in the country around, while the people, ignoring the fortified garrison, content themselves with repairing the damaged houses and burying the dead, which are the result of the raids of the marauders. So, generally speaking, is the situation in medicine today; nothing more than the patching up of those attacked and the burying of those who are slain, without a thought being given to the real stronghold.

用目前唯物主義的方法，疾病是絕不可能被治癒及根除的。理由很簡單，因為疾病的本質並非物質性的。我們所認知的疾病，只不過是顯示在身體上的最終結果、是長久而深遠的習性之最終產物罷了。即便身體的治療已有明顯成效，若未能將真正的根源移除，也只不過獲得短暫的舒解而已。近代醫藥技術潮流依其對疾病本質的不當詮釋，以及著重在肉體物質層面上的探討，而逐漸擴張了它的勢力。首先，這分散人們對認知疾病真實本質的注意力，因此忽略了真正有效的治癒方法；再者，將所有的注意力集中在身體上，不僅蒙蔽了療癒的真實希望，還挑起人們對疾病的莫大恐懼，而這原本應該是不存在的。

Disease will never be cured or eradicated by present materialistic methods, for the simple reason that disease in its origin is not material. What we know as disease is an ultimate result produced in the body, the end product of deep and long acting forces, and even if material treatment alone is apparently successful this is nothing more than a temporary relief unless the real cause has been removed. The modern trend of medical science, by misinterpreting the true nature of disease and concentrating it in materialistic terms in the physical body, has enormously increased its power, firstly, by distracting the thoughts of people from its true origin and hence from the effective method of attack, and secondly, by localising it in the body, thus obscuring true hope of recovery and raising a mighty disease complex of fear, which never should have existed.

疾病的本質，是靈魂與心智爭戰後的結果；唯有透過精神與心理層面的努力，才能真正根除。這樣的努力，如果是在正確的理解下進行（稍後我們將做探討），將可以經由根除那些基本因素，也就是疾病產生的主因，來加以預防並治癒疾病。任何單獨針對身體所進行的治療，最多只能做到表面修護而已，但卻使其無法痊癒，因為造成疾病的根源還在伺機而動，且不知何時會再次以不同的面貌顯現。事實上，許多時候，顯著的康復反而是有害的，會讓病人察覺不到問題的真正原因，同時只滿足於表面上重新獲得的康復；疾病產生的真正要素將因未被察覺而日益強大。相較於上述案例，那些原本就了解或是受到明智醫師指導的病人，知道這些負面精神和心理力量本質運作的結果，將造成我們肉體上所謂的疾病。如果病人直接嘗試終止這些負面力量的運作，一旦順利開始進行，健康狀況將立即獲得改善；當行動完成後，疾病就會消失。這是經由攻擊要塞、亦即攻擊造成痛苦的根源所在而獲得的真正療癒。

Disease is in essence the result of conflict between Soul and Mind, and will never be eradicated except by spiritual and mental effort. Such efforts, if properly made with understanding, as we shall see later, can cure and prevent disease by removing those basic factors which are its primary cause. No effort directed to the body alone can do more than superficially repair damage, and in this there is no cure, since the cause is still operative and may at any moment again demonstrate its presence in another form. In fact, in many cases apparent recovery is harmful, since it hides from the patient the true cause of his trouble, and in the satisfaction of apparently renewed health the real factor, being unnoticed, may gain in strength. Contrast these cases with that of the patient who knows, or who is by some wise physician instructed in, the nature of the adverse spiritual or mental forces at work, the result of which has precipitated what we call disease in the physical body. If that patient directly attempts to neutralise those forces, health improves as soon as this is successfully begun, and when it is completed the disease will disappear. This is true healing by attacking the stronghold, the very base of the cause of suffering.

現代醫藥技術中唯一例外的物質療法,是由同類療法始祖－偉大的哈尼曼(註1)創立的療法,他體認到造物主的慈悲大愛,以及人類內在所具有的神性,經由研究病患面對生命、環境及自身疾病的態度,試圖從自然界的藥草中,去尋找不僅能治療病患身體、同時也能提升他們心靈層次的藥方。期望對人類心懷真誠大愛的醫生們,能夠延續並拓展他的科學研究。

One of the exceptions to materialistic methods in modern medical science is that of the great Hahnemann, the founder of Homoeopathy, who with his realisation of the beneficent love of the Creator and of the Divinity which resides within man, by studying the mental attitude of his patients towards life, environment and their respective diseases, sought to find in the herbs of the field and in the realms of nature the remedy which would not only heal their bodies but would at the same time uplift their mental outlook. May his science be extended and developed by those true physicians who have the love of humanity at heart.

耶穌誕生前的五百年,即便當時的外科技術已相當純熟,甚至超越現在,而受到佛陀啟示的古印度行醫者,便已將療癒的藝術發展到可將外科手術完全廢除的境界。還有像提出偉大療癒理念的希波克拉底(註2)、肯定人類具有神性的帕拉塞爾蘇斯(註3),以及體認到人類疾病根源是超越生理層面的哈尼曼等人,他們對病痛真正的本質

及療法都有相當程度的認知。如果後代能追隨這些先知先賢們的教誨，那麼人類就能免去這廿甚或廿五個世紀以來無以數計的苦難。但就如同其他事物一般，西方世界長久以來被唯物主義所主導，致使這些深知真理的先知們所提出的忠告，被抱持現實主義的阻礙者聲浪所掩蓋了。

Five hundred years before Christ some physicians of ancient India, working under the influence of Lord Buddha, advanced the art of healing to so perfect a state that they were able to abolish surgery, although the surgery of their time was as efficient, or more so, than that of the present day. Such men as Hippocrates with his mighty ideals of healing, Paracelsus with his certainty of the divinity in man, and Hahnemann who realised that disease originated in a plane above the physical - all these knew much of the real nature and remedy of suffering. What untold misery would have been spared during the last twenty or twenty-five centuries had the teaching of these great masters of their art been followed, but, as in other things, materialism has appealed too strongly to the Western world, and for so long a time, that the voices of the practical obstructors have risen above the advice of those who knew the truth.

在此做個簡短說明：疾病，表面看起來那麼地殘酷，而本身卻是仁慈的、是為我們好的，如能正確理解，它將引導我們找出自身根本的錯誤。如果妥善處理，它將是我們去除自身錯誤、使自己比過去更臻良善的主要依據。苦難是一個矯正法門，它為我們指出人生中尚未實踐的功課；除非我們真正地學得了這門功課，否則苦難永遠無法消除。我們還必須知道的是，對於那些懂得並能夠解讀疾病前兆重要性的人，若能經由精神及心理層面的努力來改正，便能在疾病形成之前加以預防，或在疾病剛形成之時便將它去除。我們也毋需感到沮喪，不論情況多麼嚴重，只要肉體仍一息尚存，就表示主宰著我們的靈魂沒有放棄希望。

Let it here be briefly stated that disease, though apparently so cruel, is in itself beneficent and for our good and, if rightly interpreted, it will guide us to our essential faults. If properly treated, it will be the cause of the removal of those faults and leave us better and greater than before. Suffering is a corrective to point out a lesson which by other means we have failed to grasp, and never can it be eradicated until that lesson is learnt. Let is also be known that in those who understand and are able to read the significance of premonitory symptoms disease may be prevented before its onset or aborted in its earlier stages if the proper corrective spiritual and mental efforts be undertaken. Nor need any case despair, however severe, for the fact that the individual is still granted physical life indicates that the Soul who rules is not without hope.

（註1）哈尼曼：（Hahnemann Samuel；1755－1843）
德國醫師，同類療法（homeopathy）的創始人，主張以能使健康人產生同種疾病症狀的藥物來治療疾病。1796年發表此定律。4年後，進一步發展「潛效強化理論」，確認小劑量藥物即可有效地發揮醫療作用。其主要作品《合理療法的原則》（Organon der rationellen Heillkunst,1810），將上述原理擴展成為一個醫療體系，稱之為同類療法。

（註2）希波克拉底：（Hippocrates；B.C. 460－377）
古希臘醫生，傳統上被視為醫學之父。他將身體視為一個「整體」的機體，其醫療實務來自於有關身體各部分的資訊，成為一個包容性的概念，隨後又將整體分為不同的構成部分。他個人對於醫學的發展，以及對於醫生的理想和道德操守，都產生了恆久的影響。

（註3）帕拉賽爾蘇斯：（Paracelsus；1493－1541）
德國醫師、煉金士，發現並使用了多種新藥，促進了藥物化學的發展，對現代醫學，包括精神病治療的興起有著極大的貢獻。

◎第一章　重點摘錄

全新的醫學觀念

　　「自我療癒」這整本書的核心思想，其實在第一章就已經闡述明白了；甚至可以說，能夠看懂並領悟第一章的內容，就等於體會了巴赫醫師「自我療癒」的意涵，以及花精療法的精神。而其中最重要且能夠完整說明自我療癒精神內涵的一句話就是：「從自己的內在找到疾病產生的真正原因，幫助他們達到自我療癒。」當時巴赫醫師的自我療癒，主要是針對醫事同業人員而寫的。他希望社會上原本就從事療癒工作的人，不論是從事生理或心理的醫事人員或神職人員，能夠接受這個嶄新的醫學理念，然後透過這些人，將自我療癒的觀念傳播出去。巴赫醫師在這一章所要提倡的，就是一個新的醫學觀念：他認為醫生應該從物質的治療轉變為心理或精神的治療。

　　所有學習花精的人，除了要懂得巴赫花精這門學問之外，更重要的是要能把這種愛散播出去，並教導其他人，讓他們皆能受惠於巴赫花精；這也就是我們一直強調的健康的四大要素之一：「活在愛的氛圍裡」。不只在服用花精時能感受到愛的氛圍，而且是當我們把花精愛的訊息傳播出去後，其所回饋的大愛，才算是真正活在愛的氛圍裡。所以短短一段話裡就蘊涵了如此廣的意涵。

　　第二和第三段的重點在說明人們當前對疾病治療的態度常常是頭痛醫頭、腳痛醫腳，也就是沒有治療到根本，所以無法真正根治疾病。接著巴赫醫師說明了疾病產生的原因；

然而醫學太進步的結果，讓表面上痛苦的症狀很容易就獲得緩解，但這對病人來說反而是有害的。正如巴赫醫師所說的，就因為不是從疾病的源頭加以擊潰，因此，疾病可能會再一次以更強烈的方式在生理的其他部分顯現。

巴赫醫師也在第一章提出了根除疾病的方法；就是要從靈性及心智層面去根除。而他所謂的根除行動，則是他在之後的章節中加以闡述的，亦即培養相對的美德。

從第一章開始，即可強烈感受到巴赫醫師是那麼急切地要告訴世人，他找到了一個解決人類疾病根源的方法。越到文章後面，就越能發現巴赫醫師的急切，以及他是多麼地循循善誘、苦口婆心要告訴人們，趕快去開始自我療癒吧。因此，巴赫醫師在這一章的第六段中，特別提出了古代印度及希臘的先聖先賢－佛陀、希波克拉底、帕拉賽爾蘇斯等，來強調他所說的以「愛」為出發的療癒理念。

古代的先聖先賢們早就發現也提倡了，只是物質主義日益興盛，使得這些原本是最重要、最偉大的療癒藝術不再為人們所依循，因此人類才遭逢了長達廿甚至有廿五個世紀之久的苦難，而這也是巴赫醫師內心的吶喊！至於文章中所提到的同類療法創立者哈尼曼醫師，巴赫醫師在他後來的著作《人因自己而受苦》（Ye Suffer From Yourselves）當中，就已不再贊同同類療法的精神了。因為他認為同類療法製劑的作法，其實是用仇恨治療仇恨，但巴赫醫師認為應該要用愛來治療仇恨才是根本。哈尼曼本人在晚年時也發現，要從

根本治療疾病，應該要作用在人體更精微的部分，也就是後來巴赫醫師所發現的：我們的高層自我及靈魂。這也是為什麼哈尼曼晚年時一直針對「再稀釋」和「再振盪」做研究的原因，但在大部分人的眼裡，他根本是瘋了。

最後一段文字，是許多講巴赫花精的人最常引述的話：「疾病，表面看起來是那麼地殘酷，而本身卻是仁慈的、是為我們好的，如能正確理解，它將引導我們找出自身根本的錯誤。」但事實上，能夠體會巴赫醫師這句話的人並不多。如前面所提到的，這一章其實就是巴赫醫師的整個花精系統；也就是其基本的核心理念－自我療癒，其內涵的主要精神，在本章都已全說明白了。

第 2 章
Chapter Two

> 只要我們的靈魂與人格處於和諧的狀態
> 那麼一切將是喜樂與和平、快樂與健康
> 我們的人格一旦偏離了靈魂所舖陳的道路
> 衝突由此而生
> 這個衝突是疾病與不快樂的根源

要了解疾病的本質，就必須對一些基本事實有所認知。

To understand the nature of disease certain fundamental truths have to be acknowledged.

首先：人擁有靈魂，也就是他的真我 – 一個神聖、偉大的生命，萬物的造物主之子；而靈魂所在的肉身，雖然是這個靈魂現世的廟宇，但也不過是其極微小的反射。而時時伴隨著我們的靈魂與神性，依照祂希望的方式，舖陳我們的人生；只要我們允許，祂將隨時指引、保護並鼓勵我們，謹慎而慈愛地引領著我們，向最能利益我們的方向走去。而祂，我們的高層自我，是全能者的靈光閃現，因此是不朽而無可匹敵的。

The first of these is that man has a Soul which is his real self; a Divine, Mighty Being, a Son of the Creator of all things, of which the body, although the earthly temple of that Soul, is but the minutest reflection : that our Soul, our Divinity Who resides in and around us, lays down for us our lives as He wishes them to be ordered and, so far as we will allow, ever guides, protects and encourages us, watchful and beneficent to lead us always for our utmost advantage: that He, our Higher Self, being a spark of the Almighty, is thereby invincible and immortal.

第二項原則是：我們，亦即在這個世上所認知的自己，來到人世間的目的，是要經由物質的存在，去獲得所有的知識與經驗，以發展

我們所欠缺的美德，然後剷除內在所有的錯誤，好讓我們的天性能臻至完美。靈魂知道什麼樣的環境及狀況最能達到這個目的，因此，祂將我們安置在最適合那個目標的人生支脈中。

The second principle is that we, as we know ourselves in this world, are personalities down here for the purpose of gaining all the knowledge and experience which can be obtained through earthly existence, of developing virtues which we lack and of wiping out all that is wrong within us, thus advancing towards the perfection of our natures. The Soul knows what environment and what circumstances will best enable us to do this, and hence He places us in that branch of life most suited for that object.

第三：我們必須了解到，在這世上的短暫旅程，而所謂的人生，只不過是進化過程的一瞬間，猶如在學校的一天；雖然現在只能經驗及理解這一天，但內在的直覺告訴我們，出生離我們的初始無限遙遠，而死亡離我們的結束也無限遙遠。我們的靈魂，也就是真正的自己，是不朽的，而我們所覺知且短暫的身體，只不過是我們騎著去旅行的馬匹，或用以完成一項工作的器具罷了。

Thirdly, we must realise that the short passage on this earth, which we know as life, is but a moment in the course of our evolution, as one day at school is to a life, and although we can for the present only see and comprehend that one day, our intuition tells us that birth was infinitely far from our beginning and death infinitely far from our ending. Our Souls, which are really we, are immortal, and the bodies of which we are conscious and temporary, merely as horses we ride to go a journey, or instruments we use to do a piece of work.

接下來第四項偉大的原則是：只要我們的靈魂與人格處於和諧的狀態，那麼一切將是喜樂與和平、快樂與健康。我們的人格一旦偏離

了靈魂所舖陳的道路，不論是出自世俗的慾望或被他人所說服，衝突便由此而生。這個衝突是疾病與不快樂的根源。不論我們在世上從事的行業為何，擦鞋匠或修士、地主或農民，不論富有或貧窮，只要遵照靈魂的指示去執行那個特定的工作，就能平安無事；我們可以更加地確定，不論被放置在人生的哪個位置，高尚還是卑微，都包含了我們這一刻進化所需的教誨與經驗，並且給予了自我發展上絕佳的優勢。

Then follows a fourth great principle, that so long as our Souls and personalities are in harmony all is joy and peace, happiness and health. It is when our personalities are led astray from the path laid down by the Soul, either by our own worldly desires or by the persuasion of others, that a conflict arises. This conflict is the root cause of disease and unhappiness. No matter what our work in the world – bootblack or monarch, landlord or peasant, rich or poor - so long as we do that particular work according to the dictates of the Soul, all is well; and we can further rest assured that in whatever station of life we are placed, princely or lowly, it contains the lessons and experiences necessary at the moment for our evolution, and gives us the best advantage for the development of ourselves.

下一項偉大的原則是對於萬物一致性的理解：萬物的造物者是愛，而我們所意識到的一切，這無以數計的形式表徵，都是那個愛的展現，不論它是一顆星球或是一粒小石，一顆星星或一顆露珠，是人類或是最低等的生命形態。我們或許可以這樣來一窺這個觀點：想像我們的造物者，是一顆閃耀著恩慈與愛的太陽，從中心向各方散射出無以數計的光束，而我們以及一切所覺知的事物，是這個光束末端的微小粒子，被派去學習經驗與知識，但最終要回到那偉大的中心。雖然對我們來說，每道光線看起來是分散而有區別的，卻是這偉大太陽中心的實質體現。它是不可分割的，因為光束一旦來源被截斷，即不再存在。因此我們便稍稍了解到這個不可切割的事實，

縱使每個光線都有其獨特性，它終究是偉大中心創造力的一部分。所以任何與自我或他人對立的行為，都會影響到整體，因為任何部分所造成的不完美，將反映在整體上，整體中的每個粒子最終都要趨至完美。

The next great principle is the understanding of the Unity of all things: that the Creator of all things is Love, and that everything of which we are conscious is in all its infinite number of forms a manifestation of that Love, whether it be a planet or a pebble, a star or a dewdrop, man or the lowest form of life. It may be possible to get a glimpse of this conception by thinking of our Creator as a great blazing sun of beneficence and love and from the centre an infinite number of beams radiate in every direction, and that we and all of which we are conscious are particles at the end of those beams, sent out to gain experience and knowledge, but ultimately to return to the great centre. And though to us each ray may appear separate and distinct, it is in reality part of the great central Sun. Separation is impossible, for as soon as a beam of light is cut off from its source it ceases to exist. Thus we may comprehend a little of the impossibility of separateness, as although each ray may have its individuality, it is nevertheless part of the great central creative power. Thus any action against ourselves or against another affects the whole, because by causing imperfection in a part it reflects on the whole, every particle of which must ultimately become perfect.

所以我們發現了兩個最可能產生的根本錯誤：一、靈魂與人格之間的分離，二、殘酷或惡意地對待他人；這都是違背一致性的罪過。兩者皆將導致衝突，因而產生疾病。去了解我們在哪裡犯了錯（其實我們經常都沒有意識到），並誠摯地付諸心力而改正這個錯誤，不僅能帶給我們一生的喜悅與寧靜，也將帶來健康。

So we see there are two great possible fundamental errors: dissociation between our Souls and our personalities, and cruelty or wrong to others, for this is a sin against Unity. Either of these brings conflict, which leads to disease. An understanding of where we are making an error (which is so often not realised by us) and an earnest endeavour to correct the fault will lead not only to a life of joy and peace, but also to health.

疾病本身是仁慈的，是為了要找回靈魂的神聖意志而存在的；所以我們可以知道它是可預防及可避免的，只要能發現自己所犯的錯誤，並經由精神與心理的手段去改正，就不用接受痛苦的嚴苛教訓。神聖的力量會在疼痛與磨難降臨之前，給予所有補正過去行為的機會，作為最終的依靠，修正自己的道路。今天我們正在對抗的，或許並不是這一生的錯誤；雖然我們在這物質世界的意志下，或許覺察不到受苦的原因，因而認為這磨難對我們來說，是那麼地殘酷且沒有道理；然而，我們的靈魂（也就是我們自己）知道它真正的用意，而且正引領我們向自身最大的利益走去。無論如何，了解並改正錯誤，將可減少我們的病痛，帶給我們健康。認知靈魂的意旨並且順從它，意謂著能自現世的磨難及悲痛中解脫，並讓我們在喜樂中自在地展開進化。

Disease is in itself beneficent, and has for its object the bringing back of the personality to the Divine will of the Soul; and thus we can see that it is both preventable and avoidable, since if we could only realise for ourselves the mistakes we are making and correct these by spiritual and mental means there would be no need for the severe lesson of suffering. Every opportunity is given us by the Divine Power to mend our ways before, as a last resort, pain and suffering have to be applied. It may not be the errors of this life, this day at school, which we are combating; and although we in our physical minds may not be conscious of the reason of our suffering, which may to us appear cruel and without reason, yet our Souls (which are ourselves) know the full purpose and are guiding us to our best advantage. Nevertheless, understanding and correction of our errors would shorten our illness and bring us back to health. Knowledge of the Soul's purpose and acquiescence in that knowledge means the relief of earthly suffering and distress, and leaves us free to develop our evolution in joy and happiness.

有兩項嚴重的錯誤是存在的：第一、無法聽從及遵照靈魂的指示，第二、違反一致性的行為。基於第一項原因，絕對不要去評判他人，因為在一方看起來是對的，對另一方而言卻是錯的。商人的工作是要建立龐大的交易，不僅為了自己的利益，還要照顧到員工，因而去學得效率及控制的知識，並發展其相關的美德，這是必要的，而他所需要的能力與美德和擔任護士的需求必然不同，護士是為了照顧病患而奉獻自己；然而只要兩者都是遵從各自靈魂的指示，就是正確習得了進化時所需的特質。重要的是，去遵循靈魂與高層自我的指示，就是以覺知、本能與直觀的方式去學習。

There are two great errors: first, to fall to honour and obey the dictates of our Soul, and second, to act against Unity. On account of the former, be ever reluctant to judge others, because what is right for one is wrong for another. The merchant, whose work it is to build up a big trade not only to his own advantage but also to that of all those whom he may employ, thereby gaining knowledge of efficiency and control and developing the virtues associated with each, must of necessity use different qualities and different virtues from those of a nurse, sacrificing her life in the care of the sick; and yet both, if obeying the dictates of their Souls, are rightly learning those qualities necessary for their evolution. It is obeying the commands of our Soul, our Higher Self, which we learn through conscience, instinct and intuition, that matters.

　　我們因而明白，就疾病最根本的原則及本質而言，疾病不但是可預防的，也是可治癒的。所以靈性治療師及醫師的職責是除了物質的治療之外，還要能提供人們認知造成自身生活苦難的錯誤所在，以及根除這些錯誤的方法，進而引領病人重獲健康與喜樂。

Thus we see that by its very principles and in its very essence, disease is both preventable and curable, and it is the work of spiritual healers and physicians to give, in addition to material remedies, the knowledge to the suffering of the error of their lives, and of the manner in which these errors can be eradicated, and so to lead the sick back to health and joy.

◎第二章　重點摘錄

所有真理其實都相通，許多宗教教義與人生哲理，都能和
巴赫醫師「自我療癒」中所提到的觀點相互印證。

內在的本質－靈魂與神性

　　從本章第一段就能看出，巴赫醫師在宗教學及神學領域
的研究上是非常透徹的。一開始就說明了人來到世上所應該
學習的事情，以及我們生而為人所要具備的事實。所以他說：
「要了解疾病的本質，就必須對一些基本事實有所認知。」
因為大家都忘記了真我，遇到事情都只會外求。巴赫醫師
相信靈魂的存在，擁有和造物主同樣偉大的神性，此即道出
了佛學中所講的「人人皆有佛性」的道理。

　　一般人如果沒有在宗教學或心靈學上有研究，會很難
理解所謂的靈魂、高層自我、神聖本性等到底在講什麼；
解釋這些名詞其實很困難，因為很多部分只能留待個人實際
體驗。這段文章中的重點是：「靈魂與神性依照祂所希望
我們依循的方式，來舖陳我們的人生；只要我們允許，祂將
隨時引領、保護並鼓勵著我們……」，這才是巴赫醫師所要
傳達的重點。他要我們相信，靈魂會在我們走錯路時加以
指引，看顧著我們。而「只要我們允許」則道盡了自我療癒
的精髓，也是花精使用最重要的一件事；每個人都有自主
權，一旦已經準備好面對問題時，才會允許自己接受花精的
能量，啟動自我療癒系統。

靈魂與人格的不可分割

第一段內容主要在說明我們所擁有的神性；第二段則說明了在人世間受後天影響所發展而成的性格，為什麼我們需要透過物質經驗的過程去學習，然後獲得每個人在此生所需要的獨特知識與經驗。並再次強調：我們必須認清肉身之所以受苦，是沒有聽從靈魂神性的指引，因此必須要去發展相對的美德以掃除自己內在的錯誤。所以他要人們放心地把自己交給靈魂引導，如此就一定不會有錯。

第三段則點出了從整個宇宙時空來看，我們存在於人世的時間其實是很短暫的。而肉身，只不過是學習這個階段的人生功課所使用的媒介罷了。一旦功課完成了，媒介就必須要丟棄；而這一生雖然短暫，但並不表示就可以不認真。從以上內容可以隱約看出巴赫醫師有「靈魂輪迴轉世」的觀念，但他並沒用文字清楚表達出來，或許是考慮到當時人們的宗教信仰很難接受這個觀念吧。

第四段則再次強調第一章所說的：「疾病的本質，是靈魂與心智爭戰的結果；唯有透過精神與心理層面的努力，才能真正根除！」巴赫醫師只是用另一種說法再次強調：人要健康喜樂，就要與靈魂處於和諧狀態。當我們能完全到達平和喜樂的境界時，疾病就再也沒有存在的必要了。所以要記住，當疾病出現時，是在警惕我們：我們自己的心靈尚未達到真正平和喜樂的境界；這也同時表示，我們還沒能把思想和行為矯正過來，美德還沒培養出來，所以疾病還有存在的理由和價值，它提醒我們仍需繼續努力。

宇宙的中心－愛

　　第五段巴赫醫師提出了兩項重要的人生哲理:「一致性」與「愛」。他先說明我們皆來自於同一個偉大的中心,這個中心就是愛,而我們只是這偉大中心的一小部分。來到人世間,就是要學習我們所欠缺的美德,讓自己更加完美;如果我們這個小部分產生了缺失,破壞了愛的定律,基於一致性的法則,將使整體產生不完美。透過這段內容可以了解,我們被送到這人世間來,目的就是要學習愛。

　　第六段在說明,違背了一致性,就是疾病產生的原因;而疾病是要告訴我們去察覺錯誤並且努力改正,如此就能獲得健康、喜樂與寧靜。以上是更深入地說明靈魂與人格的分離,以及殘酷和惡意地對待他人,同樣都違背了一致性原則。我們皆來自一個本體,當人格與靈魂產生衝突,其實就是破壞了這個本體。當我們開始使用花精,來讓靈魂與人格能夠諧和,就是讓這個本體更完美。因此我們會發現,在使用花精之後,家庭氣氛變得愈來愈融洽,因為家庭是這個整體的一部分;當我們變完美了,家庭整體也因此而變好,亦即人與人之間的關係,都處於這個和諧的一致性當中。

苦難與疾病的真諦

　　巴赫醫師又從另一個角度說明疼痛和苦難存在的必要性,過去我們對疾病的認知太過表面了;他要大家去解讀疾病的意義及仁慈所在,認清靈魂所要給予的警惕與教訓,

只要有了這樣的領悟，就能獲得真正的平靜與健康。同時他也給予我們希望，為我們說明真相，好讓我們不再沮喪失望；亦即當我們發現苦難與疾病時，事實上就是看見了希望。

新的醫病關係

最後他提出了一個新觀點：「我們可從疾病最根本的原則及本質看出，疾病是可預防及可治癒的。而靈性治療者及醫師的職責是除了物質的治療之外，還要能提供人們認知造成自身生活苦難的錯誤所在，以及根除這些錯誤所需的行為，進而引領病人重獲健康與喜樂。」巴赫醫師一再強調，醫師與治療師要成為引領者，不只給魚吃，而還要給病人一支釣竿；一個人要獲得真正的健康，責任在於自己，而非靠醫生和治療師的專業，這是一種全新的醫病關係。

巴赫醫師當年提出這些觀念其實需要有相當的勇氣，因為他得罪了許多人，也斷送了許多人的生計。就像現今學習靈修的課程和門派相當多，但能夠提出自我療癒且不依賴任何治療師的觀念的人實在很少，或者是只提出這個觀念，但作法卻與觀念背道而馳，純綷希望人們能夠臣服在他們的權威之下，所以要評估自己所皈依的老師是否真正得道，可用這個簡單的方法加以檢視。

第 3 章
Chapter Three

疾病的預防與治療
可以經由找出自身的錯誤
以及真心誠意地培養美德來根除錯誤
不是去對抗錯誤
而是要引進其相對美德的洪流
將錯誤自我們的天性中掃除

我們所謂的疾病，其實是更深層失衡的最終階段。為了獲得真正完整而成功的治療，顯而易見地，除非同時移除其根本原因，否則僅針對最終結果去處理，將達不到全面性的成效。人類會犯下的一個主要錯誤，也就是違反一致性的行為，而它源自於自私自利。所以也可以說，只有一種主要的苦惱存在－不安適，或疾病。誠如違反一致性的行為可以分成幾種不同的類型，疾病－這些行為的結果－對應於它們的起因，也可以分成幾個主要的族群。認識疾病最原始的本質，將有助於指引我們找到違反愛的神聖定律及一致性的行為類型。

What we know as disease is the terminal stage of a much deeper disorder, and to ensure complete success in treatment it is obvious that dealing with the final result alone will not be wholly effective unless the basic cause is also removed. There is one primary error which man can make, and that is action against Unity; this originates in self-love. So also we may say that there is but one primary affliction - discomfort, or disease. And as action against Unity may be divided into various types, so also may disease - the result of these actions – be separated into main groups, corresponding to their causes. The very nature of an illness will be a useful guide to assist in discovering the type of action which is being taken against the Divine Law of Love and Unity.

如果我們天性中能存有對萬物充足的愛，那麼就不會造成傷害；因為這樣的愛，能讓我們停止一切可能會對他人造成傷害的行動及心念。但我們都還沒到達那個完美的境界；如果有的話，就不會在

愛、自由與療癒｜*Heal Thyself*

這裡了。其實我們都在朝那個境界去追求及前進，而我們當中承受著身心煎熬的人，正是在這個煎熬的帶領下，往那個理想的狀態前進；只要我們能正確地解讀，不只加快了往那個目標前去的腳步，也能夠免除自身的疾病與苦難。自學得教訓及錯誤根除的那一刻起，就再也不需要修正了，因為我們必須記住，苦難的本身是慈善的，會在我們走錯路時給予指引，並加速進化的過程，以到達那榮耀的完美境地。

If we have in our nature sufficient love of all things, then we can do no harm; because that love would stay our hand in any action, our mind at any thought which might hurt another. But we have not yet reached that state of perfection; if we had, there would be no need for our existence here. But all of us are seeking and advancing towards that state, and those of us who suffer in mind or body are by this very suffering being led towards that ideal condition; and if we will but read it aright, we may not only hasten our steps towards that goal, but also save ourselves illness and distress. From the moment the lesson is understood and the error eliminated there is no longer need for the correction, because we must remember that suffering is in itself beneficent, in that it points out to us when we are taking wrong paths and hastens our evolution to its glorious perfection.

人類最原始的疾病是驕傲、殘酷、仇恨、自私自利、無知、意志不堅及貪婪等這一類的缺點；仔細想想，會發現這些都是違反了一致性的行為。套用現代的語彙，這一類缺點才是真正的疾病；當我們有能力意識到這些是錯誤的行為時，它們已經年累月並根深蒂固地存在了，並在身體上促成了傷害性的結果，也就是我們所謂的疾病。

The real primary diseases of man are such defects as pride, cruelty, hate, self-love, ignorance, instability and greed; and each of these, if considered, will be found to be adverse to Unity. Such defects as these are the real diseases (using the word in the modem sense), and it is a continuation and persistence in such defects after we have reached that stage of development when we know them to be wrong, which precipitates in the body the injurious results which we know as illness.

之所以會驕傲，首先是因為沒有認知到人格的渺小，以及對靈魂的絕對依賴，而所獲得的成就亦非個人所有，實為神聖本性所賜予。其次，忘記自己是屬於整體的一部分，是宇宙萬物體系中最微乎其微的一部分。因為驕傲，使人拒絕以謙卑及順從的態度服膺於偉大造物主的意願，而作出違背那個意願的行為。

Pride is due, firstly, to lack of recognition of the smallness of the personality and its utter dependence on the Soul, and that all the successes it may have are not of itself but are blessings bestowed by the Divinity within; secondly, to loss of the sense of proportion, of the minuteness of one amidst the scheme of Creation. As Pride invariably refuses to bend with humility and resignation to the Will of the Great Creator, it commits actions contrary to that Will.

殘酷是拒絕承認萬物的一致性，並且無法了解到任何不利於他人的行為，就是與整體對立，因此也是與一致性相違背的行為。沒有人會讓自己親近及珍愛的人受到這種傷害，且基於一致性的原則，我們必須繼續成長，直到我們了解到每個人因為是整體的一部分，最終都會成為我們所親近及珍愛的人，甚至直到能對迫害我們的人同樣升起愛與憐憫的心為止。

Cruelty is a denial of the unity of all and a failure to understand that any action adverse to another is in opposition to the whole, and hence an action against Unity. No man would practise its injurious effects against those near and dear to him, and by the law of Unity we have to grow until we understand that everyone, as being part of a -Whole, must become near and dear to us, until even those who persecute us call up only feelings of love and sympathy.

恨是愛的反面，與萬物的法則相違逆。它違反了整個神聖體系，也否定了造物主。恨只會帶出違背一致性的行為與思想，而與這些相反的，將是由愛所支配的行為。

Hate is the opposite of Love, the reverse of the Law of Creation. It is contrary to the whole Divine scheme and is a denial of the Creator; it leads only to such actions and thoughts which are adverse to Unity and the opposite of those which would be dictated by Love.

自私自利同樣是對一致性的否定，也違背了我們對四海兄弟的責任，而將自身的利益置於人性良善及對週遭需要照顧與保護的人們之上。

Self-love again is a denial of Unity and the duty we owe to our brother men by putting the interests of ourselves before the good of humanity and the care and protection of those immediately around us.

無知是不去學習，是當認知真理的機會來臨時卻拒絕接受，因而導致許多只存在於黑暗中的錯誤行為；當真理及知識的光芒與我們同在，這些錯誤是不可能產生的。

Ignorance is the failure to learn, the refusal to see Truth when the opportunity is offered, and leads to many wrong acts such as can only exist in darkness and are not possible when the light of Truth and Knowledge is around us.

當人格拒絕接受高層自我的指引時，就會產生對自己的決心不確定、猶豫不決與意志薄弱的結果，致使我們因為軟弱而背叛了他人。如果內在具備了那不被征服、無可匹敵的神聖本性的知識，亦即真正的本我，這種情形是不可能發生的。

Instability, indecision and weakness of purpose result when the personality refuses to be ruled by the Higher Self, and lead us to betray others through our weakness. Such a condition would not be possible had we within us the knowledge of the Unconquerable, Invincible Divinity which is in reality ourselves.

貪婪會導致對權力的渴望。它否定了每個靈魂的自由與獨特性。貪婪的人格，不但無法認清每個人來到世間是要遵照靈魂的指示，並在自己的界限內自由地發展，同時要增強自己的獨特性，毫無阻礙及自由地工作；卻渴望著指使、塑造及命令，掠奪了造物者的權力。

Greed leads to a desire for power. It is a denial of the freedom and individuality of every soul. Instead of recognising that everyone of us is down here to develop freely upon his own lines according to the dictates of the soul alone, to increase his individuality, and to work free and unhampered, the personality with greed desires to dictate, mould and command, usurping the power of the Creator.

這些都是真正疾病的例證，我們苦難及不幸的根源。所有這些缺點，如果一再因違背高層自我的聲音而存在，將造成衝突，並在生理上產生必然的反應，形成其自身特定的疾病型態。

Such are examples of real disease, the origin and basis of all our suffering and distress. Each of such defects, if persisted in against the voice of the Higher Self, will produce a conflict which must of necessity be reflected in the physical body, producing its own specific type of malady.

於是我們發現，任何使我們受苦的疾病型態，是如何引領我們去發現潛在衝突背後的錯誤。舉例來說，驕傲是心智的無知及僵化造成的，會引發身體僵直及硬化的疾病。疼痛是殘酷的結果，因此病患得以經由自身的疼痛，學到不將痛苦施加於他人身上的道理，不論是

從肉體或心智的觀點來看。憎恨的懲罰是孤獨、無法控制的暴戾之氣、突發性心智失控及歇斯底里的情況。過度自省的疾病－神經炎、神經衰弱及類似的症狀－會掠奪生活中諸多樂趣，是極度自私所引起的。無知及缺乏智慧會讓自己在日常生活中陷入困境。此外，若機會來臨時，卻一再地拒絕看清真相，近視、視力及聽力損壞將是必然的結果。意志不堅，會在身體上導致類似各種影響行動及協調的失調狀況。貪婪及對他人索求無度的結果，將使自己的身體擺脫不了某些習慣，而慾望與企圖心將因疾病而受抑制。

We can now see how any type of illness from which we may suffer will guide us to the discovery of the fault which lies behind our affliction. For example, Pride, which is arrogance and rigidity of mind, will give rise to those diseases which produce rigidity and stiffness of the body. Pain is the result of cruelty, whereby the patient learns through personal suffering not to inflict it upon others, either from a physical or from a mental standpoint. The penalties of Hate are loneliness, violent uncontrollable temper, mental nerve storms and conditions of hysteria. The diseases of introspection - neurosis, neurasthenia and similar conditions - which rob life of so much enjoyment, are caused by excessive Self-love. Ignorance and lack of wisdom bring their own difficulties in everyday life, and in addition should there be a persistence in refusing to see truth when the opportunity has been given, short-sightedness and impairment of vision and hearing are the natural consequences. Instability of mind must lead to the same quality in the body with those various disorders which affect movement and co-ordination. The result of greed and domination of others is such diseases as will render the sufferer a slave to his own body, with desires and ambitions curbed by the malady.

此外，受疾病侵襲的身體部位絕非偶然，只不過是依循因果定律的法則，且再一次地成為協助我們的指引。例如：心臟，是生命的泉源，因此也是愛的泉源，當掌管人類愛的天性的面相未被開展或被誤用時，

就會受到侵襲；手部的病症，意謂著行動上的失敗或錯誤；如果作為控制中心的大腦受病痛折磨，則象徵著缺乏自我控制的能力。我們必須遵循這些既定的法則。我們不得不承認，在大發雷霆或聽聞惡耗受到驚嚇之後所伴隨而來的許多後果；如果平常這些瑣事都將對身體造成影響，那麼可以想見的是，靈魂與身體之間長久以來的衝突，不就更加地嚴重與根深蒂固；我們還會對如此結果所造成的嚴重不適，也就是我們今天所面對的這些疾病而感到訝異嗎？

Moreover, the very part of the body affected is no accident, but is in accordance with the law of cause and effect, and again will be a guide to help us. For example, the heart, the fountain of life and hence of love, is attacked when especially the love side of the nature towards humanity is not developed or is wrongly used; a hand affected denotes failure or wrong in action; the brain being the centre of control, if afflicted, indicates lack of control in the personality. Such must follow as the law lays down. We are all ready to admit the many results which may follow a fit of violent temper, the shock of sudden bad news; if trivial affairs can thus affect the body, how much more serious and deep-rooted must be a prolonged conflict between soul and body. Can we wonder that the result gives rise to such grievous complaints as the diseases amongst us today?

然而，我們也沒有沮喪的必要。疾病的預防與治療，可以經由找出自身的錯誤，以及真心誠意地培養美德來根除錯誤，進而加以摧毀；不是去對抗錯誤，而是要引進其相對美德的洪流，將錯誤自我們的天性中移除。

But yet there is no cause for depression. The prevention and cure of disease can be found by discovering the wrong within ourselves and eradicating this fault by the earnest development of the virtue which will destroy it; not by fighting the wrong, but by bringing in such a flood of its opposing virtue that it will be swept from our natures.

◎第三章　重點摘錄

疾病的產生－違反了「一致性」和「神性大愛」

　　巴赫醫師說：「疾病的產生，主要是因為人類犯了兩個主要錯誤：一是無法依照靈魂的指揮、違背靈魂的指引，另一則是違反神聖愛的定律跟宇宙整體的一致性。」然而追根究底，違背靈魂的指示在本質上仍是違反一致性的行為。所以我們可以說，所有疾病的根本原因，就是「違反一致性」。

　　我們常說一切的答案都是愛，而這個愛的本源來自於造物主。所以花精要能發揮最佳效果，就是要讓我們的大愛能透過花精協助而展現出來，然後經由一致性原則，將這個神性大愛回歸到我們最終的本源，再經過愛的本源使愛再度回饋到我們身上，如此我們才能獲得真正的療癒。我們不可以只是獨善其身，還必須要兼善天下，所以巴赫醫師在第一段即強調：「我們衍生出許多類型的苦惱，重點是這些苦惱皆違背了一致性行為，亦即自私自利、自私自愛。」

　　我們同樣來自於一個共同的本體、共同的造物主，而這個本體的中心就是愛，所以當你的行為與這個本體相違背時，就是破壞一致性、破壞了這個愛的中心。那麼，什麼才是符合一致性的行為呢？就是要自愛愛人，巴赫醫師並沒指出哪些行為才符合愛，但是他告訴我們，如果沒有犯了以下幾個主要錯誤，就不會違反一致性，那就是符合愛的行為。此外，巴赫醫師也沒有對愛提出太多解釋，他只說哪些行為不是愛；而當你將這些錯誤行為去除後，愛就產生了。

七個主要錯誤

　　第三段開始，巴赫醫師提出七個人類的主要疾病，也就是七個主要錯誤。而在之後幾段中，他其實都提供了一個對應於這些錯誤的救贖途徑，就在每一段的最後一句話！

　　巴赫醫師後來發現的三十八種花精，都可對應到這裡所提出的七項錯誤行為；它們的負向情緒和行為表現，其實都是違反了一致性以及神性大愛的原則：

- 驕傲：馬鞭草、葡萄藤、菊苣、山毛櫸、岩水、
  　　　水堇與鳳仙。
- 殘酷：馬鞭草、葡萄藤、菊苣、岩水（對自己殘酷）、
  　　　山毛櫸以及冬青。
- 恨：冬青、楊柳。
- 自私自利：菊苣、石楠、水堇。
- 無知：紫金蓮（水蕨）、栗樹芽苞、角樹、落葉松、
  　　　荊豆、龍膽草、野玫瑰、鐵線蓮、忍冬。
- 猶豫不決：「恐懼」及「懷疑」的花精族群都會有
  　　　　　猶豫不決的行為。
- 貪婪：菊苣、岩水、葡萄藤、馬鞭草、山毛櫸。

　　第三章最後四段，以例證的方式舉出，犯下錯誤會引發的生理疾病。「這些都是真正疾病的例證，我們的苦難及不幸的根源。如果所有這些缺點一再因違背高層自我的聲音而存在，將會造成衝突，並在生理上產生必然的反應，形成

其自身特定的疾病型態。」從上面這句話看來，巴赫醫師似乎把負面情緒和身體疾病做了連結，再次以另一種說法來說明，負面情緒是所有疾病產生的原因，是靈魂與心智失衡造成的結果；但是在這個部分，巴赫中心曾提出說明，認為巴赫醫師後來將這些觀點全部都捨棄推翻了，因為他認為花精療法必須忽略掉所有的生理症狀與反應。而我們也發現，同一種負面情緒可能在身體不同部位產生不同的生理病徵，而傳統醫學上所說的同一種疾病，其背後的負面情緒糾結可能非常多樣化，並且比想像中還要複雜。

自我療癒這本書，其實就是巴赫醫師反覆以不同方式，用不同語彙在講同樣的一件事。

第 4 章
Chapter Four

> 最終而完整的療癒
> 終究是要來自於內在　來自於靈魂本身
> 只要願意
> 就能因著祂的仁慈
> 讓人格散發出全然和諧的光芒

　　於是我們發現，不論意外事故的類型或是身體受侵襲的部位為何，其本質上不應被視為疾病；疾病和其他能量的結果一樣，也是依循著因果定律的法則而運作。某些疾病可能因直接的身體傷害而引發，例如與毒物、意外和外傷以及暴行有關；但一般來說，疾病是因我們體質上的某些基本錯誤而造成，誠如先前所舉的例子。

So we find that there is nothing of the nature of accident as regards disease, either in its type or in that part of the body which is affected; like all other results of energy it follows the law of cause and effect. Certain maladies may be caused by direct physical means, such as those associated with some poisons, accidents and injuries, and gross excesses; but disease in general is due to some basic error in our constitution, as in the examples already given.

　　因此，要獲得完整的治療，不僅需採用物質的方法；而且一定要選用療癒藝術中最為人所知的最佳方法；但我們自己也必須竭盡所能地付諸心力去移除天性中的缺點；因為最終且最完整的療癒，終究要來自內在，來自靈魂本身，只要願意，就能因著祂的仁慈，讓人格散發出全然和諧的光茫。

And thus for a complete cure not only must physical means be used, choosing always the best methods which are known to the art of healing, but we ourselves must also endeavour to the utmost of our ability to remove any fault in our nature; because final and complete healing ultimately comes from within, from the Soul itself, which by His beneficence radiates harmony throughout the personality, when allowed to do so.

就因所有疾病都肇因於一個最主要的根源，也就是自私自利，那麼要脫離所有苦難的不二法門－就是將自私自利轉變成對他人的奉獻。只要我們不斷為周遭的人付出愛與關懷，並從中充分地發展出犧牲自我的本質，沈浸在那獲得知識與幫助他人的壯麗冒險中，我們個人的悲傷及苦難將立即結束。這偉大的終極目標就是：在服務人群中放棄自身利益。我們的神性到底要把我們放在人生中的那一站，這並不重要。不管是從商或成為專業人士、富有或貧窮、是修士或乞丐，大家都能夠在完成各自天職的同時，透過傳遞同胞之間的神聖大愛，而成為週遭的人名符其實的恩賜。

As there is one great root cause of all disease, namely self-love, so there is one great certain method of relief of all suffering, the conversion of self-love into devotion to others. If we but sufficiently develop the quality of losing ourselves in the love and care of those around us, enjoying the glorious adventure of gaining knowledge and helping others, our personal griefs and sufferings rapidly come to an end. It is the great ultimate aim: the losing of our own interests in the service of humanity. It matters not the station in life in which our Divinity has placed us. Whether engaged in trade or profession, rich or poor, monarch or beggar, for one and all it is possible to carry on the work of their respective vocations and yet be veritable blessings to those around by communicating to them the Divine Love of Brotherhood.

但絕大多數的人，在到達那個完美的境界之前，都還有一段路要走；任何人一旦開始認真地往這個方向努力，他的進步就會神速地令人訝異。倘若他不單只是信任自己那貧乏的人格，而有全然的信念，那麼，依照世上偉大聖賢們的模範與教悔，他就能與自己的靈魂，亦即內在的神性結合，這時一切都變得可能。大多數的人都存在著一個或多個特別阻礙前進的缺點，這就是我們必須從自己的內在去找

出的缺點，然後努力培養天性中愛的一面，並將它擴展到世界，同時竭盡所能地以天性中相對美德的洪流，來洗去那個缺點。起初可能會有些困難，但也只是在剛開始的時候，因為不可思議的是，一個真正受到鼓舞的美德，將會多麼迅速地增長，再與內在神性協助下的知識相連結；只要我們堅持到底，絕不可能失敗。

But the vast majority of us have some way to travel before we can reach this state of perfection, although it is surprising how rapidly any individual may advance along these lines if the effort is seriously made, providing he trusts not in his poor personality alone but has implicit faith, that by the example and teaching of the great masters of the world he may be enabled to unite himself with his own Soul, the Divinity within, when all things become possible. In most of us there is one, or more, adverse defect which is particularly hindering our advancement, and it is such defect, or defects, which we must especially seek out within ourselves, and whilst striving to develop and extend the love side of our nature towards the world, endeavour at the same time to wash away any such defect in particular by the flooding of our nature with the opposing virtue. At first this may be a little difficult, but only just at first, for it is remarkable how rapidly a truly encouraged virtue will increase, linked with the knowledge that with the aid of the Divinity within us, if we but persevere, failure is impossible.

在自身內在宇宙大愛的發展上，我們必須學著更加了解，每個人不論多麼卑微，都是造物者之子，有一天，且在不久的將來，將會提升至我們期望到達的完美境界。任何人或生物，不論多麼卑下，我們必須記住，內在皆存在著神性的靈光，它將慢慢地但也穩當地成長，直到造物者的榮光照耀了那個生命。

In the development of Universal Love within ourselves, we must learn to realise more and more that every human being, however lowly, is a son of the Creator, and that one day and in due time he will advance to perfection just as we all hope to do. However base a man or creature may appear, we must remember that there is the Divine Spark within, which will slowly but surely grow until the glory of the Creator irradiates that being.

　　此外，關於對與錯、善與惡的問題，完全是相對的。對自然演化的原始聚落而言是對的事情，在我們這樣高度理性的文明社會看來就可能是錯的；又對一個已達到靈性修持的人來說是項美德的行為，在我們看來卻是不適當而因此是錯的。我們所謂的錯或惡，事實上只是不在適當位置的善，也因此這完全是相對的。我們要記得，即使是對於理想的標準，也同樣是相對的；對動物來說，我們就像至高的上帝一般，但相較於那些偉大聖賢的精神，以及他們為我們所立下的典範，事實上我們距離那樣的標準還差得遠呢。因此，必須對比我們卑微的生命付出憐憫與同情，就算我們自認為早已從那個階段一路進化過來了，其實我們也不過是那麼地渺小；況且在到達祖先們的標準之前，還有好長一段路要走；他們的榮光在每個時代裡遍照著世界。

Moreover, the question of right or wrong, of good and evil, is purely relative. That which is right in the natural evolution of the aboriginal would be wrong for the more enlightened of our civilisation, and that which might even be a virtue in such as ourselves might be out of place, and hence wrong, in one who has reached the stage of discipleship. What we call wrong or evil is in reality good out of place, and hence is purely relative. Let us remember also that our standard of idealism again is relative; to the animals we must appear as veritable gods, whereas we in ourselves are very far below the standards of the great White Brotherhood of Saints and Martyrs who have given their all to be examples to us. Hence we must have compassion and sympathy for the lowliest, for whilst we may consider ourselves as having advanced far above their level, we are in ourselves minute indeed, and have yet a long journey before us to reach the standard of our older brothers, whose light shines throughout the world in every age.

當驕傲襲來，讓我們試著了解，我們的人格是卑微的，無法作出什麼了不起的工作或令人滿意的貢獻，也沒有能力阻擋黑暗力量，除非藉助來自上層的光 — 我們靈魂的榮光；盡力去領會和窺見造物者那全能而不可思議的力量，祂以一滴水造就了世界，並建構了宇宙系統中的系統；也試著去領會我們所欠缺的相對謙卑，以及對祂的絕對依賴。我們學會向人類的上師致敬並給予尊重；然而，在偉大的宇宙創造者面前，更是要以最謙卑的心去認知到自己的脆弱。

If Pride assails us, let us try to realise that our personalities are in themselves as nothing, unable to do any good work or acceptable service, or to resist the powers of darkness, unless assisted by that Light which is from above, the Light of our Soul; endeavour to comprehend a glimpse of the omnipotence and unthinkable mightiness of our Creator, Who makes in all perfection a world in one drop of water and systems upon systems of universes, and try to realise the relative humility we owe and our utter dependence upon Him. We learn to pay homage and give respect to our human superiors; how infinitely more should we acknowledge our own frailty with utmost humility before the Great Architect of the Universe!

當殘酷或恨阻礙了進步的路，讓我們記住，愛是宇宙萬物的基礎，在每個生命體中都存在著些許良善，而絕大多數的人也存在著些許惡念。透過尋求彼此間的良善，即便是那些曾經傷害過我們的人，至少也能讓我們學到發展一些同情心，並希望他們能發現更適當的方式，那麼便自然而燃起協助自我提升的渴望。最終的勝利，將是透過愛與和善來獲得；當我們充分地發展了這項兩樣特質之後，就沒有任何事能擊倒我們，因為我們將充滿了愛心，不再企圖抵抗，然而這也是依循著相同的因果定律法則- 抵抗會造成損害。我們人生的目的，是要遵照高層自我的指示，不因他人的影響而有所阻礙。這只能經由和緩的方式前進而達到，但同時絕不能去干預任何人，

或者以殘酷或恨的手段，去造成任何一點傷害。我們必須努力學習對他人的愛，也許從一個對象或一隻動物開始，然後讓這個愛發展，並擴展到更寬更廣的範圍，直到所有相對的缺點自動消失為止。愛衍生愛，如同恨衍生恨。

If Cruelty, or Hate, bar our way to progress, let us remember that Love is the foundation of Creation, that in every living soul there is some good, and that in the best of us there is some bad. By seeking the good in others, even in those who at first offend us, we shall learn to develop, if nothing more, some sympathy and a hope that they will see better ways, then it follows that the desire will arise to help them to that uplift. The ultimate conquest of all will be through love and gentleness, and when we have sufficiently developed these two qualities nothing will be able to assail us, since we shall ever have compassion and not offer resistance; for again by the same law of cause and effect it is resistance which damages. Our object in life is to follow the dictates of our Higher Self, undeterred by the influence of others, and this can only be achieved if we gently go our own way, but at the same time never interfere with the personality of another or cause the least harm by any method of cruelty or hate. We must strive to learn love of others, beginning perhaps with one individual or even an animal, and let this love develop and extend over a wider and wider range, until its opposing defects will automatically disappear. Love begets Love, as Hate does Hate.

要有效治療自私自利，是將投注於自我的關心與注意轉而付出予他人，逐漸專注於對他人的福祉上，直到我們在那樣的奉獻中忘記了自己。誠如四海內兄弟情誼的名言中所闡述的：「只有在同伴苦惱的時刻給予救助與安慰，自身的苦難才得以找到慰藉！」。因此，治療自私自利以及隨之而來的失序，沒有比這個還要牢靠的方法了。

The cure of self-love is effected by the turning outwards to others of the care and attention which we are devoting to ourselves, becoming so engrossed in their welfare that we forget ourselves in that endeavour. As one great order of Brotherhood expresses it, "to seek the solace of own distress by extending relief and consolation to our fellow creatures in the hour of their affliction," and there is no surer way of curing self-love and the disorders which follow it than by such a method.

建立自主自決可以改善意志不堅的情況，下定決心，並且以果決的態度處理事情，而不是猶豫跟徬徨。儘管一開始我們有時會犯錯，但為了獲得決心，付諸行動總比讓機會流失要來得好。決心很快會增長；對於投入生活所感到的恐懼將會消失，而從中獲得的經驗，將引導我們的心去作出更好的判斷。

Instability can be eradicated by the development of self-determination, by making up the mind and doing things with definiteness instead of wavering and hovering. Even if at first we may sometimes make errors, it were better to act than to let opportunities pass for the want of decision. Determination will soon grow; fear of plunging into life will disappear, and the experiences gained will guide our mind to better judgement.

要根除無知，而再一次地，讓我們不要對經驗感到害怕，但一定要保持頭腦清醒，張大眼睛和耳朵，去吸取在所有的事物中可能獲得的知識。同時保有活絡的思緒，以免先入為主的觀念及過往的成見，剝奪了增廣見聞的機會。我們應該隨時樂意去拓展心智，並摒除任何成見。不論它是如何地牢固根植，一個真正偉大的真理，自然會在更廣泛的經驗下不證自明。

To eradicate Ignorance, again let us not be afraid of experience, but with mind awake and with eyes and ears wide open take in every particle of knowledge which may be obtained. At the same time we must keep flexible in thought, lest preconceived ideas and former convictions rob us of the opportunity of gaining fresh and wider knowledge. We should be ever ready to expand the mind and to disregard any idea, however firmly rooted, if under wider experience a greater truth shows itself.

　　貪婪跟驕傲一樣，對我們的進步造成極大的阻礙，兩者都必須硬下心腸加以掃除。貪婪的結果是相當嚴重的，因為那會導致我們去阻礙他人靈魂的進化。我們必須知道，所有的生命來到這裡，是要依循個人靈魂的指示，去發展自身的進化，而也只能依循其靈魂本身。其他人所能做的，是在其他弟兄們的發展上不斷地給予鼓勵。我們必須協助他抱持希望，如果能力所及，還要增長他的見識，並給予他世俗的機會去得到進步。就如同希望他人協助我們越過生命中崎嶇的山路一般，讓我們隨時願意伸出援手，並將增廣見聞的經驗提供給比我們弱小的弟兄們。這樣的態度，包括父母對孩子、主人對僕人或同事對同事之間的關係，儘可能地依他們的需要與利益，去付出關懷、愛與保護。但絕不能在任何時刻，對他人天性的發展有所干涉。因為，這必須是來自靈魂的指示。

Like Pride, Greed is a great obstacle to advancement, and both of these must be ruthlessly washed away. The results of Greed are serious indeed, because it leads us to interfere with the soul development of our fellow-men. We must realise that every being is here to develop his own evolution according to the dictates of his Soul, and his Soul alone, and that none of us must do anything but encourage our brother in that development. We must help him to hope and, if in our power, increase his knowledge and worldly opportunities to gain his advancement. Just as we would wish others to help us up the steep and difficult mountain path of life so let us be ever ready to lend a helping hand and give the experience of our wider knowledge to a weaker or younger brother. Such should be the attitude of parent to child, master to man or comrade to comrade, giving care, love and protection as far as may be needed and beneficial, yet never for one moment interfering with the natural evolution of the personality, as this must be dictated by the Soul.

　　我們許多人在孩童時期或生命的早期，都比長大後更接近自己的靈魂。在那個階段，我們對於在生命中要做的事，也有較明顯的概念。

像是我們所期待要付出的努力，以及我們需要發展的性格。之所以會這樣，是因為我們這個時代裡的唯物主義與環境，以及我們所交往的人，都逐漸把我們拉離我們高層自我的聲音，並將我們牢牢地捆綁在缺乏創意的平凡之中，這種情形在社會文明中隨處可見。請為人父母、為人上司以及為人同事者 — 這些都是擁有絕佳權力及動用其影響力機會的人們，一定要不斷努力鼓勵他人去增長高層自我。但請務必要給予別人自由，就如同自己也希望被賦予自由一樣。

Many of us in our childhood and early life are much nearer to our own Soul than we are in later years, and have then clearer ideas of our work in life, the endeavours we are expected to make and the character we are required to develop. The reason for this is that the materialism and circumstances of our age, and the personalities with whom we associate, lead us away from the voice of our Higher Self and bind us firmly to the commonplace with its lack of ideals, all too evident in this civilisation. Let the parent, the master and the comrade ever strive to encourage the growth of the Higher Self within those over whom they have the wonderful privilege and opportunity to exert their influence, but let them ever allow freedom to others, as they hope to have freedom given to them.

所以我們可以用類似的方法，去找出自身內在的錯誤，然後透過發展相對的美德來將錯誤掃除。這樣就能將造成人格與靈魂之間衝突的原因，也就是造成疾病的主要根源，自我們的天性中移除。病患若能抱持信念與毅力，僅僅這個行動的本身，就能帶來慰藉、健康與喜樂，至於意志不夠堅定的病患，這樣的作為，也將對世俗醫師們的工作產生實質的幫助，進而得到相同的效果。

So in a similar way may we seek out any faults in our constitution and wash them out by developing the opposing virtue, thus removing from our nature the cause of the conflict between Soul and personality, which is the primary basic cause of disease. Such action alone, if the patient has faith and strength, will bring relief, health and joy, and in those not so strong will materially assist the work of the earthly physician in bringing about the same result.

　　我們必須依照靈魂的指示，誠摯地學習發展自我，不懼怕任何人，並且了解到，沒有人可以干涉或勸阻我們對於自身進化的發展、任務的完成，以及對同伴的協助。切記，愈是進步，就愈能成為周圍人們的恩賜。在給予他人協助時，不論對象是誰，都要特別留意，要確認這個助人的渴望，是來自於內在自我的指示，而不是受另一個強勢者的建議或勸說而造成的錯誤判斷。這是現代社會規範下所衍生的悲劇性結果之一，那成千上萬受阻的生命、無以數計錯失了的機會，與因之而來的悲傷與磨難，實在難以估計。無數的子女基於責任感，多年來都可能必須照顧病弱的父母，而這些父母唯一的疾病，其實只是貪戀於被照顧。想想那些成群的男人女人們，他們的人格被另一個人所箝制，但卻也沒有勇氣向對方爭取自由，更阻礙了去從事對人類而言可能是重大而有意義的工作；孩童在年幼時便知道並渴望命運的召喚，然而因為環境艱困、被他人勸阻而削弱了意志，便漸漸地流失在其他的人生支脈中。在那裡，他們既不快樂，也無法發展原本可以達到的個人進化。只有良知的指引能夠告訴我們，自己的責任到底在哪裡、有哪些，我們又應該為哪些人服務；然而不論答案是什麼，都應該盡力去聽從那個指示。

We must earnestly learn to develop individuality according to the dictates of our own Soul, to fear no man and to see that no one interferes with, or dissuades us from, the development of our evolution, the fulfilment of our duty and the rendering of help to our fellow-men, remembering that the further we advance, the greater blessing we become to those around. Especially must we be on guard in the giving of help to other people, no matter whom they are, to be certain that the desire to help comes from the dictates of the Inner Self and is not a false sense of duty imposed by the suggestion or persuasion of a more dominant personality. One tragedy resulting from modern convention is of such a type, and it is impossible to calculate the thousands of hindered lives, the myriads of missed opportunities, the sorrow and the suffering so caused, the countless number of children who from a sense of duty have perhaps for years waited upon an invalid parent when the only malady the parent has known has been greed of attention. Think of the armies of men and women who have been prevented from doing perhaps some great and useful work for humanity because their personality has been captured by some one individual from whom they have not had the courage to win freedom; the children who in their early days know and desire their ordained calling, and yet from difficulties of circumstance, dissuasion by others and weakness of purpose glide into some other branch of life, where they are neither happy nor able to develop their evolution as they might otherwise have done. It is the dictates of our conscience alone which can tell us whether our duty lies with one or many, how and whom we should serve; but whichever it may be, we should obey that command to the utmost of our ability.

最後，讓我們毫不畏懼地投入生活；我們是來獲得經驗與知識的，除非能面對現實，並竭盡所能地向內在探求，否則能學到的也是有限。這樣的經驗可以在任何地方獲得，即使在鄉間小屋，也能夠像在喧擾的都市裡一樣，實際地獲得大自然及人性的真理，也許還更好。

Finally, let us not fear to plunge into life; we are here to gain experience and knowledge, and we shall learn but little unless we face realities and seek to our utmost. Such experience can be gained in every quarter, and the truths of nature and of humanity can be won just as effectively, perhaps even more so, in a country cottage as amongst the noise and hustle of a city.

◎第四章　重點摘錄

　　有許多人會問，意外災難所造成的身體病症，難道也跟負面心理情緒有關嗎？花精對於這些病症有效嗎？巴赫醫師在第一段就提出了關於意外的問題，他說意外造成的身體損傷，和他在本書中所要談論的－因人格與靈魂衝突所造成的疾病是不同的，這也就是為什麼他會說：「意外的本質不能被視為疾病。」因為他所主張的自我療癒的觀點，要關照的是我們人格與靈魂失衡的部分，這才是一般人所謂的疾病，因此在一開始就先提出來做釐清，以免混淆。不過確實很多因意外而造成的身體損傷，在使用過花精之後，達到很好的調理效果。

個人的意願－自我療癒的主要關鍵

　　在本章裡，巴赫醫師提出獲得療癒的主要關鍵，就在於個人的意願和主動性，而最終的療癒都是來自於我們的內在。先前已經討論過關於花精的效用何時能夠發揮最大功效，那就是當病人自己有病識感，並且願意而主動得到療癒的時候，所以，巴赫醫師在書中一再重複告訴大家：「當你應許時…」、「只要我們願意…」等等。

「愛」能量的流動

　　當我們對別人付出了愛之後，透過宇宙整體的一致性，得到最多愛的回饋也是自己，這就是一種愛的流動。事實上，許多負面情緒的產生，是因為在愛的流動上出現問題，比如菊苣、水堇，而每一種花精人格的負面情緒失衡，追根

究底都出在自私自利的問題上，致使愛的能量無法流動，因而產生了疾病。我們可以用佛教哲理來加以說明：大乘佛教要人往菩薩道的境界去追求，才得以終結悲傷與磨難；也就是說，最終疾病要真正獲得療癒，其實是要把我們的愛傳播出去，透過整體的一致性，愛的能量不斷回饋，愛的氛圍會越來越廣，讓我們沐浴在療癒的大愛能量之中。

這也就是為什麼佛教徒剛開始是走在小乘佛教追求個人修為的羅漢道，但最終仍要走上大乘佛教的菩薩道去為人群服務。同樣地，巴赫醫師自我療癒的觀點，首先要能把自己的身心修養好，然後才將大愛傳播出去，引導和協助他人走向療癒之路，這也是他一再在自我療癒中提到的—「四海之內皆兄弟的情誼」。

從內在去尋找—自我療能的啟動

巴赫醫師在這一章第四段中提到：要從內在去找出阻礙我們進步的缺點，然後努力培養相對的美德，就能把缺點從天性中完全根除。而其中這一段話：「起初可能會有些困難，但也只是在剛開始的時候，因為不可思議的是，一個真正受到鼓勵的美德，將會多麼迅速地發展，而再與內在神性協助下的知識相連結，只要我們堅持到底，絕不可能失敗。」

這段話非常重要，初用花精的人，一開始要踏出這一步，其實是很困難的。有一種人是想用花精但不相信它，所以踏不出去；另一種人是願意相信，可是花精沒效，

於是就不用了。為什麼沒效？因為這一類的人在使用花精時，只把花精當作藥物，沒能領會花精使用真正的精髓，因此無法真正得到花精的協助。要真能得到花精的協助，就要如同巴赫醫師所說的，要向內心去探求，這時內在的療癒系統才能真正啟動，也是一個真正的修行過程。許多人學了花精，會一直想幫助別人，甚至想用花精改造別人，但自己卻不願意使用。或許要看清自己的問題確實是最困難的，但巴赫醫師重視自我療癒，凡事都得要先治療自己，然後再去治療別人；這一點相當困難，但也最重要。

有些人會對花精卡的使用存疑，但在使用花精初期，這也是可以找出內在問題的工具，它能協助我們達到內省的功夫，大多數的人在沒有任何具體工具的協助下，比較難以立刻做到內觀自省這一步。

善惡、對錯的問題

一直以來，我們受到社會價值觀引導，而建立起是非價值的概念。正如巴赫醫師所強調的，我們自以為是好的事，會因不同時空、不同文化而有所差異，甚至可能是錯的；從整個宇宙時空來看，我們是如此渺小，所以不應該看不起較低等或卑微的生命。我們所要發展的慈悲心，也是要從這些地方著手，因為我們也曾如此地卑微，所以對於還未進化到同等階段的生物，都要給予憐憫心，因為我們的全部只是這漫漫長河中的一環而已。

第 5 章
Chapter Five

缺乏自主性

與疾病的產生有著極重要的關係

而這經常發生在人生初期

自由的取得

亦即贏得個人的獨立與自主

大多需要很大的勇氣與信心

　　正因為缺乏自主性（亦即允許人格被干預，這樣的干預會阻礙其遵從高層自我的指示）與疾病的產生有著極重要的關係，而這經常發生在人生初期；現在讓我們來仔細思考一下，父母與孩子以及教師與學生之間真正的關係。

As lack of individuality (that is, the allowing of interference with the personality, such interference preventing it from complying with the demands of the Higher Self) is of such great importance in the production of disease, and as it often begins early in life, let us now consider the true relation between parent and child, teacher and pupil.

　　基本上，父母的職責，是經由行使這個權力的方式（當然，它應該被視為一個神賜的特權），讓一個靈魂基於進化的緣故，而得以和這個世界有所聯繫。如能正確理解，人類世界大概沒有任何一個被賦予的機會能像它一樣偉大，就是作為靈魂其物質性誕生的媒介，以及讓這個年輕的生命，在人世間的最初幾年當中獲得照料。整個親職的態度，應該盡其所能地提供這個新到來的小訪客，所有靈性、心智及物質上的引導，並要時時謹記，這個小小的個體，是一個特有的靈魂，來到這裡，是因他自身高層自我的指示，並用這個方式來獲得經驗與知識，所以要給予他最大的自由，好讓他能毫無阻礙地發展。

Fundamentally, the office of parenthood is to be the privileged means (and, indeed, it should be considered as divinely privileged) of enabling a soul to contact this world for the sake of evolution. If properly understood, there is probably no greater opportunity offered to mankind than this, to be the agent of the physical birth of a soul and to have the care of the young personality during the first few years of its existence on earth. The whole attitude of parents should be to give the little newcomer all the spiritual, mental and physical guidance to the utmost of their ability, ever remembering that the wee one is an individual soul come down to gain his own experience and knowledge in this own way according to the dictates of his Higher Self, and every possible freedom should be given for unhampered development.

父母的職責是項神聖的義務，應該像任何其他被要求去承擔的義務一般受到重視，甚至更加尊重。就因為它是一種犧牲，所以要打從心裡去認知，絕不可以向子女要求任何回報，其主要的目的是付出，而且只有付出奉獻、慈愛、保護以及引導，直到他的靈魂接管了這個年輕的生命為止。在孩子的生命當中，一開始就應該要教導自主、獨立和自由，越早鼓勵他們以自己的方式表現言行舉止越好。父母應該要逐步交出支配權，因為孩子自我管理的能力會發展，且之後也不得以任何約束，或對父母的責任之謬論為由，去阻礙孩子靈魂的指揮。

The office of parenthood is one of divine service, and should be respected as much as, or perhaps even more than, any other duty we may be called upon to undertake. As it is one of sacrifice, it must ever be borne in mind that nothing whatever should be required in return from the child, the whole object being to give, and give alone, gentle love, protection and guidance until the soul takes charge of the young personality. Independence, individuality and freedom should be taught from the beginning, and the child should be encouraged as early as possible in life to think and act for himself. All parental control should be relinquished step by step as the ability for self-management is developed, and later on no restraint or false idea of duty to parenthood should hamper the dictates of the child' s soul.

　　為人父母是生命中一代傳一代的職務，本質上是在短期間內付出暫時的引導與保護，時間一到就要停止這些作為，讓他們自由發展。一定要記得，不論我們成為哪個孩子暫時的守護者，他們的靈魂都可能比我們的靈魂還要古老且偉大，在靈性上是前輩，所以支配與保護應該僅限於這個年輕生命的需求範圍內。

　　Parenthood is an office in life which passes from one to another, and is in essence a temporary giving of guidance and protection for a brief period, after which time it should then cease its efforts and leave the object of its attention free to advance alone. Be it remembered that the child for whom we may become a temporary guardian may be a much older and greater soul than ourselves, and spiritually our superior, so that control and protection should be confined to the needs of the young personality.

　　父母的職責是神聖的使命，是個暫時且代代相傳的角色。本質上除了奉獻之外別無其他，更不能要求子女回報，因為他們應該要以自己的方式去自由發展，且在日後儘可能恰如其分地去完成相同的任務。因此，孩子不應被限制、沒有義務且不應受父母的阻撓，要知道先前父母所被賦予的親職義務，同樣也可能是自己要向別人履行的任務。

　　Parenthood is a sacred duty, temporary in its character and passing from generation to generation. It carries with it nothing but service and calls for no obligation in return from the young, since they must be left free to develop in their own way and become as fitted as possible to fulfil the same office in but a few years' time. Thus the child should have no restrictions, no obligations and no parental hindrances, knowing that parenthood had previously been bestowed on his father and mother and that it may be his duty to perform the same office for another.

父母們應該要特別留意自身的慾望，不要以任何自己的觀念或期望，去影響年輕的生命，更應避免因個人的喜好，而有任何過分的控制或指使，因為作為父母這項天性義務與神聖殊榮，是協助靈魂與世界接觸的媒介。任何想要控制的慾望，或基於個人的動機，而想要去影響年輕的生命，都是極度貪婪的形式，永遠都不該被鼓勵，因為那會根植在這些即將為人父母者的心目中，並使他們在將來變成名符其實的吸血鬼。只要有一絲想要支配的慾望，就應該從源頭加以檢視。我們一定要拒絕被貪婪所奴役，它會迫使我們升起掌控他人的慾望。我們必須激發自己內在奉獻的藝術，並不斷地加強，直到以犧牲奉獻來洗去我們所有負面行為的蹤跡。

Parents should be particularly on guard against any desire to mould the young personality according to their own ideas or wishes, and should refrain from any undue control or demand of favours in return for their natural duty and divine privilege of being the means of helping a soul to contact the world. Any desire for control, or wish to shape the young life for personal motives, is a terrible form of greed and should never be countenanced, for if in the young father or mother this takes root it will in later years lead them to be veritable vampires. If there is the least desire to dominate, it should be checked at the onset. We must refuse to be under the slavery of greed, which compels in us the wish to possess others. We must encourage in ourselves the art of giving, and develop this until it has washed out by its sacrifice every trace of adverse action.

身為教師要銘記在心的是，他的職責僅在於給予年輕人指引，並且成為給予年輕人學習有關世界與人生事物機會的媒介，如此每個孩子便能以自己的方式去吸收知識；如果給予自由，他就能用直覺選出成就人生所需的事物。那麼同樣地，要讓學生能夠獲得所需的知識，只要付出真心與引領他們就可以了。

The teacher should ever bear in mind that it is his office merely to be the agent of giving to the young guidance and an opportunity of learning the things of the world and of life, so that each child may absorb knowledge in his own way and, if allowed freedom, instinctively choose that which is necessary for the success of his life. Again, therefore, nothing more than the gentlest care and guidance should be given to enable the student to gain the knowledge he requires.

孩子應該記住一件事：父母的職責，是創造大能的象徵，其使命是神聖的，但不表示可以在任何發展上有所限制，也不應基於義務而迫使他們在靈魂指揮下的生活及工作受到阻礙。那些在當今文明社會中無數的磨難、受羈絆的天性及逐漸形成的強勢性格，實在難以估計，這都是因為缺乏覺知而衍生的事實。幾乎所有家庭中的父母與孩子，都因全然錯誤的動機及錯誤的親子觀念，而將彼此監禁起來。這樣的禁錮阻擋了自由、羈絆了生活、阻礙了天性發展，並在各方面帶來痛苦，而讓這些人深陷心理、神經甚至身體失調的折磨，當然這就是這個時代的疾病了。

Children should remember that the office of parenthood, as emblematical of creative power, is divine in its mission, but that it calls for no restriction of development and no obligations which might hamper the life and work dictated to them by their own Soul. It is impossible to estimate in this present civilisation the untold suffering, the cramping of natures and the developing of dominant characters which the lack of a realisation of this fact produces. In almost every home parents and children build themselves prisons from entirely false motives and a wrong conception of the relationship of parent and child. These prisons bar the freedom, cramp the life, prevent the natural development and bring unhappiness to all concerned, and the mental, nervous and even physical disorders which afflict such people from a very large proportion indeed of the sickness of our present time.

　　我們多數人並沒有很確切地了解到，每個靈魂化身來到這個世上，主要目的是為了獲得經驗與認知，同時依照靈魂為他鋪設的理想典範，讓人格更臻完美。不論我們彼此之間的關係是什麼，夫妻、親子、兄妹或師徒，如果因一己之私而妨礙了他人靈魂的進化，就是違反造物者以及父兄的罪行。我們唯一的任務就是去遵循自身良知的指引，而這一點都不容許另一個人的支配。請大家記住，每個人的靈魂都為自己安排了獨特的工作，如果沒有完成，縱然是不自覺的，亦將無可避免地造成靈魂與人格之間的衝突，也必然會以生理失衡的形式反應出來。

　　It cannot be too firmly realised that every soul in incarnation is down here for the specific purpose of gaining experience and understanding, and of perfecting his personality towards those ideals laid down by the soul. No matter what our relationship be to each other, whether husband and wife, parent and child, brother and sister, or master and man, we sin against our Creator and against our fellow men if we hinder from motives of personal desire the evolution of another soul. Our sole duty is to obey the dictates of our own conscience, and this will never for one moment brook the domination of another personality. Let everyone remember that his Soul has laid down for him a particular work, and that unless he does this work, though perhaps not consciously, he will inevitably raise a conflict between his Soul and personality which of necessity reacts in the form of physical disorders.

　　是的，也許有些人的使命是要為某一個人奉獻自己的生命，但在這麼做之前，請完全確定這是來自他靈魂的指示，而不是被某個強勢者提出的建議過度慫恿，或是被錯誤的責任感所誤導。還必須記住，我們來到這世界，是為了要贏得勝利，是要抵抗控制我們的人以獲得力量，並且要進化到以下的境界：也就是當我們經歷人生時，安靜而平和地完成我們的工作，不受任何生命體的妨礙與影響，永遠沈著地

依循著我們高層自我的聲音。對許多人來說，最大的爭戰將是在自己的家庭中；在戰勝世界獲得個人的自由之前，必須從最親近的親屬們有害的支配與控制中解放自己。

True, it may be the calling of any one individual to devote his life to one other alone, but before doing so let him be absolutely certain that this is the command of his Soul, and that it is not the suggestion of some other dominant personality over-persuading him, or false ideas of duty misdirecting him. Let him also remember that we come down into this world to win battles, to gain strength against those who would control us, and to advance to that stage when to pass through life doing our duty quietly and calmly, undeterred and uninfluenced by any living being, calmly guided always by the voice of our Higher Self. For very many their greatest battle will be in their own home, where before gaining their liberty to win victories in the world they will have to free themselves from the adverse domination and control of some very near relative.

任何人，不管大人還是小孩，對於此生的功課部分，是要從他人的強勢控制中解放自我，而且應該要記住以下的話：首先，要把可能成為壓迫者的人，看做是運動場上競爭的對手，或是一個跟他一起參與人生遊戲的人，不帶一絲痛苦的痕跡；因為如果沒有這些對手，我們將會失去發展勇氣與自我的機會。其次，人生中真正的勝利是來自愛與慈善，而且在這樣的競賽中，絕不可以使用任何形式的暴力；經由在天性中穩定地滋長出憐憫、仁慈以及熱情，如果可以的話，或者，能夠滋長出對敵人的愛的話更好，他可以這樣地成長，時候一到，就能非常溫和、沈靜且不受任何阻礙地去遵循內在良知的召喚。

Any individual, whether adult or child, part of whose work it is in this life to free himself from the dominant control of another, should remember the following: firstly, that his would-be oppressor should be regarded in the same way as we look upon an opponent in sport, as a personality with whom we are playing the game of Life, without the least trace of bitterness, and that if it were not for such opponents we should be lacking the opportunity of developing our own courage and individuality; secondly, that the real victories of life come through love and gentleness, and that in such a contest no force whatever must be used; that by steadily growing in his own nature, bearing sympathy, kindness and, if possible, affection - or, even better, love towards the opponent, he may so develop that in time he may very gently and quietly follow the call of conscience without allowing the least interference.

至於那些具有優勢的人，需要更多協助與引導，使他們明白關於一致性的偉大宇宙真理，以及體會到四海兄弟情誼的喜樂。錯失了這些，等於是錯失了人生中真正的幸福；只要我們能力所及，就要盡力去協助這些人。是我們的軟弱，讓他們得以擴張影響力，而這樣對他們一點幫助也沒有；溫和地拒絕他們的控制，而且努力讓他們領悟到，付出的喜樂，會在他們自我提升的路上提供協助。

Those who are dominant require much help and guidance to enable them to realise the great universal truth of Unity and to understand the joy of Brotherhood. To miss such things is to miss the real happiness of Life, and we must help such folk as far as lies within our power. Weakness on our part, which allows them to extend their influence, will in no way assist them; a gentle refusal to be under their control and an endeavour to bring to them the realisation of the joy of giving will help them along the upward path.

自由的取得，亦即贏得個人的獨立與自主，大多需要很大的勇氣與信心。但在最黑暗的時刻，當成功彷彿遙不可及時，讓我們謹記，上帝的子民應該永不畏懼，我們的靈魂只會給予能力所及的任務；因此，只要我們對內在的神性保有勇氣與信心，勝利必將來到努力不懈的人們面前。

The gaining of our freedom, the winning of our individuality and independence, will in most cases call for much courage and faith. But in the darkest hours, and when success seems well-nigh impossible, let us ever remember that God's children should never be afraid, that our Souls only give us such tasks as we are capable of accomplishing, and that with our own courage and faith in the Divinity within us victory must come to all who continue to strive.

◎第五章　重點摘錄

　　《自我療癒》（Heal Thyself）一書，對於研究花精療法的人來說，或許是一本必須潛心研讀的聖經，而其中的內容和道理，也是巴赫醫師的人生經歷和個人對生命的體會。他體驗到人因缺乏自主性，會將自己和週遭的親友禁錮在互相羈絆的關係之中，而獲得自主性的最大障礙，也經常來自於給我們最大溫暖和支持的家庭之中，這是疾病產生的一大原因，因此巴赫醫師特別強調追尋個人自由的重要性，所以後來又寫了《讓自己自由》（Free Thyself）一書。以下這首紀伯倫的詩，可以完全說明第五章的重點。

　　孩子
　　一個胸前懷抱著乳兒的婦人說，對我們說說孩子吧。
　　於是他說：
　　你的孩子並不是你的。
　　他們是「生命」對他自身的渴慕所生的子女。
　　他們經你而生，卻不是你所造生。
　　雖然他們與你同在，但是並不屬於你。
　　你可以給他們你的愛，卻非你的思想。
　　因為他們擁有自己的思想。

　　你能供給他們身體安居之所，
　　卻不可以藏置他們的靈魂，
　　因為他們的靈魂居住在明日的住所中，
　　而那是非你所能觀覽的地方，甚至不在你的夢中。

你可以奮勉以求與他們相像，
但是不要設法使他們肖似你。
因為生命不能回溯，也不滯戀昨日。

你是弓，而你的孩子好比有生命的箭借你而送向前方。
那射手看到了無限之路上的標靶，
於是用祂的大力來拉彎你，以使祂的箭能射的快且遠。

愉悅地屈服在祂的手中吧！
因為正如祂愛那飛馳的箭，
同樣的祂也愛靜存於掌中的弓。

　　　　　　　　　　　　　—語出紀伯倫《先知》

第 6 章
Chapter Six

生命並未要求我們作出想像不到的犧牲

它要我們帶著滿心的喜悅踏上旅程

並且成為週遭人們的恩賜

因此當我們離開這個世界的時候

就算在這次旅程中

只有一點點的進步

那麼也算是完成工作了

　　現在，親愛的兄弟姐妹們，當我們領悟到愛與一致性是宇宙萬物的偉大基礎，而我們本身因為是神性大愛的子民，因此所有錯誤與磨難的最終戰疫，都將被仁慈與愛所征服；當體悟到這一切之後，我們還能在這樣美麗的畫面中，放上活體解剖及動物腺體移植的種種實驗嗎？我們仍是如此地未開化、如此地異教徒式，且仍相信藉由動物的犧牲，就能逃脫掉因我們自身錯誤及失敗所造成的結果？大約2500 年前，佛陀就已向世人昭示了犧牲低等物種的謬誤。人類已虧欠那些遭我們折磨與殘殺的偉大動物太多太多了，而這樣不人道的行為，不但沒為人類帶來任何好處，反而為人類及動物世界帶來了傷害與損失。我們西方人離那遠古印度母親的完美典範多麼遙遠啊！那時對地球萬物的愛是那麼偉大，人們不僅接受過動物疾病與外傷醫治的精密訓練，更包括了對鳥類的治療。當時更是大量設置容納各式生命型態的庇護所，而且人們對傷害較低等生物的行為非常反感，任何曾經獵殺過動物的人，一旦生病了，連醫生都不願意照護他，除非他誓言不再這樣做。

And now, dear brothers and sisters, when we realise that Love and Unity are the great foundations of our Creation, that we in ourselves are children of the Divine Love, and that the eternal conquest of all wrong and suffering will be accomplished by means of gentleness and love, when we realise all this, where in this beauteous picture are we to place such practices as vivisection and animal gland grafting? Are we still so primitive, so pagan, that we yet believe that by the sacrifice of animals we are enabled to escape the results of our own faults and failings? Nearly 2,500 years ago the

Lord Buddha showed to the world the wrongness of sacrificing the lower creatures. Humanity already owes a mighty debt to the animals which it has tortured and destroyed, and far from any good resulting to man from such inhuman practices, nothing but harm and damage can be wrought to both the human and animal kingdoms. How far have we of the West wandered from those beautiful ideals of our mother India of old times, when so great was the love for the creatures of the earth that men were trained and skilled to attend the maladies and injuries of not only the animals, but also the birds. Moreover, there was vast sanctuaries for all types of life, and so averse were the people to hurting a lower creature that any man who any hunted was refused the attendance of a physician in time of sickness until he had vowed to relinquish such a practice.

我們姑且不要去反對進行活體解剖的人，因為他們許多人是基於真正的人道主義原則下工作，期望及努力為人們尋找解除痛苦的方法，他們的動機是良善的，但智慧卻是貧乏的，而且對生命的意義並沒有太多的了解。不管有多正確，只有動機是不夠的；它必須結合智慧與知識才是。

Let us not speak against the men who practise vivisection, for numbers of these are working with truly humanitarian principles, hoping and striving to find some relief for human suffering; their motive is good enough, but their wisdom is poor, and they have little understanding of the reason of life. Motive alone, however right, is not enough; it must be combined with wisdom and knowledge.

關於使用動物腺體移植的恐怖巫術，我們根本就不必提起了，但懇求每個人將它視為比瘟疫還要可怕千萬倍般地避開它，因為它是違反了神、人與動物的罪過。

Of the horror of the black magic associated with gland-grafting let us not even write, but implore every human being to shun it as ten thousand times worse than any plague, for it is a sin against God, man and animal.

除了少數一兩個例外的情況，實在沒有理由老是停留在現代醫藥科學的貧乏中；破壞是無用的，除非能夠重建雄偉的建築，而在醫學上的新建築基礎已經奠定了，我們只要專心地在那個廟宇上增添一磚一石即可。當今來自同業的負面批評也是沒有意義的，主要的錯誤來自制度本身，而不在人身上；因為這樣的制度讓醫師僅從經濟面來考量，沒有時間進行安靜詳和的治療，或是給予人們機會進行必要的冥想與思考，而這（冥想與思考）應該是那些奉獻自身生命照料病患者的智慧結晶。正如帕拉塞爾蘇斯所言，明智的醫生一天醫治五名病患，而不是十五名－這對時下一般的執業醫師來說，是個不切實際的理想。

With just such one or two exceptions there is no point in dwelling on the failure of modern medical science; destruction is useless unless we rebuild a better edifice, and as in medicine the foundation of the newer building is already laid, let us concentrate on adding one or two stones to that temple. Neither is adverse criticism of the profession today of value; it is the system which is mainly wrong, not the men; for it is a system whereby the physician, from economic reasons alone, has not the time for administering quiet, peaceful treatment or the opportunity for the necessary meditation and thought which should be the heritage of those who devote their lives to attendance on the sick. As Paracelsus said, the wise physician attends five, not fifteen patients in a day – an ideal impracticable in this age for the average practitioner.

一個療癒藝術上嶄新而美好的曙光已經來臨。一百年前哈尼曼的同類療法，猶如劃破漫漫長夜的第一道曙光，對於未來的醫學領域也將扮演著重要的角色。此外，目前對於生命品質的改善，以及提供更純粹而潔淨的飲食控制，是疾病預防的一大進展；而能引領人們注意到心靈失衡與疾病有關，以及能經由心智的完整而獲得療癒的這些行動，正指示了在明亮陽光的照耀之下，疾病所帶來的黑暗將會消失。

The dawn of a new and better art of healing is upon us. A hundred years ago the Homoeopathy of Hahnemann was as the first streak of the morning light after a long night of darkness, and it may play a big part in the medicine of the future. Moreover, the attention which is being given at the present time to improving conditions of life and providing purer and cleaner diet is an advance towards the prevention of sickness; and those movements which are directed to bring to the notice of the people both the connection between spiritual failings and disease and the healing which may be obtained through perfection of the mind, are pointing the way towards the coming of that bright sunshine in whose radiant light the darkness of disease will disappear.

讓我們記得，疾病是共同的敵人，是任何一個人所要征服的部分，這不僅幫助了自己，也幫助了全人類。在我們完全打敗疾病之前，耗費相當的能量是一定要的；讓大家一起來為這個結果奮鬥。至於那些比其他人優秀而堅強的人，不僅要盡自己的一份力量，還要實際地去協助其他較弱勢的弟兄們。

Let us remember that disease is a common enemy, and that everyone of us who conquers a fragment of it is thereby helping not only himself but the whole of humanity. A certain, but definite, amount of energy will have to be expended before its overthrow is complete; let us one and all strive for this result, and those who are greater and stronger than the others may not only do their share, but materially assist their weaker brothers.

顯然地，預防疾病散播及擴大的第一個方法是，讓我們停止做出會使它增強的行為；第二，要掃除我們天性中的缺點，因為它會造成進一步的侵害。這樣的成就絕對是一項勝利；那麼，既然解放了自己，我們就可以自在地去協助他人。而它並不會像一開始時看起來那麼困難，只要盡我們所能去做就好了，而且我們知道，只要能夠聆聽內在靈魂的指示，每個人都可能做到。生命並未要求我們作出想像不到

的犧牲；它要我們帶著滿心的喜悅踏上旅程，並且成為週遭人們的恩賜，因此當我們離開這個世界的時候，就算在這次旅程中，只有那麼一點點的進步，也算是完成工作了。

Obviously the first way to prevent the spread and increase of disease is for us to cease committing those actions which extend its power; the second, to wipe out from our natures our own defects, which would allow further invasion. The achievement of this is victory indeed; then, having freed ourselves, we are free to help others. And it is not so difficult as it may at first appear; we are but expected to do our best, and we know that this is possible for all of us if we will but listen to the dictates of our own Soul. Life does not demand of us unthinkable sacrifice; it asks us to travel its journey with joy in our heart and to be a blessing to those around, so that if we leave the world just that trifle better for our visit, then have we done our work.

若能好好地解讀教義，它懇求我們：「捨棄一切，跟隨我。」意指將自己完全交給高層自我去作主，但這並不像一些人所想像的那樣，要拋棄家庭與安適、愛與樂趣，完全不是這樣的。統御國土的王子，擁有著華麗的宮殿，對他的人民以及他的國家－哦不，甚至對全世界來說，這或許真的是上天給予的賞賜與祝福；如果王子想像自己的職責是要進修道院修行，那他所失去的將何其多。每一個階層的生命任務，從最低下到最高貴，都必須要去完成，而我們生命中的神性指導者，知道什麼位置對我們最好；我們要做的，只是認真地、愉快地去完成那個任務。工廠的板凳上，或船艦上的鍋爐室裡同樣都會有聖人，他們和從事宗教神職人員中的高僧沒兩樣。這世上沒有任何人會被要求去做超出他能力範圍的事，如果我們努力去保有內在最好的一面，永遠聽從高層自我的指引，那麼每個人都能得到健康與喜樂。

The teachings of religions, if properly read, plead with us "to forsake all and follow Me," the interpretation of which is to give ourselves entirely up to the demands of our Higher Self, but not, as some imagine, to discard home and comfort, love and luxury; very far from this is the truth. A prince of the realm, with all the glories of the palace, may be a Godsend and a blessing indeed to his people, to his country - nay, even to the world; how much might have been lost had that prince imagined it his duty to enter a monastery. The offices of life in every branch, from the lowliest to the most exalted, have to be filled, and the Divine Guide of our destinies knows into which office to place us for our best advantage; all we are expected to do is to fulfil that duty cheerfully and well. There are saints at the factory bench and in the stokehold of a ship as well as among the dignitaries of religious orders. Not one of us upon this earth is being asked to do more than is within his power to perform, and if we strive to obtain the best within us, ever guided by our Higher Self, health and happiness is a possibility for each one.

過去這兩千多年來的大部分時間裡，西方文明歷經了極度唯物主義的時代，我們天性中靈性層面與存在的領悟大幅消失了，取而代之的則是財富、野心、慾望及歡愉的心態，超越了生命中真實的事物。人類存在於世上的真義，被急切地只想從肉身得到世俗利益所蒙蔽。而一度因缺乏真正的慰藉、鼓勵及昇華，讓生活變得非常困頓，但這些必須經由對偉大事物的領悟得來，而非來自世俗界。在過去幾個世紀裡，宗教對人們來說，更像是與他們無關的神話，而不是與他們存在的真正本質有關。除了現在的這一生外（物質的慾望），高層自我的真正本質以及前世與來世的知識，對我們來說，一直都不具太大的意義，然而它們反而是所有行為的指引與激勵。我們寧願避開這些偉大的事物，藉由將超自然的部分自心靈中排除，只是讓生活儘可能地安逸，並且依賴世俗的歡愉來補償我們的試煉。因此擁有地位、名聲、財富與世俗的財產，成為這些世紀以來的目標；就因為

這些東西都是無常的，並且只能經由許多的渴望，以及專注在物質事物上去獲得，這就是為什麼，在過去幾個世代裡，真正內在的平靜與喜樂，是遠遠的低於人類本來所應擁有的。

For the greater part of the last two thousand years Western civilisation has passed through an age of intense materialism, and the realization of the spiritual side of our natures and existence has been greatly lost in the attitude of mind which has placed worldly possessions, ambitions, desires and pleasures above the real things of life. The true reason of man's existence on earth has been overshadowed by his anxiety to obtain from his incarnation nothing but worldly gain. It has been a period when life has been very difficult because of the lack of the real comfort, encouragement and uplift which is brought by a realisation of greater things than those of the world. During the last centuries religions have to many people appeared rather as legends having no bearing on their lives instead of being the very essence of their existence. The true nature of our Higher Self, the knowledge of previous and later life, apart from this present one, has meant but very little to us instead of being the guide and stimulus of our every action. We have rather shunned the great things and attempted to make life as comfortable as possible by putting the superphysical out of our minds and depending upon earthly pleasures to compensate us for our trials. Thus have position, rank, wealth and worldly possessions become the goal of these centuries; and as all such things are transient and can only be obtained and held with much anxiety and concentration on material things, so has the real internal peace and happiness of the past generations been infinitely below that which is the due of mankind.

當實踐心靈成長的功課時，靈魂與心智真正的平靜是與我們同在的，而不是單單藉由聚集財富就能獲得，不論財富有多少。但時代正在改變，很多跡象顯示，現代文明已經從純粹物質性的追求，過渡到對宇宙實相與真理的渴望。目前人們對於追求超自然真相知識的

興趣，已普遍和快速地增長了，從愈來愈多人渴望了解生命的過去與
未來、經由信仰及靈性的手段尋找克服疾病的方法，以及向古代與
東方探求教誨與智慧等作為來看，顯示當前人們已經窺見了事情的
真相。因此，我們可以理解到，在面對療癒的問題時，也必須要跟上
時代的腳步，將大量使用唯物主義的方針，轉變成基於真理實相的
科學，以及支配人類天性的相同法則。療癒將由以物質方法為主的
身體治療取向，轉變為精神與靈性的療癒，也就是經由靈魂與心智
之間獲得和諧，而根絕造成疾病的基本原因，然後才去使用這些能
達到身體完整康復所需的物理療法。

The real peace of the Soul and mind is with us when we are making
spiritual advance, and it cannot be obtained by the accumulation of
wealth alone, no matter how great. But the times are changing, and the
indications are many that this civilisation has begun to pass from the age
of pure materialism to a desire for the realities and truths of the universe.
The general and rapidly increasing interest exhibited today for knowledge
of superphysical truths, the growing number of those who are desiring
information on existence before and after this life, the founding of methods
to conquer disease by faith and spiritual means, the quest after the ancient
teachings and wisdom of the East all these are signs that people of the
present time have glimpsed the reality of things. Thus, when we come to the
problem of healing we can understand that this also will have to keep pace
with the times and change its methods from those of gross materialism to
those of a science founded upon the realities of Truth and governed by the
same Divine laws which rule our very natures. Healing will pass from the
domain of physical methods of treating the physical body to that of spiritual
and mental healing, which by bringing about harmony between the Soul
and mind will eradicate the very basic cause of disease, and then allow such
physical means to be used as may be necessary to complete the cure of the
body.

　　由此可見，唯有醫藥專業人士能理解這些事實，並促使人們靈性增長，療癒的藝術才有可能交到宗教修持者，以及存在每個世代中真正的療癒者的手中；這些人截至目前為止，都還不能真正自我覺察地活著，因為傳統觀念的束縛，而無法跟隨他們天性的呼喚。因此，未來的醫師們有兩項偉大的目標：第一，協助病患了解自己，並且為他們指出所犯的錯誤、個性中應彌補的缺失，以及天性中必須根除的缺點，然後以相對的美德來取代。這樣的醫師，本身必須是人類天性法則下的優秀學生，如此他才能看出，造成所有來到他面前的人們其自身靈魂與人格間衝突的要素。他必須能為受苦的人提出讓他們獲致心靈和諧的建議，而哪些行為違反了一致性，他們必須不再犯；又必須去發展哪些必要的美德，以掃除他們自身的缺點。每個個案都需要仔細研究；也只有那些奉獻畢生心力於人類知識研究，且內心充滿著助人渴望的人，才有可能成功地為人類承擔這光耀而神聖的工作，去幫助受苦的人開啟眼界，並啟發他們個人存在的理由，還要喚起希望、慰藉與信念，好讓他們能戰勝疾病。

It seems quite possible that unless the medical profession realises these facts and advances with the spiritual growth of the people, the art of healing may pass into the hands of religious orders or into those of the trueborn healers of men who exist in every generation, but who yet have lived more or less unobserved, prevented from following their natural calling by the attitude of the orthodox. So that the physician of the future will have two great aims. The first will be to assist the patient to a knowledge of himself and to point out to him the fundamental mistakes he may be making, the deficiencies in his character which he should remedy, and the defects in his nature which must be eradicated and replaced by the corresponding virtues. Such a physician will have to be a great student of the laws governing humanity and of human nature itself, so that he may recognise in all who come to him those elements which are causing a conflict between the Soul and personality. He must be able to advise the sufferer how best to bring about the harmony required, what actions against Unity he must cease to perform and the necessary virtues he must develop to wipe out his defects. Each case will need a careful study, and it will only be those who have devoted much of their life to the knowledge of mankind and in whose heart burns the desire to help, who will be able to undertake successfully this glorious and divine work for humanity, to open the eyes of a sufferer and enlighten him on the reason of his being, and to inspire hope, comfort and faith which will enable him to conquer his malady.

醫師們的第二項任務，將是去執行能讓物質的身體獲得力量、並協助心智得到平靜的療法，擴展它的前景，並努力向完美境地前進，如此才能為整個人格帶來平靜與和諧。這樣的療法存在於大自然之中，是神聖的造物者，為了療癒與慰藉人類而有的仁慈賜予；這有些是為人所知的，而有更多則是當前世界各地的醫師們正在找尋的，尤其是在我們的母國印度，且毫無疑問地，當這樣的研究能更進一步地發展時，我們將重拾更多兩千多年前便已為人熟知的知識，而未來的治療師，將能自由地發揮這美好且自然的療方，這些是上天為了解除人類疾患而安排的。

The second duty of the physician will be to administer such remedies as will help the physical body to gain strength and assist the mind to become calm, widen its outlook and strive towards perfection, thus bringing peace and harmony to the whole personality. Such remedies there are in nature, placed there by the mercy of the Divine Creator for the healing and comfort of mankind. A few of these are known, and more are being sought at the present time by physicians in different parts of the world, especially in our Mother India, and there is no doubt that when such researches have become more developed we shall regain much of the knowledge which was known more than two thousand years ago, and the healer of the future will have at his disposal the wonderful and natural remedies, which were divinely placed for man to relieve his sickness.

　　因此，疾病的剷除，將依賴人類對於宇宙恆久不變法則其真理的體悟，並讓自己以謙卑的心去服膺於這些法則之下，因而帶來自己與靈魂之間的平靜，並獲致生命中真正的喜樂與幸福。而醫師這一方，則要協助受苦的人去認知這個真理，為他指出獲得心靈和諧的途徑，鼓勵他對內在神性的信心，這是我們克服一切事物所仰賴的。然後，去施行那些能幫助人格和諧與身體療癒的物理療法。

Thus the abolition of disease will depend upon humanity realising the truth of the unalterable laws of our Universe and adapting itself with humility and obedience to those laws, thus bringing peace between its Soul and itself, and gaining the real joy and happiness of life. And the part of the physician will be to assist any sufferer to a knowledge of such truth and to point out to him the means by which he can gain harmony, to inspire him with faith in his Divinity which can overcome all, and to administer such physical remedies as will help in the harmonising of the personality and the healing of the body.

◎第六章　重點摘錄

　　巴赫醫師在本章提到活體解剖、動物腺體移植等問題，目的是要人們認清我們與大自然萬物是一體的，而這些方式是一種破壞整體性的行為，到後來種種傷害也會反撲到人類身上。人類並不是最崇高的物種，不應傷害其他生物來救治人類的生命。要治療疾病，最終還是要依靠我們的愛與仁慈，才能獲得真正全面性的勝利。

　　「疾病是共同的敵人，我們任何所要征服的部分，這不僅幫助了自己，也幫助了全人類。」這句話很值得深思，因為當個人變完美了，宇宙也跟著變好，同樣地它也呼應了本章的第一節：如果我們每天讓自己逐漸變好，將對全人類有所助益，所以不應該小看自己每天的努力。這也是巴赫醫師一再想要告訴大家的：我們都具有神性，都來自同一個宇宙的大愛中心，最後都要回歸到那個中心，因此，我們的好壞與整體宇宙的好壞有關，只要把自己做好，世界也會跟著變好。進一步地，巴赫醫師要我們在能力許可時，盡自己的那一份力量，分享自己的經驗，以及在各方面提供實質的協助給弱勢者。

第 7 章
Chapter Seven

－真正的喜樂－
存在生活中最單純的事物中
因為愈單純的事物
愈是接近偉大的真理

現在我們面臨最重要的問題是，我們如何幫助自己？如何讓心智與身體保持和諧的狀態，不讓疾病輕易攻擊我們；因為沒有衝突的人格，的確可免於疾病的侵襲。

And now we come to the all-important problem, how can we help ourselves? How can we keep our mind and body in that state of harmony which will make it difficult or impossible for disease to attack us, for it is certain that the personality without conflict is immune from illness.

首先讓我們想想心智。我們已經花了很長的篇幅去討論，為何需要從自己的內在找尋致使我們違反一致性的缺點，還有探求因無法聽從靈魂指揮而失衡的原因，並且發展相對的美德來根除這些缺點。這可依循先前所陳述的內容達到，而誠實地自我檢視，將為我們揭露出自身錯誤的本質。我們靈性的指引者、真正的醫師與親密的朋友，的確可以幫助我們認識自己的真實面貌，但學習這個功課最完美的途徑，是要透過冷靜的思考與冥想，藉由將自己帶到那種平靜的氛圍之中，靈魂便能透過良知和直覺與我們對話，並依照祂的期望來引導我們。如果，每天能抽出一點時間，在儘可能安靜的地方獨處，遠離外在的干擾，然後只是靜靜地坐著或躺著，不管是讓頭腦暫時放空或平靜地思考著這一生的工作；經過一些時日後會發現，我們會像是在知識與指引的靈光乍現這樣的時刻裡獲得很大的幫助。我們會發現，人生中許多難以解答的問題，都有了清楚的答案，於是我們變得有自信去選擇正確的方向。在這些時刻裡，心中應該保有為人類服務奉獻的誠摯渴望，然後依照靈魂的指示行事。

First let us consider the mind. We have already discussed at some length the necessity of seeking within ourselves those defects we possess which cause us to work against Unity and out of harmony with the dictates of the Soul, and of eliminating these faults by developing the opposing virtues. This can be done on the lines already indicated, and an honest self-examination will disclose to us the nature of our errors. Our spiritual advisers, true physicians and intimate friends should be able to assist us to obtain a faithful picture of ourselves, but the perfect method of learning this is by calm thought and meditation, and by bringing ourselves to such an atmosphere of peace that our Souls are able to speak to us through our conscience and intuition, and to guide us according to their wishes. If we can only set aside a short time every day, quite alone and in as quiet a place as possible, free from interruption, and merely sit or lie quietly, either keeping the mind a blank or calmly thinking of one's work in life, it will be found after a time that we get great help at such moments and, as it were, flashes of knowledge and guidance are given to us. We find that the questions of the difficult problems of life are unmistakably answered, and we become able to choose with confidence the right course. Throughout such times we should keep an earnest desire in the heart to serve humanity and work according to the dictates of our Soul.

切記，找到錯誤時，治療的方法不在於抗爭，也不是以任何意志力來壓抑這個錯誤，而是持續穩定地發展出相對的美德，因而在不自覺中洗去天性中所有違規的跡象，這是求進步真正且自然的方法，也是征服錯誤的方法，這要比去對抗任何一個特定的缺點還要來得簡單而有效。與錯誤對抗，只會增強它的力量，讓注意力無法集中在它的存在上，反而為我們帶來了一場戰役；我們所能得到的成效，也只不過是經由壓抑的方式得到了征服，而這個結果實在是差強人意，因為敵人仍與我們同在，將在我們軟弱時再度現身。忘卻缺點，然後有意識地努力培養相對美德，就不會讓這樣的情況發生，這才是真正的勝利。

Be it remembered that when the fault is found the remedy lies not in a battle against this and not in a use of will power and energy to suppress a wrong, but in a steady development of the opposite virtue, thus automatically washing from our natures all trace of the offender. This is the true and natural method of advancement and of the conquest of wrong, vastly easier and more effective than fighting a particular defect. To struggle against a fault increases its power, keeps out attention riveted on its presence, and brings us a battle indeed, and the most success we can then expect is conquest by suppression, which is far from satisfactory, as the enemy is still with us and may in a weak moment show itself afresh. To forget the failing and consciously to strive to develop the virtue which would make the former impossible, this is true victory.

舉例來說，要是大自然中存在著殘酷，我們或許可以一直這麼說：「我不要成為殘酷的人」，來防止在這方面犯錯，但這樣的成功依靠的是心智的力量，只要意志有一丁點兒削弱，就可能暫時忘了真正的決心。另一方面來說，如果能發展對人們真正的憐憫之心，這樣的能力將使殘酷無法生存，因為升起的同情心，將讓我們以惶恐的心去迴避這樣的行為。這不應帶有壓力，也不會有敵人在我們休息時刻突然跑出來，因為憐憫之心，將從我們的天性中根絕所有可能造成他人傷害的行為。

For example, should there be cruelty in our nature, we can continually say, "I will not be cruel," and so prevent ourselves erring in that direction; but the success of this depends on the strength of the mind, and should it weaken we might for the moment forget our good resolve. But should we, on the other hand, develop real sympathy towards our fellow-men, this quality will once and for all make cruelty impossible, for we should shun the very act with horror because of our fellow-feeling. About this there is no suppression, no hidden enemy to come forward at moments when we are off our guard, because our sympathy will have completely eradicated from our nature the possibility of any act which could hurt another.

如同先前所看到的一樣，肉體疾病的本質，將實質地協助我們指出心智的不諧和，亦即造成疾病的基本原因；而另一個成功的重要因素是，我們必須擁有對生命的熱情，不只將生存看成是一種義務，而是要帶著最大的耐心，在我們這趟世界的冒險旅程中去發展真正的喜樂。

As we have previously seen, the nature of our physical maladies will materially help in pointing out to us the mental disharmony which is the basic cause of their origin; and another great factor of success is that we must have a zest for life and look upon existence not merely as a duty to be borne with as much patience as possible, developing a real joy in the adventure of our journey through this world.

唯物主義中最大的悲劇，恐怕是造成了人們厭世的態度，與內心真正喜樂的喪失；它教導人們在煩惱的時候，從世俗的歡愉及娛樂中去尋找滿足與補償，而這樣只不過是暫時地忘卻了我們的困境。一旦想從那些娛樂丑角的手上去尋求補償，來代替自己應有的試煉，就開始落入了惡性循環之中。趣味、娛樂與放鬆對大家來說的確很好，但不是持續地依賴它來減輕我們的煩惱。每一種世俗的娛樂為了要保持新奇，必然會不斷地增加強度，而今天的興奮，將成為明天的無聊。於是，我們不斷尋求其他更大的刺激，直到我們變得飽足，且不再從那個方向去獲得舒解。因為對世俗娛樂某種形式或程度上的依賴，讓我們全都變成了浮士德（註：將靈魂賣給了魔鬼的煉金師）。雖然在有意識的自我裡，或許並不是完全的覺知，但人生對我們來說，已經變成不得不忍耐的責任，而所有真正的熱情與喜悅，是每個人從孩提到生命最後的時日都應該擁有的特權，但卻已離我們遠去。現今社會的科學研究，已經往返老還童和延長自然的生命狀態，以及增加感官享樂的方向去極度發展，並且以非常極端的手法來達成。

Perhaps one of the greatest tragedies of materialism is the development of boredom and the loss of real inner happiness; it teaches people to seek contentment and compensation for troubles in earthly enjoyments and pleasures, and these can never bring anything but temporary oblivion of our difficulties. Once we begin to seek compensation for our trials at the hands of the paid jester we start a vicious circle. Amusement, entertainment and frivolity are good for us all, but not when we persistently depend upon these to alleviate our troubles. Worldly amusements of every kind have to be steadily increased in their intensity to keep their hold, and the thrill of yesterday becomes the bore of tomorrow. So we go on seeking other and greater excitements until we become satiated and can no longer obtain relief in that direction. In some form or another reliance on worldly entertainment makes Fausts of us all, and though perhaps we may not fully realise it in our conscious self, life becomes for us little more than a patient duty and all its true zest and joy, such as should be the heritage of every child and be maintained until our latest hours, departs from us. The extreme stage is reached today in the scientific efforts being evolved to obtain rejuvenation, prolongation of natural life and increase of sensual pleasures by means of devilish practices.

處於厭倦的狀態，其實會讓自己比平常更容易生病，而且這種情形在生命的早期就已逐漸開始了，因此與厭倦有關的疾病，似乎傾向於在年輕的時候就產生。如果我們能認知到內在神聖本質的真相，亦即我們在世的使命，以及由此而擁有汲取經驗與助人的喜樂時，那麼這種情形就不可能發生了。救治厭倦無聊的解藥，就是去對我們週遭的人事物擁有積極與強烈的興趣，整天都浸淫在對生命的學習之中，從同胞的身上與生活中的事件，一直不斷地去學習再學習，習得所有事物背後蘊涵的真理，並在獲得知識與經驗的藝術中逐漸忘卻自己，並留意一有機會就要用它來利益我們的同伴。因此，我們每一刻的工作及遊戲，將是帶著熱誠的學習，渴望去經驗真實事物的

感受，從事真實而有價值的冒險與行動；在發展這樣的能力時，將發現自己正在重獲自微小事物中得到喜樂的能力，而先前一直被視為平常、無聊且單調的事件，將成為我們去發掘與冒險的機會。真正的喜樂存在於生活中最單純的事物中－因為愈單純的事物，愈是接近偉大的真理。

The state of boredom is responsible for the admittance into ourselves of much more disease than would be generally realised, and as it tends today to occur early in life, so the maladies associated with it tend to appear at a younger age. Such a condition cannot occur if we acknowledge the truth of our Divinity, our mission in the world, and thereby possess the joy of gaining experience and helping others. The antidote for boredom is to take an active and lively interest in all around us, to study life throughout the whole day, to learn and learn and learn from our fellow-men and from the occurrences in life the Truth that lies behind all things, to lose ourselves in the art of gaining knowledge and experience, and to watch for opportunities when we may use such to the advantage of a fellow-traveller. Thus every moment of our work and play will bring with it a zeal for learning, a desire to experience real things, real adventures and deeds worth while, and as we develop this faculty we shall find that we are regaining the power of obtaining joy from the smallest incidents, and occurrences we have previously regarded as commonplace and of dull monotony will become the opportunity for research and adventure. It is in the simple things of life - the simple things because they are nearer the great Truth - that real pleasure is to be found.

屈從於人生，會讓人變成只不過是在生命的旅途中毫無覺知的旅客而已，而且等於是對未知而有害的影響敞開了大門；然而，如果我們一直都能將冒險的喜樂與精神帶入日常事物當中，這種影響根本就不會有機可趁。不論我們的身分是什麼，城市裡擁擠人群中的工人，或山丘上孤獨的牧羊人，讓我們一起努力地把單調變成樂趣，讓平凡

無奇的工作變成是可以快樂冒險的機會，然後，把日常生活變成對人性以及對偉大宇宙法則的研究。每一個角落，都充滿了觀察造物法則的機會，不論是山丘或河谷，或在我們的同袍之間。首先，讓我們將人生變成吸收樂趣的探險，當無聊厭倦無處容身時，就能透過從中獲得的知識，去找到身心的和諧，以及與神聖萬物之間偉大的一致性。

Resignation, which makes one become merely an unobservant passenger on the journey of life, opens the door to untold adverse influences which would never have an opportunity of gaining admittance as long as our daily existence brought with it the spirit and joy of adventure. Whatever may be our station, whether a worker in the city with its teeming myriads or a lonely shepherd on the hills, let us strive to turn monotony into interest, dull duty into a joyous opportunity for experience, and daily life into an intense study of humanity and the great fundamental laws of the Universe. In every place there is ample opportunity to observe the laws of Creation, either in the mountains or valleys or amongst our brother men. First let us turn life into an adventure of absorbing interest, when boredom will be no longer possible, and from the knowledge thus gained seek to harmonise our mind with our Soul and with the great Unity of God's Creation.

另一個對我們有實質幫助的方法，就是要能拋棄所有的恐懼。恐懼，其實是不應見容於人類世界的；既然內在的神性本質，也就是我們自己，是無可匹敵而不朽的，只要能真正地了解到這點，我們－上帝的子民－應永不畏懼。在唯物主義的時代裡，恐懼會因我們對世俗財富重視的程度而相對地增加（不管是身體本身或外在的財富），因為如果這是我們身處世界真正的情況，那麼由於這些物質事物本身是短暫的、是難以掌控的，而且連一刻都無法真正保有，我們惟恐機會將隨時從手中流逝，而激起了極大的焦慮不安，因此必然會自覺或不自覺的持續活在這樣的恐懼當中，因為在內心深處，我們知道這些世俗的擁有隨時都可能被奪走，而我們也只是短暫地擁有罷了！

Another fundamental help to us is to put away all fear. Fear in reality holds no place in the natural human kingdom, since the Divinity within us, which is ourself, is unconquerable and immortal, and if we could but realise it we, as Children of God, have nothing of which to be afraid. In materialistic ages fear naturally increases in proportion to the amount of importance we place on earthly possessions (whether they be of the body itself or external riches), for if such things be our world, since they are so transient, so difficult to obtain and so impossible to hold save for a brief spell, they arouse in us the utmost anxiety lest we miss an opportunity of grasping them while we may, and we must of necessity live in a constant state of fear, conscious or sub-conscious, because in our inner self we know that such possessions may at any moment be snatched from us and that at the most we can only hold them for a brief life.

在這個時代裡，對疾病的恐懼，已經發展到極具殺傷力，那是因為它讓我們對生活中懼怕的事物敞開了大門，使疾病得以輕易地入侵。這樣的恐懼，其實是利己主義的表現，因為如果我們誠摯地投注心力在他人的福祉時，是不可能有時間為個人疾病擔憂的。恐懼是現今讓疾病惡化最大的因素，加上現代科技將其發現藉由媒體傳播給一般大眾知道，反而把人們對事物驚怖的範圍給擴大了；事實上，那些發現卻也只是部分的真相而已。至於細菌與各種微生物和疾病之間有關的訊息，也讓成千上萬人的心智陷於混亂之中，就因為這種從內心升起的恐懼，使他們變得更容易受到疾病的侵襲。雖然像細菌這一類的低等生命形態，也許在某一部分扮演著與生理疾病相關的角色，但這並不代表它就是造成問題的所有事實，這也不是經由科學實驗，或在日常生活中就能看得出來的。有一些因素是科學無法從物質的層面去解釋的，這也是為什麼縱使兩種不同情況的人，同樣都暴露在可能受感染狀態下，而有些人會受到疾病侵襲，但有些人卻不會。

In this age the fear of disease has developed until it has become a great power for harm, because it opens the door to those things we dread and makes it easier for their admission. Such fear is really self-interest, for when we are earnestly absorbed in the welfare of others there is no time to be apprehensive of personal maladies. Fear at the present time is playing a great part in intensifying disease, and modern science has increased the reign of terror by spreading abroad to the general public its discoveries, which as yet are but half-truths. The knowledge of bacteria and the various germs associated with disease has played havoc in the minds of tens of thousands of people, and by the dread aroused in them has in itself rendered them more susceptible of attack. While lower forms of life, such as bacteria, may play a part in or be associated with physical disease, they constitute by no means the whole truth of the problem, as can be demonstrated scientifically or by everyday occurrences. There is a factor which science is unable to explain on physical grounds, and that is why some people become affected by disease while others escape, although both classes may be open to the same possibility of infection.

有一個超越物質層次的因素，是唯物主義所忽略的，而不論疾病的本質是什麼，在平凡的生命過程中，是這個因素，左右了任何特定個體面對疾病時的狀態，是被保護還是任由疾病侵襲。恐懼，藉由在心理上引起的沮喪作用，造成我們生理與磁性身體的不和諧，為入侵行動鋪了路；又如果細菌跟物質是疾病產生真正及唯一的因素，那麼就應該多少能減輕人們的恐懼才對。然而，當我們了解到即便是最可怕的傳染病，也只有部分暴露在感染源之下的人受到了侵襲；況且我們也已經發現到，疾病產生的真正原因，與自身人格有關，是我們能控制的。當了解到治療的方法在於我們自己，那麼，還有什麼理由對疾病感到恐懼與害怕的呢？我們可以把物質因素是造成疾病唯一原因的所有恐懼，全都拋諸在腦後，並了解到這樣的焦慮不安，只會讓我們變得更容易受侵襲。如果把心力投注在為自身人格帶來

寧靜和諧的努力之中，那麼我們對疾病所預期的擔憂，不應該比害怕被雷擊，或被隕石碎片打中還要來得大才對啊。

Materialism forgets that there is a factor above the physical plane which in the ordinary course of life protects or renders susceptible any particular individual with regard to disease, of whatever nature it may be. Fear, by its depressing effect on our mentality, thus causing disharmony in our physical and magnetic bodies, paves the way for invasion, and if bacteria and such physical means were the sure and only cause of disease, then indeed there might be but little encouragement not to be afraid. But when we realise that in the worst epidemics only a proportion of those exposed to infection are attacked and that, as we have already seen, the real cause of disease lies in our own personality and is within our control, then have we reason to go about without dread and fearless, knowing that the remedy lies with ourselves. We can put all fear of physical means alone as a cause of disease out of our minds, knowing that such anxiety merely renders us susceptible, and that if we are endeavouring to bring harmony into our personality we need anticipate illness no more than we dread being struck by lightning or hit by a fragment of a falling meteor.

現在，讓我們來談談身體。絕對不要忘了，它只不過是靈魂藉著它來與世界接觸的物質居所，並且為了獲得經驗與知識，而在此做短暫停留。不要與身體有太多牽扯，我們需要的是尊重它與照顧它，保持身體健康，好讓我們能完成此生的工作。任何時候都不應變得全神貫注，或過度熱衷在身體上，最好是儘量學著不去察覺它的存在，而把它當成靈魂與心智的工具，是我們操控意志時的僕人。外在與內在的清潔是很重要的，就前者而言，我們西方人用的水，溫度都太高了，這樣會讓皮膚張開而使污物進入。此外過度使用肥皂，會讓皮膚表面黏黏的。使用涼的或微溫的水，像沖澡一樣讓水一直流動，或更換幾次水，這樣都是較接近自然的方法，也更能保持身體健康；用適量的肥皂來洗淨明顯的髒污就好了，之後一定要用清水沖洗乾淨。

Now let us consider the physical body. It must never be forgotten that this is but the earthly habitation of the Soul, in which we dwell only for a short time in order that we may be able to contact the world for the purpose of gaining experience and knowledge. Without too much identifying ourselves with our bodies we should treat them with respect and care, so that they may be healthy and last the longer to do our work. Never for one moment should we become engrossed or over-anxious about them, but learn to be as little conscious of their existence as possible, using them as a vehicle of our Soul and mind and as servants to do our will. External and internal cleanliness are of great importance. For the former we of the West use our water too hot; this opens the skin and allows the admission of dirt. Moreover, the excessive use of soap renders the surface sticky. Cool or tepid water, either running as a shower bath or changed more than once is nearer the natural method and keeps the body healthier; only such an amount of soap as is necessary to remove obvious dirt should be used, and this should afterwards be well washed off in fresh water.

內在的純淨取決於節制的飲食，我們應該要選擇乾淨、健康及新鮮的食物，最好是天然的水果、蔬菜及核果。應該要避免肉類：首先，它會在身體造成許多毒素；再者，它會激起不正常及過多的食慾；第三，它造成了對動物界必然的殘殺。要淨化身體，就需要大量液體，像是水、天然的酒，以及許多直接在大自然環境下製作的產品，避免太多人工蒸餾的飲料。睡眠也不應過度，因為我們多數的人，醒來比睡著時有更多的自制力。古諺有云：「該翻身時，就該起床。」這句話是我們何時該起床的最佳指引。衣服儘量輕便，但也要穿的暖和，必須讓空氣能夠接觸到身體，皮膚要儘可能地接觸到陽光與新鮮空氣。水和日光浴是健康與活力的最佳來源。

Internal cleanliness depends on diet, and we should choose everything that is clean and wholesome and as fresh as possible, chiefly natural fruit, vegetables and nuts. Animal flesh should certainly be avoided: first, because it gives rise to much physical poison in the body; secondly, because it stimulates an abnormal and excessive appetite; and thirdly, because it necessitates cruelty to the animal world. Plenty of fluid should be taken to cleanse the body, such as water and natural wines and products made direct from Nature's storehouse, avoiding the more artificial beverages of distillation. Sleep should not be excessive, as many of us have more control over ourselves whilst awake than when asleep. The old saying, "Time to turn over, time to turn out," is an excellent guide as to when to rise. Clothing should be as light in weight as is compatible with warmth; it should allow air to reach the body, and sunshine and fresh air should be permitted to contact the skin on all possible occasions. Water and sun bathing are great donors of health and vitality.

所有事物都應該要激發歡樂，而且我們都應該拒絕被疑惑與沮喪所壓迫，請一定要記得，那絕對不是真正的自我，因為我們的靈魂所認知的，只有喜樂與幸福。

In all things cheerfulness should be encouraged, and we should refuse to be oppressed by doubt and depression, but remember that such are not of ourselves, for our Souls know only joy and happiness.

◎第七章　重點摘錄

　　本章前三段已經很明白地告訴我們應如何達到自我療癒。首先，要透過精神層面的努力，然後利用冷靜的思考與冥想，去找到我們生活中所面臨的困境，以及主要的問題癥結。給自己一段安靜獨處的時間，且不要與缺點抗爭，這些是巴赫花精療法的重點所在。而現今大部分的人缺乏給予自己安靜獨處的時間，而且很多人在獨處時，常常出現沒耐性的情況，例如打坐時無法靜下來心，一直覺得找不到自己的關鍵問題，於是轉而依賴抽花卡、隨機取用花精或使用人體感應等方式，來幫助自己找到合適的花精，但卻不去自我省思。然而習慣採取這些方式之後，就會變得愈來愈不能與自己內在的靈魂對話，久而久之，這種能力也會愈來愈弱。

　　通篇內容提到了一件很重要的事，那就是愛滋長愛、恨滋長恨，所以不要用對抗的方式去面對錯誤與缺點，而是要培養相對的美德，也就是滋長愛，升起我們的憐憫之心，我們就不會對別人造成傷害。

　　本章還提到了一般人面對痛苦時習慣用尋找娛樂的方式，來彌補我們所遭受到的痛苦，而這樣只是惡性循環的開始。許多人經常把生存看成是一項義務，覺得來到這個世界，每天只是工作、賺錢，察覺不到生命的意義，抱怨命運，甚至逃避，於是落入「楊柳」的失衡狀態中；之後對生命更失去了熱情，凡事逆來順受，放棄了生命的挑戰，這時又落入了「野玫瑰」的失衡狀態。以上情況，讓人們對娛樂的刺激需求愈來愈高、愈來愈多，也讓人們對生命更加地麻木沒感覺，因而走入惡性循環。

　　現代社會到底有哪些問題，造成人們不斷地去尋求刺激和娛樂呢？巴赫醫師在文章中提到：「唯物主義中最大的悲劇，恐怕是造成了人們厭世的態度，與內心真正喜樂的喪失…」這就是癥結所在。因為這樣的心理狀態，會讓很多人想要嘗試吸毒、嗑藥，或從事犯罪行為，目的都是想要尋求更大更多的刺激，讓自己處於一種亢奮的狀態。因為找不到生命的喜樂，只好藉由物質及藥物的刺激來麻醉自己。巴赫醫師又說：「…今天的興奮，將成為明天的無聊…」所以許多人前一夜歌舞狂歡，隔天醒來心情卻更加低落，接著只好再去尋找更多刺激，這樣不斷不斷地重複及循環。

　　另一個重點是，現代醫學一直在往延長生命的方向追求，但卻不試圖提升生命品質，對於這些身體已經非常虛弱的重症病患來說，生命確實被延長了，但他們的肉體和精神真的非常痛苦；這種延長生命的方式，難道是有價值的嗎？或者這只是人類為了滿足大家的私慾、安撫大家對死亡恐懼的一種消極對抗方式而已呢？其實對他們來說，這種醫療方式，好不起來也死不了，對死亡充滿了懼怕，也找不到生命的樂趣，不僅對自己身心是一種折磨，對家人來說，也是精神上的沉重負擔。因此，現代醫學這樣延長壽命的方式，到底是好還是不好？是不是反而製造了更多的社會問題？這確實值得我們深思！巴赫醫師在那個年代就已經預見了這樣的情況，真的可以說是很有遠見。

　　巴赫醫師在本章內容中，特別提出了「恐懼」對現代人的影響。恐懼事實上是現代人普遍存在的一種情緒狀態，許多的情緒失衡，其背後經常是隱藏著對事物的恐懼，或是對生存的恐懼。它呼應到我們對物質享受無法達到滿足時所產生的恐懼，也是巴赫醫師一再強調的，唯物主義帶給人們不是更好的生命品質，而是人類對物質世界極度擴張的恐懼，這些恐懼也是造成現代許多重大疾病的一大主因。

　　巴赫花精系統之所以不同於其他後來發現的花精，主要在於巴赫醫師先研究人類心理情緒上的種種問題，參悟宇宙間的真理，然後再去尋找一個對應的花精來協助處理。然而一些後來發現的花精，幾乎都是先找到一種花精，然後對應到我們所面臨的問題上，希望藉助這個花精來解決。前者是主動積極地面對情緒而改變態度，而後者則傾向於被動，依賴這個花精來幫我們解決問題。此外，有些新發現的花精，中心主旨不夠明確，一種花精好像可以處理很多種情緒問題，不容易了解花精的深層意義。然而巴赫醫師的38 種花精，都有一個最關鍵的主旨可作依循，這也是它比較容易學習的原因之一。

　　「真正的喜樂存在於生活中最單純的事物之中－因為愈單純的事物，愈是接近偉大的真理」，這句話就是巴赫花精療法的精神所在－簡單、純粹的原則。

第 *8* 章
Chapter Eight

每天花一點時間

靜心思考一下寧靜詳和之美

以及沈靜帶給我們的好處

還要認知到擔心和著急都無法成就事情

惟有冷靜、沈著的思緒

能讓我們面對事物時

行動變得更有效益

所以我們知道，唯有依靠以下的法則，才能戰勝疾病：首先，體認到內在本然的神性，以及我們具有克服所有錯誤的力量；其次，認知到疾病的根源，乃來自於人格與靈魂之間的不一致；第三，我們是否有決心及能力找出造成這些衝突的缺點；第四，培養相對的美德以剷除這些缺點。

Thus we see that our conquest of disease will mainly depend on the following: firstly, the realisation of the Divinity within our nature and our consequent power to overcome all that is wrong; secondly, the knowledge that the basic cause of disease is due to disharmony between the personality and the Soul; thirdly, our willingness and ability to discover the fault which is causing such a conflict; and fourthly, the removal of any such fault by developing the opposing virtue.

療癒的藝術的真義，將是在於協助我們找到克服自身疾病所需的知識與方法；除此之外，還要去施行可以鞏固身心，並且提供最有可能戰勝疾病的療法。那麼，我們就有能力從疾病的最源頭加以擊潰，並擁有真正成功的希望。未來的醫藥教育，將不會只對疾病的最終結果及產物特別關注，也不會在身體的機能障礙上花費太多心力，或者是給患者服用只為減輕症狀的藥材及化學製劑，這不過是次要的，而是要知道真正生病的原因，並察覺到明顯的生理結果。未來將是要把力量集中在為人們帶來身心靈的和諧，以獲得疾病的舒緩與療癒。如果能儘早進行像這樣的心智矯正，就能在疾病即將產生時就避開它。

The duty of the healing art will be to assist us to the necessary knowledge and means by which we may overcome our maladies, and in addition to this to administer such remedies as will strengthen our mental and physical bodies and give us greater opportunities of victory. Then shall we indeed be capable of attacking disease at its very base with real hope of success. The medical school of the future will not particularly interest itself in the ultimate results and products of disease, nor will it pay so much attention to actual physical lesions, or administer drugs and chemicals merely for the sake of palliating our symptoms, but knowing the true cause of sickness and aware that the obvious physical results are merely secondary it will concentrate its efforts upon bringing about the harmony between body, mind and soul which results in the relief and cure of disease. And in such cases as are undertaken early enough the correction of the mind will avert the imminent illness.

在處方的選用上，將要使用「大自然的藥房」裡最美麗的植物與藥草，它們蘊涵了療癒人類身心的神聖力量。

Amongst the types of remedies that will be used will be those obtained from the most beautiful plants and herbs to be found in the pharmacy of Nature, such as have been divinely enriched with healing powers for the mind and body of man.

至於我們的部分，則必須要學習平靜、和諧、獨立自主以及意志堅定，還要逐步增長這樣的信念；我們是來自於神性的大愛，是造物主的子民，因而具有神聖的本質，只要我們一直在這方面發展，最終一定會擁有臻至完美的力量。這樣的事實必須在內在逐漸地增長，直到它成為生活中最顯著的特徵。我們必須持續穩定地學習平靜，想像我們的心是一片隨時保持靜止的湖面，沒有一點波紋或漣漪能攪動它的平靜，持續發展這樣的寧靜狀態，直到生活中沒有任何事件、

任何境遇及任何人，能在任何情況下去吹皺那片湖水，或是在內心引起任何躁動、壓抑或懷疑的情緒。每天花一點時間，靜心思考一下寧靜詳和之美，以及沈靜所帶給我們的好處，還要認知到擔心和著急都無法成就事情；惟有冷靜、沈著的思緒，才能讓我們在面對事物時，行動變得更有效益。根據自身靈魂的期望，去統合此生所有的行為舉止，並時時維持在平靜的狀態中，不受世上任何的試煉與煩惱的干擾，這的確是一項了不起的成就，並為我們帶來那超越一切感知的平靜。起初這看起來好像是遙不可及的夢想，但它是真實的，只要有耐心及毅力，大家都做得到。

For our own part we must practice peace, harmony, individuality and firmness of purpose and increasingly develop the knowledge that in essence we are of Divine origin, children of the Creator, and thus have within us, if we will but develop it, as in time we ultimately surely must, the power to attain perfection. And this reality must increase within us until it becomes the most outstanding feature of our existence. We must steadfastly practise peace, imagining our minds as a lake ever to be kept calm, without waves, or even ripples, to disturb its tranquillity, and gradually develop this state of peace until no event of life, no circumstance, no other personality is able under any condition to ruffle the surface of that lake or raise within us any feelings of irritability, depression or doubt. It will materially help to set apart a short time each day to think quietly of the beauty of peace and the benefits of calmness, and to realise that it is neither by worrying nor hurrying that we accomplish most, but by calm, quiet thought and action become more efficient in all we undertake. To harmonise our conduct in this life in accordance with the wishes of our own Soul, and to remain in such a state of peace that the trials and disturbances of the world leave us unruffled, is a great attainment indeed and brings to us that Peace which passeth understanding; and though at first it may seem to be beyond our dreams, it is in reality, with patience and perseverance, within the reach of us all.

　　並不是所有人都被要求變成聖人或烈士或名流士紳，大多數人所被賦予的，其實都是不起眼的工作。但我們都期望能體會人生的喜樂與冒險，且期望內在神性為我們安排的這項獨特工作而充滿歡樂。

We are not all asked to be saints or martyrs or men of renown; to most of us less conspicuous offices are allotted. But we are all expected to understand the joy and adventure of life and to fulfil with cheerfulness the particular piece of work which has been ordained for us by our Divinity.

　　至於生病的人，內心的平靜與靈魂的和諧，對身體的康復最有幫助。未來的醫藥與照護，將投注更多心力在提升病人內在的層次上，而不是像現在這樣，只依賴物質科學的手段去判定病患的進展，我們常常用頻繁的體溫測量，以及許多的照顧去干擾病患，病患康復所最需要的安靜休養及身心的舒緩卻不見提升。不管是什麼病、什麼情況，如果能在疾病才剛發生的時候，花上幾小時真正地放鬆休息，並與高層自我達到和諧的狀態，疾病一定會立即終止，這是無庸置疑的。在這樣的時刻裡，我們需要把自己帶到一種完全平和的狀態，就像當時耶穌基督在暴風中踏上伽俐略湖上的船隻時，祂說：「平靜，靜下來。」

For those who are sick, peace of mind and harmony with the Soul is the greatest aid to recovery. The medicine and nursing of the future will pay much more attention to the development of this within the patient than we do today when, unable to judge the progress of a case except by materialistic scientific means, we think more of the frequent taking of temperature and a number of attentions which interrupt, rather than promote, that quiet rest and relaxation of body and mind which are so essential to recovery. There is no doubt that at the very onset of, at any rate, minor ailments, if we could but get a few hours' complete relaxation and in harmony with our Higher Self the illness would be aborted. At such moments we need to bring down into

ourselves but a fraction of that calm, as symbolised by the entry of Christ
into the boat during the storm on the lake of Galilee, when He ordered,
"Peace, be still."

我們對人生的展望，端看人格與靈魂之間密切的程度。愈是接近，
就愈能一致；愈是和諧與平靜，就愈能清晰地照見真理的光，並煥發
出高層世界的喜樂；這能讓我們在面對世界的困境與恐怖時，更加地
穩固及不驚慌，因為這些都立基於上天恆久不滅的真理之上。對於
真理的認知，同時也讓我們確信，儘管人世間有些事件看起來是那麼
不幸，它們也只不過是人類進化過程中的過渡階段；就連疾病本身也
是有益的，它是在特定的法則下，為了成就最終的利益，並帶出一股
臻至完美的持續力量所安排的一項工作。有這項認知的人，不會因那
些對一般人而言是負擔的事件而感到難受、沮喪或驚慌，所有的不安、
恐懼及失望也會永遠消失。我們如果能一直與自身的靈魂、我們的
天父保持密切的關係，那麼這將是個充滿喜樂的世界，也不會有任何
不利的事物降臨。

Our outlook on life depends on the nearness of the personality to the
Soul. The closer the union, the greater the harmony and peace, and the more
clearly will shine the light of Truth and the radiant happiness which is of the
higher realms; these will hold us steady and undismayed by the difficulties
and terrors of the world, since they have their foundations on the Eternal
Truth of God. The knowledge of Truth also gives to us the certainty that,
however tragic some of the events of the world may appear to be, they form
but a temporary stage in the evolution of man, and that even disease is in
itself beneficent and works under the operation of certain laws designed to
produce ultimate good and exerting a continual pressure towards perfection.
Those who have this knowledge are unable to be touched or depressed
or dismayed by those events which are such a burden to others, and all
uncertainty, fear and despair go for ever. If we can but keep in constant

communion with our own Soul, our Heavenly Father, then indeed is the world a place of joy, nor can any adverse influence be exerted upon us.

我們都拒絕承認自身神性的偉大，或去認清眼前的天命及壯麗的未來，其實是強大有力的；如果能承認，人生將不再是磨難、不需汲汲營營，不求論功行賞。美德就是在面對重大事物時以平常心看待，但要帶著信心與勇氣好好地生活，並具備面對這世上種種困境的能力。不論如何，我們必能透過與高層自我的溝通來保有那樣的和諧狀態，如此就能克服所有世俗的對立，並讓我們的旅程不受任何外在影響，而朝向實現天命的大道上前進，不致偏離。

We are not permitted to see the magnitude of our own Divinity, or to realise the mightiness of our Destiny and the glorious future which lies before us; for, if we were, life would be no trial and would involve no effort, no test of merit. Our virtue lies in being oblivious for the most part to those great things, and yet having faith and courage to live well and master the difficulties of this earth. We can, however, by communion with our Higher Self keep that harmony which enables us to overcome all worldly opposition and make our journey along the straight path to fulfil our destiny, undeterred by the influences which would lead us astray.

接著必須要發展獨立自主的能力，並從所有形式的物質影響中解脫，因此，只需遵從自身靈魂的指示，不因任何環境或任何人而動搖，成為自己的主宰，在波濤洶湧的人生大海中航行，堅守正確的舵位絕不放棄，也不任意將掌舵的工作交到他人手中。我們必須獲得完全且絕對的自由，這樣所有的作為、所有的行動－哦不，甚至是每一個念頭－都源自我們本身，如此才能完全按照自己的指示，自在地生活和付出。

Next must we develop individuality and free ourselves from all worldly influences, so that obeying only the dictates of our own Soul and unmoved by circumstances or other people we become our own masters, steering our bark over the rough seas of life without ever quitting the helm of rectitude, or at any time leaving the steering of our vessel to the hands of another. We must gain our freedom absolutely and completely, so that all we do, our every action - nay, even our every thought - derives its origin in ourselves, thus enabling us to live and give freely of our own accord, and of our own accord alone.

在獲得自主性的工作上，最大的困難常常是來自週遭最親近的人，尤其在這個時代裡，我們所面對的傳統恐懼與對責任的是非標準，已發展到令人無法承受的地步。然而我們必須增長自己的勇氣，因為大多數的人好像都有足夠的能力，去面對生活中看起來較重大的事物，但在面對親密關係的試煉時，卻經常遭逢失敗。我們必須客觀地判斷是非對錯，在親人或朋友的面前也要毫不畏懼。有很多人在外面的世界表現得像個英雄，回到家卻變成了儒夫！會阻礙我們完成天命的事情，或許真的很難被察覺，像虛假的情愛或是錯誤的責任感，都是讓我們變成奴隸的方式，然後把自己囚禁在他人的願望與慾念之中，而這些都必須被無情地甩開。如果我們不想受到週遭人們的阻礙，那麼自身靈魂的聲音，且只有那個聲音，是我們面對責任時唯一需要留心的。要儘可能地發展自主性，縱然生命中除了自己內在的靈魂外，沒有其他人可以給我們指引與協助，我們還是得學會往前走，去享受在所有事物中獲致知識與經驗的自由。

Our greatest difficulty in this direction may lie with those nearest to us in this age when the fear of convention and false standards of duty are so appallingly developed. But we must increase our courage, which with so many of us is sufficient to face the apparently big things of life but which yet fails at the more intimate trials. We must be able with impersonality to determine right and wrong and to act fearlessly in the presence of relative or friend. What a vast number of us are heroes in the outer world, but cowards at home! Though subtle indeed may be the means used to prevent us from fulfilling our Destiny, the pretence of love and affection, or a false sense of duty, methods to enslave us and keep us prisoners to the wishes and desires of others, yet must all such be ruthlessly put aside. The voice of our own Soul, and that voice alone, must be heeded as regards our duty if we are not to be hampered by those around us. Individuality must be developed to the utmost, and we must learn to walk though life relying on none but our own Soul for guidance and help, to take our freedom to gain every particle of knowledge and experience which may be possible.

我們同時還必須留意，要給予每個人相同的自由，不要企求他人的施予；相反地，要隨時準備好，在他人遇到困難與需要時，伸出援手扶他們一把。所以，我們在人生中遇見的每一個人，不論是母親、丈夫、孩子、陌生人或朋友，都成了旅程上的同伴，而他們任何一個人在靈性的層次上，或許比我們高或比我們低；但我們全都是四海一家之內共同的成員，在同一個偉大的共同體之下，經歷同樣的旅程，並懷抱著相同的美麗遠景。

At the same time we must be on our guard to allow to everyone their freedom also, to expect nothing from others but, on the contrary, to be ever ready to lend a helping hand to lift them upwards in times of their need and difficulty. Thus every personality we meet in life, whether mother, husband, child, stranger or friend, becomes a fellow-traveller, and any one of them may be greater or smaller than ourselves as regards spiritual development; but all of us are members of a common brotherhood and part of a great community making the same journey and with the same glorious end in view.

　　我們要下定決心獲得勝利，以不屈不撓的意志登上山峰；就算在中途失足，也不必有任何悔恨。所有大幅前進的步伐，都必定經歷過錯誤與失足，要把這些當成是幫助我們在未來不至於步伐踉蹌的經驗。不要因過去所犯的錯誤而感到沮喪；它們都過去了、結束了，從而獲得的知識，將幫助我們不再重蹈覆轍。我們必須堅定地向前邁進，不懊悔也不回顧，即便只是過去的一個小時，也都已經離我們而去，而壯麗的未來，總是以它耀眼的光芒照亮在我們面前。所有恐懼都應被逐退；它原本就不該存在人類的心智裡，只有在我們無法照見內在神性的時候，才會出現。我們的本性中並不存在恐懼，因為我們是造物主之子、神聖生命的靈光閃現，是不朽的、不可摧毀而無可匹敵的。疾病顯然是很殘酷的，因為它是錯誤的想法與錯誤行為的懲罰，最後必然會造成我們以殘酷的方式去對待他人。這就是為什麼一定要竭盡所能地去發展愛，以及我們天性中友愛的一面，只有這樣才能避免日後殘酷的行為。

　　We must be steadfast in the determination to win, resolute in the will to gain the mountain summit; let us not give a moment's regret to the slips by the way. No great ascent was ever made without faults and falls, and they must be regarded as experiences which will help us to stumble less in the future. No thoughts of past errors must ever depress us; they are over and finished, and the knowledge thus gained will help to avoid a repetition of them. Steadily must we press forwards and onwards, never regretting and never looking back, for the past of even one hour ago is behind us, and the glorious future with its blazing light ever before us. All fear must be cast out; it should never exist in the human mind, and is only possible when we lose sight of our Divinity. It is foreign to us because as Sons of the Creator, Sparks of the Divine Life, we are invincible, indestructible and unconquerable. Disease is apparently cruel because it is the penalty of wrong thought and wrong action, which must result in cruelty to others. Hence the necessity of developing the love and brotherhood side of our natures to the utmost, since this will make cruelty in the future an impossibility.

　　愛的增長，為我們帶來了一致性的體現，體悟了我們都來自同一個造物主的真理。

The development of Love brings us to the realisation of Unity, of the truth that one and all of us are of the One Great Creation.

　　我們所有的煩惱都起因於自私與分別心，而當愛與偉大一致性的認知變成我們天性中的一部分時，這就會立即消逝無蹤。宇宙是神的體現；宇宙的誕生即神的再生；宇宙的終止即是神最終極的發展。人類也是這樣的，肉體是人自身的具象化，其內在本質的物質性表現，是自身的表達，是內在意識特質的實體化。

The cause of all our troubles is self and separateness, and this vanishes as soon as Love and the knowledge of the great Unity become part of our natures. The Universe is God rendered objective; at its birth it is God reborn; at its close it is God more highly evolved. So with man; his body is himself externalised, an objective manifestation of his internal nature; he is the expression of himself, the materialisation of the qualities of his consciousness.

　　西方文明中有極佳的例證、完美的最佳典範，以及耶穌基督的教誨能引領我們。祂扮演著人格與靈魂之間協調者的角色。祂在世上的使命，是教導我們與內在高層自我、與天父達到和諧與共融，然後依照偉大造物主的意旨去獲致完美。

In our Western civilisation we have the glorious example, the great standard of perfection and the teachings of The Christ to guide us. He acts for us as Mediator between our personality and our Soul. His mission on earth was to teach us how to obtain harmony and communion with our Higher Self, with Our Father which is in Heaven, and thereby to obtain perfection in accordance with the Will of the Great Creator of all.

佛陀與其他偉大的聖賢們，也是這樣教導我們的，他們不時來到人世間，就是為了指引人類趨向完美的道路。對人類而言，沒有所謂的折衷路途。真理必然要被獲得，而人類必須讓自己與造物大愛的無限體系相結合。

Thus also taught the Lord Buddha and other great Masters, who have come down from time to time upon earth to point out to men the way to attain perfection. There is no halfway path for humanity. The Truth must be acknowledged, and man must unite himself with the infinite scheme of. Love of his Creator.

所以，去吧！我所有的兄弟姐妹們，到你們神性知識閃耀的陽光下，誠摯穩健地前行，加入獲得喜樂與傳遞幸福的偉大行列吧！連結四海之內兄弟的偉大情誼，他們為了服膺神的旨意而存在，而他們最大的喜樂，則來自於為其他弱小的弟兄們奉獻自我。

And so come out, my brothers and sisters, into the glorious sun shine of the knowledge of your Divinity, and earnestly and steadfastly set to work to join in the Grand Design of being happy and communicating happiness, uniting with that great band of the White Brotherhood whose whole existence is to obey the wish of their God, and whose great joy is in the service of their younger brother men.

◎第八章　重點摘錄

巴赫花精系統的總結

　　這一章的第一段內容，可說是這本書的總結、巴赫花精系統的精隨所在，也可以說闡釋了自我療癒的真正精神。我們要戰勝疾病，第一：深信每個人內在都有療癒的能力；第二：我們之所以會生病，是因為我們人格與靈魂已經產生了衝突；第三：要有決心找出造成衝突的缺點，經由找出缺點，花精的使用才會有效；第四：透過花精的協助，把我們需要的美德逐漸地提升起來，以剷除疾病。大多數的人在治療上遇到障礙，都是因為缺乏第一點和第二點的認知，很多人都沒認知到自己內在的神性是可以克服疾病的，也不認為自己生病是因為人格與靈魂產生了衝突，因此就算醫生幫你找到了生病的原因，卻還是無法治癒。

　　過去我們在為病人診察時，在發現到某種花精的身體反應區後，就會立刻為病人進行花精貼敷調理，讓病患能儘快解除病痛。但近年來，我們逐漸改變這種模式，而讓病人自己去尋找所需要的花精。因為讓病人找出自己合適的花精，絕對比別人替他找出來更有效。這裡又再次印證了第八章第一段所提到的療癒的四個重要階段。如果我們在使用花精時，是由諮詢師來協助處方，病人很容易忽略以下兩個重要的認知：一、內在就具有療癒的能力；二、疾病的根源來自人格與靈魂的不一致。這兩個過程若忽略了，內在的自我療癒系統就難以被啟動。

巴赫醫師提到了不要去在意自己是否能成為聖人烈士，事實上，聖人與烈士是現代人特意造就與定義出來的。我們在小時候經常被提醒，當論及遠大的夢想時，似乎要每個人都去成為聖人或偉人。然而，就如同巴赫醫師所說的，並不是每個人生來就被要求成為聖人，然而現今社會卻在無形中暗示人們，要成為像耶穌、達賴喇嘛那樣，才算是神聖和被尊敬的人。但巴赫醫師卻說：「即使是工廠的板凳上或船艦上的鍋爐室裡，都會有聖人，他們跟宗教神職人員中的高僧是一樣的。」意思是，每個人只要能在自己的崗位上，好好地把自己的工作做好，那就足夠了。

他強調的是，每個人要認知到自己內在是具有神性的，來到這個物質世界，都有特定的工作要完成；當我們真正盡了自己的本份後，就算只成就了一件微小的事，也算完成了此生的任務。同時，巴赫醫師也提醒我們不應對自己太苛責，而花精中也有許多是太過完美主義類型的，要求別人跟自己都要完美，例如：岩水、松、馬鞭草就是。

巴赫醫師在本章也預言了未來的醫療體系應該走的方向。第六段的內容對醫生來說衝擊是很大的，因為醫生在面對病人時，第一件事就是想趕快檢查出病人身體上的病變，利用各種最先進的儀器和藥物去診療疾病。然而，巴赫醫師在這裡卻說：「…內心的平靜與靈魂的和諧，對身體的康復最有幫助。」這也就是說，給病人一個身心安適的空間環境，才是真正讓病人儘速得到緩解的不二法門，

這段話非常值得我們去學習和體會。此外，還有一個重要的意義就是，現在很多人會用各式各樣的檢測方式，來幫病人找到合適的花精，但卻忽略了提供病人得到內心平靜的時間和環境，也忽略了病人必須自省的內在功夫，讓他們有機會找出自身的錯誤所在，這才是使用花精的重點。

在第五章裡，巴赫醫師提出每個人獲得自主性及自由的重要性，到了第八章，他又再度強調，可以看出他在為下一本著作《讓自己自由》（Free Thyself）作準備，因為他發現多數人最大的問題，仍在於無法擺脫種種束縛，無法讓自己的靈魂獲得自由。

Part Ⅱ

人因自己受苦

Ye Suffer From Yourself

【譯者序】
自內在療癒自我

黃韋睿

　　三年前我因為身體上的病痛，而有了接觸巴赫花精的契機，也慢慢地明白了巴赫醫師所說的疾病背後的意義，它讓我省思自身的問題，從最初的只求外力醫療的介入，到後來懂得沈靜地自內在療癒自我。

　　記得在學習完 38 種花精之後，對於巴赫醫師的醫學理念充滿了探知的熱忱，除了針對花精的闡述之外，也開始閱讀巴赫醫師的一些著作，如 ˋHeal Thyselfˊ、ˋFree Thyselfˊ 和 ˋYe Suffer From Yourselfˊ。第一次閱讀時印象是，覺得書中所陳述的都是些簡單的道理，直到後來重新閱讀和翻譯時，才發現看似簡單的道理，其背後實存在著很重要的見解，可說是對人生和處世態度相當受用的「教科書」。

　　在這次翻譯的過程中，我發現巴赫醫師的文筆流暢優美，在傳達理念時，描繪了許多讓人深感共鳴的動人例子，且之後的每一次翻閱，都能得到不同的體會。我覺得這些美好的字句，很適合在任何時刻隨手翻閱，在其文字的循循善誘之下，成為一個健康、平衡而有智慧的人。

【譯者簡介】黃韋睿先生，現任職專利事務所，畢業於國立清華大學資工研究所碩士，曾任資訊業軟體工程師。

【導讀】

完美的醫療體系

李穎哲

　　本文是巴赫醫師針對同類療法醫師演說的演講稿，目的是要告訴同儕真正完美的醫療方式。巴赫花精於 1993 年列入英國的同類療法的藥典中 (British Homeopathic Pharmacopoeia；dilution as 5x，using ethanol 22%)，所以很多人會以為巴赫花精屬於同類療法藥物，所以在製作花精或調配花精處方時，會以為將它們震盪之後，其臨床療效會更好。不過您是否思考過，當年巴赫醫師為什麼放棄同類療法而自創花精療法呢？花精到底和同類療法藥物有什麼不同？

　　巴赫醫師受到哈尼曼和帕拉賽爾蘇斯兩人的影響很大，因為他們同樣都認為「精神和心靈層面達到和諧，則疾病不復存在」，此外，花精療法跟同類療法最終皆是想要達到人類精神與心靈層面的和諧。然而，同類療法原則上還是認為疾病是邪惡的，必須利用方法來啟動人體的療癒系統，將疾病完全地消滅；因而選取會讓人產生類似疾病症狀的藥材，經過稀釋、震盪的勢能化過程，把藥材的性質完全改變，然後再拿來治療疾病，其目的只是要驅趕疾病，並無法認清疾病真正的本質。

　　巴赫醫師說：「…不再需要以疾病戰勝疾病；不再需要以疾病的產物來對抗疾病；也不需要用會引起疾病的物質來引發疾病。相反地，要找出疾病的根源來治療疾病。」巴赫醫師認為，當我們無法遵循靈魂的指揮，以及違法宇宙一致性和愛的原則時，疾病將會產生；然而疾病的出現，目的不是要置我們於死地，而是要提醒我們已經偏離了人生的方向，唯有透過愛、慈悲和同理心，才能讓我們看清自己的目標，消除仇恨、殘酷、

恐懼等種種的負面情緒。哈尼曼利用同類療法的勢能化作用，致力於將錯誤轉為正確，或將毒素轉成良藥，但本質仍然是以仇恨來壓抑仇恨，而巴赫花精則是直接使用大自然中被上天賜福的美麗花朵，是一種愛、完美而良善的療方。

因此，從本篇演講稿中，你可以完全的了解花精和同類療法藥物的差別，也可以知道為什麼巴赫醫師放棄了同類療法的治療方式；但文中巴赫醫師仍然相當推崇哈尼曼的理念，他很謙卑地說，自己只不過是將哈尼曼的工作延續到下個階段而已，他也鼓勵所有的醫療人員繼續研究下去，不要侷限在理論或是傳統的認知之內，要能夠超越所有唯物層面與唯物法則。

每一種醫療均有其值得稱許和優越的地方，在今日疾病日趨嚴重複雜的時代裡，或許我們可以採用每一種醫療體系的優點，來找到身心真正的健康與喜樂。

人因自己受苦
Ye Suffer From Yourself

· ·

1931 年 2 月巴赫醫師
於南波特 (Southport) 發表的一篇演說

今晚要來對各位演講，實在不是一件容易的事情。

In coming to address you this evening, I find the task not an easy one.

各位都是醫界人士，我本身也是個醫生，然而今晚我要談的這種藥，和現代正統醫學大相逕庭，一般醫療場所 (診療室、醫護室或是病房) 也不常見。

You are a medical society, and I come to you as a medical man: yet the medicine of which one would speak is so far removed from the orthodox views of today, that there will be little in this paper which savours of the consulting room, nursing home, or hospital ward as we know them at present.

哈尼曼在醫學領域上大幅超越了過去兩千年來奉行蓋林 (Galen) (註 1) 理論的正統醫學界人士。要不是各位都是哈尼曼 (Hahnemann) 的門生，不然我現在也很難在這裡啟齒。

Were it not that you, as followers of Hahnemann, are already vastly in advance of those who preach the teachings of Galen, and the orthodox medicine of the last two thousand years, one would fear to speak at all.

（註 1）蓋林：（Galen 或 Aelius Galenus；大約 129 － 200 年）
羅馬時期實驗生醫學的創始者，認為精確的解剖才是瞭解疾病的基礎。
他是對抗療法的鼻祖。他的解剖知識建立在以動物解剖來臆測人體內、
血液、心臟、肝臟或肺臟之功能。

你們偉大的尊師及其後進的教誨，已充分彰顯疾病的本質，並且開啟了一條正確導向的療癒之路。而我相信，各位已準備好跟著我向前更進一步走上了解全然健康的榮耀，以及疾病和治療之真正本質的道路。

But the teaching of your great Master and his followers has shed so much light upon the nature of disease, and opened up so much of the road which leads to correct healing, that I know you will be prepared to come with me further along that path, and see more of the glories of perfect health, and the true nature of disease and cure.

哈尼曼的見解給了被唯物主義矇蔽的人們一盞明燈，因為人們認為疾病純然是唯物問題，只能以唯物方法才能舒解及治療疾病。

The inspiration given to Hahnemann brought a light to humanity in the darkness of materialism, when man had come to consider disease as a purely materialistic problem to be relieved and cured by materialistic means alone.

哈尼曼和帕拉賽爾蘇斯 (Paracelsus)（註 2）同樣都認為：「如果我們的精神和心靈層面達到和諧，則疾病不復存在。」於是他開始尋找可以治癒心靈的療方，為我們帶來平和與健康。

He, like Paracelsus, knew that if our spiritual and mental aspects were in harmony, illness could not exist: and he set out to find remedies which would treat our minds, and thus bring us peace and health.

（註 2）帕拉賽爾蘇斯（Paracelsus；1493.11.11 — 1541.9.24）
　　　　企圖將醫學和煉金術結合成一種新的醫學化學科學，當時稱之為的
　　　　醫療化學。

哈尼曼在這方面的成就相當大，帶領我們向前邁進一大步，但畢竟他能夠努力的時間就只有他的一生而已；現在換我們來繼承他未竟的事業，在他已完成的全然療癒之架構基礎上補足更多，以期建立完整體系。

Hahnemann made a great advance and carried us a long way along the road, but he had only the length of one life in which to work, and it is for us to continue his researches where he left off: to add more to the structure of perfect healing of which he laid the foundation, and so worthily began the building.

同類療法已排除正統醫學中許多不必要以及不重要的部分，然而它仍有一段很長的路要走。我知道你們想了解更多，因為不論是過去或是當今的知識，仍不足以滿足真理追求者。

The homoeopath has already dispensed with much of the unnecessary and unimportant aspects of orthodox medicine, but he has yet further to go. I know that you wish to look forward, for neither the knowledge of the past nor the present is sufficient for the seeker after truth.

帕拉賽爾蘇斯和哈尼曼教導我們不要太過注意疾病本身，而是要治療人格和內心；要能領悟：只有心靈和諧了疾病才會自然消失。他們兩位的偉大思想基礎，正是我們必須延續的基本論調。

Paracelsus and Hahnemann taught us not to pay too much attention to the details of disease, but to treat the personality, the inner man, realising that if our spiritual and mental natures were in harmony disease disappeared. That great foundation to their edifice is the fundamental teaching which must continue.

　　哈尼曼接著探討如何達成這樣的和諧。他使用傳統醫學上的藥物，或是他所挑選出來的元素和植物，以同類療法勢能化（註3）的特殊製藥法，讓原來有致病性的物質轉化其作用方式，而只要少許用量，就能治療特定的症狀。

Hahnemann next saw how to bring about this harmony, and he found that among the drugs and the remedies of the old school, and among elements and plants which he himself selected, he could reverse their action by potentisation, so that the same substance which gave rise to poisonings and symptoms of disease, could—in the minutest quantity—cure those particular symptoms when prepared by his special method.

李穎哲：

　　巴赫醫師受到哈尼曼和帕拉賽爾蘇斯兩人的影響很大，因為他們同樣都認為「精神和心靈層面達到和諧，則疾病不復存在」；巴赫醫師的花精療法就是要做到這一點，而花精作用的方式就是在心靈和精神層次上。

陳慧玲：

　　不懂…什麼叫做喚醒藥物原來的潛在能量？

（註3）同類療法勢能化（Potentisation）乃使用物理方法，喚醒藥物原來的潛在能量並加以發揮。當其處於生藥狀態時，常呈惰性而不活潑；若採取勢能化的程序，能讓患者減少服用的藥物量，並且使其相反的能量性質大增。

李穎哲：

　　譬如說喝咖啡，原來會造成的影響可能有心悸、睡不著、焦躁，這種狀態下的咖啡，在同類療法裡可以歸類成尚未活化的物質或藥材，可以稱之為「生藥」。生藥經過同類療法的勢能化，也就是將之稀釋到極度微小的量，並經過震盪之後，讓原來的藥物效能變得活化，結果其作用的功效會與原來的生藥完全相反，亦即本來咖啡會造成心悸、睡不著、焦躁，現在反而可以用來治療以上的症狀。

　　因此形成了他另一項重要的生命基本原則：相似治療相似。這讓我們得以延續他的研究工作。

　　Thus formulated he the law of 'like cures like' : another great fundamental principle of life. And he left us to continue the building of the temple, the earlier plans of which had been disclosed to him.

　　如果我們依循這項原則研究下去，會領悟到一個事實，那就是疾病本身也是「相似治療相似」。疾病是錯誤行為所致，也是身體和靈魂不和諧的自然結果，也就是所謂的「相似治療相似」，因為每種疾病都是為了制止我們繼續犯下錯誤的行為；同時，也是在教導我們去改正自身的錯誤，並藉由探索心靈讓生活達到和諧。

　　And if we follow on this line of thought, the first great realisation which comes upon us is the truth that it is disease itself which is 'like curing like' : because disease is the result of wrong activity. It is the natural consequence of disharmony between our bodies and our Souls: it is 'like curing like' because it is the very disease itself which hinders and prevents our carrying our wrong actions too far, and at the same time, is a lesson to teach us to correct our ways, and harmonise our lives with the dictates of our Soul.

疾病是錯誤思想和錯誤行為的結果，只有思想和行為都正確了，疾病才會消失。當我們從痛苦、折磨和憂傷中學到教訓時，疾病已經沒有存在的必要，自然就會消失了。

Disease is the result of wrong thinking and wrong doing, and ceases when the act and thought are put in order. When the lesson of pain and suffering and distress is learnt, there is no further purpose in its presence, and it automatically disappears.

這是哈尼曼沒有完全見到的真理，正所謂的「相似治療相似」。

This is what Hahnemann incompletely saw as 'like curing like'.

李穎哲：

　　所以剛剛咖啡的例子，本來咖啡會造成焦躁頭暈，經過同類療法的製程後就可以拿來治療焦躁和頭暈，所以說是「相似治療相似」。

吳謝興：

　　為什麼這邊會說哈尼曼沒有完全見到「相似治療相似」的真理？

李穎哲：

　　因為巴赫醫師認為經過這種勢能化的過程，然後把物質的性質改變再拿來治療疾病，無法認清楚疾病真正的本質，目的還是在驅趕疾病，同類療法原則上仍然認為疾病是邪惡的，稍後巴赫醫師會點出應該是用「愛」與「慈悲」去詮釋和了解相似治療相似。

魏愛娟：

　　我覺得巴赫醫師會這樣說，是因為哈尼曼沒有領悟到我們應該從痛苦、折磨和憂傷中去學教訓，他還是從疾病等於邪惡的觀點去看。

李穎哲：

　　嗯，雖然哈尼曼認為身而為人，精神和心靈層面應該要達到平衡和諧，但當他在治病時卻還是從疾病的角度去看；可是巴赫醫師認為，真正的療癒是要從人的立場去看，如果從疾病的角度去看，就不是真正的相似治療相似了。

讓我們進一步來看：

COME A LITTLE FURTHER ALONG THE ROAD：

　　另一個要呈現給大家的偉大觀點是，要了解真正的治療並不是以錯誤對抗錯誤，而是以「正確」取代「錯誤」、以「良善」取代「罪惡」、以「光明」取代「黑暗」。

　　Another glorious view then opens out before us, and here we see that true healing can be obtained, not by wrong repelling wrong, but by right replacing wrong: good replacing evil: light replacing darkness.

　　現在我們知道，不再需要以疾病戰勝疾病；不再需要以疾病的產物來對抗疾病；也不需要用會引起疾病的物質來引發病。相反地，要找出疾病的根源來治療疾病。

Here we come to the understanding that we no longer fight disease with disease: no longer oppose illness with the products of illness: no longer attempt to drive out maladies with such substances that can cause them: but, on the contrary, to bring down the opposing virtue which will eliminate the fault.

未來的藥師就應只使用能從疾病根源來治療疾病的藥劑，取代那些僅能抑制疾病的藥劑。

And the pharmacopoeia of the near future should contain only those remedies which have the power to bring down good, eliminating all those whose only quality is to resist evil.

的確，仇恨或許會被更多的仇恨壓制，而唯有愛才能消除仇恨；殘酷或許能夠被程度更無法想像的殘酷所阻撓，而唯有同情心和同理心才能消除殘酷；恐懼或許會因更深的恐懼而被遺忘，但只有全然的勇氣才能真正消除恐懼。

True, hate may be conquered by a greater hate, but it can only be cured by love: cruelty may be prevented by a greater cruelty, but only eliminated when the qualities of sympathy and pity have developed: one fear may be lost and forgotten in the presence of a greater fear, but the real cure of all fear is perfect courage.

因此現在我們這些醫界人士，必須將注意力集中在這些美麗的花精上，這是神賜予我們的療癒藥方；而這藥方則遍佈在鄉野間的美麗花草中。

And so now, we of this school of medicine have to turn our attention to those beautiful remedies which have been Divinely placed in nature for our healing, amongst those beneficent, exquisite plants and herbs of the countryside.

李穎哲：

　　所以說咖啡本來是可能引起疾病的，現在若依靠轉變咖啡的性質去治療這種疾病，就是從疾病的角度去考慮治療。這篇文章的觀點引發很多的爭議，大部分的同類療法醫師都不予採納，或者視而不見，畢竟這點出了同類療法的缺陷；倘若同類療法醫師採信，等於是整個同類療法系統崩盤瓦解，那不是醫學界願意面對接受的，而且目前很多國家仍將花精歸類在同類療法的藥物裡頭。

　　「相似治療相似」顯然有其本質上的錯誤；哈尼曼對真理的認知是正確的，但他詮釋的方式卻不夠完整。相似可以增強相似、相似可以退卻相似，但在真正的治療當中，相似無法治療相似。

　　It is obviously fundamentally wrong to say that 'like cures like'. Hahnemann had a conception of the truth right enough, but expressed it incompletely. Like may strengthen like, like may repel like, but in the true healing sense like cannot cure like.

　　如果你聆聽奎師那、佛祖，或是耶穌基督的教誨，你會發現他們所要傳達的絕對都是良善戰勝邪惡的思想。耶穌基督教導我們不要抵抗邪惡，而要愛我們的敵人，為迫害我們的人祈禱；這些道理都不是以相似治療相似。在真正的治療或是靈魂的進化當中，必須尋求以良善驅逐邪惡、用愛戰勝仇恨，以光明退去黑暗。因此，我們必須要避免使用任何毒害物質，只採用美好而有益的物質。

If you listen to the teachings of Krishna, Buddha, or Christ, you will find always the teachings of good overcoming evil. Christ taught us not to resist evil, to love our enemies, to bless those who persecute us – there is no like curing like in this. And so in true healing, and so in spiritual advancement, we must always seek good to drive out evil, love to conquer hate, and light to dispel darkness. Thus must we avoid all poisons, all harmful things, and use only the beneficent and beautiful.

無疑地，哈尼曼利用同類療法的勢能化，致力於將錯誤轉為正確，或將毒素轉成良藥，但最簡單的方法則是直接使用美麗、良善的治療。

No doubt Hahnemann, by his method of potentisation, endeavoured to turn wrong into right, poisons into virtues, but it is simpler to use the beauteous and virtuous remedies direct.

治療，其根本是神聖的，超越所有唯物層面與唯物法則，不應侷限在我們的習俗或是傳統的認知之內。我們必須提升自己的理想、思想、抱負，以達到偉大先知們訓示我們的崇高境界。

Healing, being above all materialistic things, and materialistic laws, Divine in its origin, is not bound by any of our conventions or ordinary standards. In this we have to raise our ideals, our thoughts, our aspirations, to those glorious and lofty realms taught and shown to us by the Great Masters.

請不要認為這在否定哈尼曼的理論，相反地，應該說是他提出了基礎法則；然而他只有一生的時間可以做研究，如果繼續研究下去，必然也會走上這條道路。我們只不過是將他的工作延續到下個階段而已。

Do not think for one moment that one is detracting from Hahnemann's work, on the contrary, he pointed out the great fundamental laws, the basis;

but he had only one life: and had he continued his work longer, no doubt he would have progressed along these lines. We are merely advancing his work, and carrying it to the next natural stage.

讓我們來思考一下，為什麼醫藥需要改革？過去兩千年來科學都將疾病視為是唯物因素，並且可以唯物方法來治療，這實在是大錯特錯。

Let us now consider why medicine must so inevitably change. The science of the last two thousand years has regarded disease as a material factor which can be eliminated by material means: such, of course, is entirely wrong.

如我們所知，身體疾病是結果，是最終的產物，也是更深層事物發展的最後階段。疾病的起源超乎了唯物層面，而比較接近於精神層面。疾病完完全全是我們靈魂與心智產生衝突的結果。當兩者無法協調時，就會產生我們所說的「疾病」；而只有兩者和諧，才能擁有全然的健康。

Disease of the body, as we know it, is a result, an end product, a final stage of something much deeper. Disease originates above the physical plane, nearer to the mental. It is entirely the result of a conflict between our spiritual and mortal selves. So long as these two are in harmony, we are in perfect health: but when there is discord, there follows what we know as disease.

疾病純粹是指標而已，它並非是要用來殘酷懲罰我們所犯下的錯誤，而是要指出錯誤，讓我們儘早改進，以免犯下更大的錯誤或做出更多傷害，並且帶領我們回到真理與光明的道路上。

Disease is solely and purely corrective: it is neither vindictive nor cruel: but it is the means adopted by our own Souls to point out to us our faults: to prevent our making greater errors: to hinder us from doing more harm: and to bring us back to that path of Truth and Light from which we should never have strayed.

所以疾病其實是為了讓我們更好、是有益的，而我們應該要透過真知與持續向善的念頭來預防疾病發生。

Disease is, in reality, for our good, and is beneficent, though we should avoid it if we had but the correct understanding, combined with the desire to do right.

無論犯下什麼錯誤，錯誤都會依其本質反應在人身上，造成我們不快樂、不舒服和痛苦。目的是要告訴我們錯誤的行為及思考所帶來的傷害，並藉著在身體上造成相似的後果來告訴我們錯誤如何帶給別人困擾，並且違背大愛和一致性。

Whatever errors we make, it re-acts upon ourselves, causing us unhappiness, discomfort, or suffering, according to its nature. The object being to teach us the harmful effect of wrong action or thought: and, by its producing similar results upon ourselves, shows us how it causes distress to others, and is hence contrary to the Great and Divine Law of Love and Unity.

有此一認知的醫生，會了解疾病本身是在彰顯衝突的本性。或許最好的解釋方式是舉例來讓你們找回這個認知：「不論你所生什麼病，都是肇因於自己與內在神性之間不和諧，而高我正試圖要改正你所犯下的錯誤。」不論是生理上或心理上的苦痛，都是殘酷的行為或信念所引發的結果；但無須擔憂！當你感受到苦痛，只要願意向內心

察看，就會發現存在於自己天性中的冷酷行為或思想；一旦將之去除，苦痛就會解除。假如一個人有肢體或關節僵硬的問題，很可能心態上也是固執的，緊抓著某些原本應該放手的想法、信條或常規；假如一個人有氣喘或呼吸的毛病，可能是抑制了某種自我性格或者缺乏踏上正途的勇氣，而使自己透不過氣來；假如一個人任由自己的天賦荒廢，那就是容許別人阻礙自己接受生命力量。

To the understanding physician, the disease itself points out the nature of the conflict. Perhaps this is best illustrated by giving you examples to bring home to you that no matter from what disease you may suffer, it is because there is disharmony between yourself and the Divinity within you, and that you are committing some fault, some error, which your Higher Self is attempting to correct. Pain is the result of cruelty which causes pain to others, and may be mental or physical: but be sure that if you suffer pain, if you will but search yourselves you will find that some hard action or hard thought is present in your nature: remove this, and your pain will cease. If you suffer from stiffness of joint or limb, you can be equally certain that there is stiffness in your mind; that you are rigidly holding on to some idea, some principle, some convention may be, which you should not have. If you suffer from asthma, or difficulty in breathing, you are in some way stifling another personality; or from lack of courage to do right, smothering yourself. If you waste, it is because you are allowing someone to obstruct your own life-force from entering your body.

即使只是身體的某個部分出現病痛，也能指出錯誤的根源：手部病痛，表示行為不當或錯誤；腳部病痛，表示未能好好協助他人；腦部病痛，表示無法控制自己；心臟病痛，表示表達不足或過度，或在愛的體現上有所缺失；眼睛病痛，表示未能正確、明白地看清眼前的真相。如此一來，就能找出病症的本質與緣由，讓病人得以學習到必要的改正。

Even the part of the body affected indicates the nature of the fault. The hand, failure or wrong in action: the foot, failure to assist others: the brain, lack of control: the heart, deficiency or excess, or wrong doing in the aspect of love: the eye, failure to see aright and comprehend the truth when placed before you. And so, exactly, may be worked out the reason and nature of an infirmity: the lesson required of the patient: and the necessary correction to be made.

讓我們來想像一下未來醫院的樣貌。

Let us now glance, for a moment, at the hospital of the future.

未來的醫院,是個和平、希望與喜悅的殿堂:不慌不亂、沒有噪音,更找不到現今那些種種嚇人的醫療器材與設備,再也聞不到會讓人聯想到痛苦與疾病的消毒藥水和麻醉藥味道;不必經常進行會打擾病人休息的體溫量測;也不需要進行會在病人心中留下疾病烙印的聽診、抽液等例行檢查;也不會因刻意感受脈搏跳動而使心跳加速。捨棄了這些之後,平和與安靜的氛圍就能讓病人趕快痊癒。甚至連病理實驗室也可以捨棄了;因為一旦我們明白需要治療的不是疾病而是病人本身,那些細微的檢查和實驗就顯得不那麼重要了。

It will be a sanctuary of peace, hope and joy. No hurry: no noise: entirely devoid of all the terrifying apparatus and appliances of today: free from the smell of antiseptics and anaesthetics: devoid of every thing that suggests illness and suffering. There will be no frequent taking of temperatures to disturb the patient's rest: no daily examinations with stethoscopes and tappings to impress upon the patient's mind the nature of his illness. No constant feeling of the pulse to suggest that the heart is beating too rapidly. For all these things remove the very atmosphere of peace and calm that is so necessary for the patient to bring about his speedy recovery. Neither will there by any need for laboratories; for the minute and microscopic examination of detail will no longer matter when it is fully realised that it is the patient to be treated and not the disease.

醫療院所的宗旨將是營造一個充滿和平、希望、喜悅和信念的環境，並致力於鼓勵病人忘卻疾病的恐懼，為健康而努力；同時讓病人瞭解自己所需學習的課題，進一步克服天生的缺點。

The object of all institutions will be to have an atmosphere of peace, and of hope, of joy, and of faith. Everything will be done to encourage the patient to forget his illness; to strive for health; and at the same time to correct any fault in his nature; and come to an understanding of the lesson which he has to learn.

如此的醫院是向上提升且完美的；病人所要尋求的庇護所將不只是能夠解除病痛而已，更要能發展出與自己靈魂更協調的生活。

Everything about the hospital of the future will be uplifting and beautiful, so that the patient will seek that refuge, not only to be relieved of his malady, but also to develop the desire to live a life more in harmony with the dictates of his Soul than had been previously done.

醫院是病人的母親，無條件地將子女擁抱在懷裡，安撫他們，帶給他們希望、信念，以及克服險阻的勇氣。

The hospital will be the mother of the sick; will take them up in her arms; soothe and comfort them; and bring them hope, faith and courage to overcome their difficulties.

李穎哲：

　　有哪一家醫院能夠做到像巴赫醫師所認為的理想療癒場所呢？

魏愛娟：

　　安寧病房…

陳慧玲：

　　某些牙醫診所…

李穎哲：

　　安寧病房真的就像這樣，它頂多是有量血壓、測體溫這些例行性的檢查工作，不過大部分安寧病房進去之後就出不來了，所以我覺得安寧病房蠻需要荊豆花精的，因為很多病人到那裡就等於在等死，太悲觀了！和巴赫醫師的理念不合。如果安寧病房能夠發揮荊豆的正向觀點，就蠻接近這裡所描述的理想醫院了，而且很多宗教或社工人員的力量，都在安寧病房發揮了很大的力量，但其實不需要到這麼嚴重的地步才去借助宗教或社工人員，好像先前的治療相當積極，到後來嚴重的時候就放棄治療，任由疾病宰割。如果說當一個病人來到醫院就開始結合傳統醫療、花精療法、宗教或者社工人員的力量，我想病患一定會痊癒的比較快。

　　我覺得這一段或許大家看起來覺得很簡單，但對醫生來說其實是很大的衝擊。這篇文章主要的演講對象是醫生，可能有很多醫生認為巴赫醫師瘋了；對大部分的醫生來說，以上這些觀念和想法根本是做不到的。

吳謝興：

其實醫學之父—希波克拉底所提倡的醫院就是像這個樣子的。

　　未來的醫生會知道自己其實並不具有療癒力量，但他若願意奉獻生命為同胞服務、研究人類天性以瞭解箇中涵意、全心期望解除痛苦、不顧一切地為病人付出，那麼，疾病的知識將得以透過醫生傳遞，幫助病人解除痛苦；他們的療癒能力將和助人的心念強度以及是否樂於助人成正比。並且他們會瞭解，健康就像生活一樣，是神性展現的一部分，而他們所運用的療方，只是在神聖藍圖中扮演著工具和媒介的角色，用以幫助病人重回神聖法則的道路。

The physician of tomorrow will realise that he of himself has no power to heal, but that if he dedicates his life to the service of his brother-men; to study human nature so that he may, in part, comprehend its meaning; to desire wholeheartedly to relieve suffering, and to surrender all for the help of the sick; then, through him may be sent knowledge to guide them, and the power of healing to relieve their pain. And even then, his power and ability to help will be in proportion to his intensity of desire and his willingness to serve. He will understand that health, like life, is of God, and God alone. That he and the remedies that he uses are merely instruments and agents in the Divine Plan to assist to bring the sufferer back to the path of the Divine Law.

　　這樣的醫生他感興趣的會是健康的真義，而非病理學和解剖學。舉例來說，他不會去在意病人的呼吸困難是肇因於結核菌、鏈球菌或其他有機體的感染，反倒會非常在意是什麼樣的錯誤造成了病人痛苦。好比像心臟疾病，醫生不會去探究是哪個瓣膜出了問題，而

是去瞭解病人在愛的發展上有什麼錯誤，這才是真正關鍵的部分。也不再需要使用 X 光儀器來檢查關節炎；病人需要深入探究的是自己的心態，找出固執之所在。

He will have no interest in pathology or morbid anatomy; for his study will be that of health. It will not matter to him whether, for example, shortness of breath is caused by the tubercle baccillus, the streptococcus, or any other organism: but it will matter intensely to know why the patient should have to suffer difficulty of breathing. It will be of no moment to know which of the valves of the heart is damaged, but it will be vital to realise in what way the patient is wrongly developing his love aspect. X-rays will no longer be called into use to examine an arthritic joint, but rather research into the patient's mentality to discover the stiffness in his mind.

李穎哲：

　　這觀念對醫生來說，又是一個很大的震撼，因為很多醫生覺得自己擁有很完美的療癒技能，但這裡卻指出，醫生其實是不具有任何療癒力量的，療癒必須完全來自於病人的內心。

　　記得之前和許麗玲老師一起參與讀書會，她曾經說過，雖然有些人可以接收來自於宇宙高次元的能量，但他們不過是宇宙能量銀行的一個出納員而已，上天只是藉由他們作為管道來接收和傳送能量訊息，就如同巴赫醫師上面所講的，我們只是媒介而已。通常在當媒介的過程中會忘記這一點，以為自己是全能的，自己就是神，可以超控生死大權，反而剝奪造物主的權利。所以吳謝興老師也常常說，要判斷一個治療師好不好很簡單，如果這個治療師希望你崇拜他，並圍繞在他身邊成為他的信徒，那麼這種治療的方法就應該捨棄。

　　而且疾病的預後將視病人改正自身錯誤和協調靈性的能力，而不再是靠身體的病症去判斷。

The prognosis of disease will no longer depend on physical signs and symptoms, but on the ability of the patient to correct his fault and harmonise himself with his Spiritual Life.

　　醫學教育要深入探討的是人性，純粹完美的真貌以及存在每個人心中的神性，並且讓他們有足夠的知識去引導那些受苦的人們，找回心靈的寧靜並重拾健康和諧的人生。

The education of the physician will be a deep study of human nature; a great realisation of the pure and perfect: and an understanding of the Divine state of man: and the knowledge of how to assist those who suffer that they may harmonise their conduct with their Spiritual Self, so that they may bring concord and health to the personality.

　　在此教育之下，醫生將有能力從病人的生活習慣和行為中，找出造成他們生病或內心無法寧靜的原因，然後進一步給予適當的建議與療方。

He will have to be able, from the life and history of the patient, to understand the conflict which is causing disease or disharmony between the body and Soul, and thus enable him to give the necessary advice and treatment for the relief of the sufferer.

　　此外，醫師還必須要親近大自然，研究自然界的法則，在熟悉大自然所蘊含的療癒力量之後，就能加以運用而造福病人。

He will also have to study Nature and Nature's Laws: be conversant with Her Healing Powers, that he may utilise these for the benefit and advantage of the patient.

說到未來的療方，將具備以下四個特點：第一，和平；第二，希望；第三，喜悅；第四，信念。

The treatment of tomorrow will be essentially to bring four qualities to the patient. First, peace: secondly, hope: thirdly, joy: and fourthly, faith.

李穎哲：

　　我覺得未來的療方所應具備的四個特點蠻有意思的，許多人都說，吃了花精之後沒什麼感覺，可是依照我個人的觀察，花精帶給人們的最大改變是，讓人們比較喜悅、心情比較平和、感覺人生比較有希望，但許多人認為這不是改變，因為他們有更多的期望。像我之前的一些癌症病人，在服用花精之後，所表現出來的就是喜悅和感謝。

陳慧玲：

　　我覺得當心靈被治癒了，身體的病痛就不那麼重要了。

李穎哲：

　　所以巴赫醫師這邊提到的「療方」，並不只是要讓肉體繼續存活下去，如此才能定義為成功的治療；對巴赫醫師來說，他的治療已經跳脫了生命的延續。然而現在許多醫療所講求的，是關注在如何將病人的生命繼續延續下去，例如我看過一些癌症病人，以傳統醫學治療之後，雖然存活了下來了，但是他們的內心仍然存在著很大的恐懼，害怕哪一天癌症又會復發。

　　所以這樣生命的延續有意義嗎？其實他們的心中沒有了和平、希望、喜悅、信念，因為隨時都害怕癌症復發而帶來

死亡，因為西醫如果說五年內存活率是 50%，那十年呢？越多年存活率越低，大部分的病人就會懷疑那我會不會是那百分之幾的其中之一呢？他已經失去了自己內在的信仰，終日活在死亡的恐懼中。回到花精療法的基本面上，或許對某些病人來說，沒有辦法完全治癒肉體的病痛，但卻帶給他們這四個特點，就像剛剛陳慧玲講的，重點不是在於生命的長短，而是在於靈魂是否真正得到了解脫。

黃韋睿：

　　我覺得醫生真的好難當，因為要懂好多事情，不只是病理，還有病人的心理和自身的修為。

李穎哲：

　　我在醫學院裡的醫學訓練，是要我們醫生負起全部的責任，要不斷地精進研究，所以為什麼很多醫生後來投入了所謂的染色體基因治療，企圖找出最終的特效藥。很多醫生沒有機會看到這篇文章，或者看到了也無法體會；我覺得我自己蠻幸運的，能夠接觸到花精療法的中心思想。

　　以前我最痛苦的就是經常要找大陸的醫學期刊，想瞭解是不是有什麼新的處方對什麼病有特效。現在有很多病都很難治，例如牛皮癬、癌症、愛滋病，以前醫師不斷地尋求特效藥，然而我發現這些很難醫治的病，都需要從心靈和情緒面去著手。像牛皮癬的病人，只服用幾瓶花精或使用急救藥膏其實是不夠的，重點是在於病人自己是不是能夠自己走向療癒。我前一陣子身體的左半邊出現牛皮癬，自己服用花精、塗平衡油來處理，到現在已經兩年多沒有復發了，因此許多頑固性的疾病，都需要往自己的心靈深處去

探索，看看問題糾結是什麼，才能找到解藥，獲得真正的痊癒。牛皮癬本身是很多負面情緒糾結所產生的結果，現在幾乎沒有醫生敢說牛皮癬可以完全被治癒。

黃韋睿：

　　那異位性皮膚炎呢？

李穎哲：

　　我覺得異位性皮膚炎的臨床療效蠻好的，因為大部分都是因為體質太寒，服用理中湯或附子理中湯等中藥、注意清潔用品的使用、塗塗救援花精乳霜，大部分都能改善。比較難治的是那種過了青春期之後的異位性皮膚炎，因為他們可能塗過不少抑制性的藥物，那種被壓抑進去的病症就比較需要花時間，而且塗過抑制性藥物的病人，剛開始接觸中藥或花精時，可能會讓病情變得很嚴重，因此很多人都撐不過去，只好繼續接受抑制性的治療方法。

　　此外，虛寒體質的病人，倘若在治療過程中吃到寒涼的食物，會讓病情惡化；但問題來了，有些病人認為維他命C太重要了，因此每天都要喝大量的蔬果汁，固執地遵崇生機飲食，他們沒有攝取食物營養素的正確觀念，反而被一些媒體的錯誤觀念誤導，讓病情反覆而難以控制，很多原因是對疾病恐懼（溝酸醬），或是無法相信內在的指引（紫金蓮）。

林鈺傑：

　　既然疾病跟情緒有關，那麼是否有專家做過研究，例如說乳癌的相關情緒為何？胃癌的相關情緒為何？

陳慧玲：

　　《創造生命的奇蹟》這本書有寫…

李穎哲：

　　《創造生命的奇蹟》算是第一本提出某某情緒跟某某疾病相關的書籍，但是我對那本書不是很認同，因為從臨床上的經驗來看，其實並沒有那麼簡單，它只是提供了一個方向，證明疾病跟情緒是有關的。像巴赫醫師所說的，某個病人得到胃炎，如果單純只是把胃炎治好，而沒有找到真正的問題，下一次可能變成喉嚨痛；再沒有解決真正的問題，下下次可能變成卵巢炎或尿道炎；所以哪個情緒會引起哪種病症，我覺得不是那麼絕對的，那本書只是一個參考。另外，很多人說花精是在平衡我們的負面情緒，我覺得這只對了一部分，其實花精的基礎理論認為疾病的生成，是心靈跟心智產生衝突，花精用在調和這部分的衝突，而不單是平衡負面情緒而已。

林筱岑：

　　我發現巴赫花精系統在台灣也發展好幾年了，可是在很多討論區所提問的問題，都是在問哪個花精可以解決我這種那種的病痛或負面情緒，好像覺得吃了花精之後，就可以解決某某病痛和負面情緒。

　　醫療的環境與重點將圍繞在這些層面上，為病人帶來健康與光明的氛圍，加速復原。同時，經詳細診斷後找出病人的缺點，加以協助與鼓勵，就能一一加以克服。

And all the surroundings and attention will be to that end. To surround the patient with such an atmosphere of health and light as will encourage recovery. At the same time, the errors of the patient, having been diagnosed, will be pointed out, and assistance and encouragement given that they may be conquered.

除此之外，這些完美的療方，已被賦予了神聖的療癒力量；用於病人身上，將為他們開啟通往靈性的道路，迎接來自靈魂深處的光芒與美德。

In addition to this, those beautiful remedies, which have been Divinely enriched with healing powers, will be administered, to open up those channels to admit more of the light of the Soul, that the patient may be flooded with healing virtue.

進一步來說，這些療方可以增加我們的心靈感應，開啟通往靈性的道路，讓我們得以學習自身所欠缺的美德，然後洗刷掉致病的錯誤。這些療方像是美妙的樂曲或是任何能夠激發靈感的美好事物一樣地突顯我們的天性，帶領我們更接近自己的靈魂，也因此有助於解除痛苦而獲得寧靜。

The action of these remedies is to raise our vibrations and open up our channels for the reception of our Spiritual Self, to flood our natures with the particular virtue we need, and wash out from us the fault which is causing harm. They are able, like beautiful music, or any gloriously uplifting thing which gives us inspiration, to raise our very natures, and bring us nearer to our Souls: and by that very act, to bring us peace, and relieve our sufferings.

它們的作用方式不是一味地攻擊疾病，而是讓較高天性的美好能量在我們體內產生共鳴，讓疾病就像冰雪遇到陽光一樣消融於無形。

They cure, not by attacking disease, but by flooding our bodies with the beautiful vibrations of our Higher Nature, in the presence of which disease melts as snow in the sunshine.

最後，醫生所要做的就是去教育病人關於疾病與健康的真理。

And, finally, how they must change the attitude of the patient towards disease and health.

人們必須捨棄「金錢能解除痛苦」的觀念，因為健康就像生命一樣，來自神聖的根源，唯有依循神聖法則才能獲得；相反地，金錢、享樂和旅行或許能改善身體外在，但卻無法讓我們獲得真正的健康。

Gone forever must be the thought that relief may be obtained by the payment of gold or silver. Health, like life, is of Divine origin, and can only be obtained by Divine Means. Money, luxury, travel, may outwardly appear to be able to purchase for us an improvement in our physical being: but these things can never give us true health.

未來的病人必須要瞭解的是：一個人只靠自己，或者是藉助於某位兄長同胞的指點和幫忙，也能為自己解除病痛。

The patient of tomorrow must understand that he, and he alone, can bring himself relief from suffering, though he may obtain advice and help from an elder brother who will assist him in his effort.

因為身心靈協調了，健康才得以存在；而也唯有協調之後才能治癒！

Health exists when there is perfect harmony between Soul and mind and body: and this harmony, and this harmony alone, must be attained before cure can be accomplished.

所以在未來，罹患疾病並不怎麼地令人得意，反倒會是件讓自己蒙羞的事。

In the future there will no pride in being ill: on the contrary, people will be as ashamed of sickness as they should be of crime.

現在我要向你們解釋兩個情況，而它們極可能是造成我國疾病增加的主因，那就是現代文明的重大過失－「貪婪」與「盲目崇拜」。

And now I want to explain to you two conditions which are probably giving rise to more disease in this country than any other single cause: the great failings of our civilisation - greed and idolatry.

疾病是為了糾正我們的錯誤，它全然是自己錯誤的行為與思想所致，正因為如此，所以我們才能改正這些錯誤，並且依循這個神聖藍圖來和諧地生活，如此疾病將無法侵擾我們。

Disease, is, of course, sent to us as a correction. We bring it entirely upon ourselves: it is the result of our own wrong doing and wrong thinking. Can we but correct our faults and live in harmony with the Divine Plan, illness can never assail us.

在我們的文明中，貪婪籠罩一切，有追求財富的貪婪、追求身分地位的貪婪、追求職位的貪婪、追求世俗榮耀的貪婪，追求舒適的貪婪和追求受歡迎的貪婪；以上種種的貪婪，雖然不似那些大剌剌和突顯於外的缺點，但卻能造成更多傷害。

In this, our civilisation, greed overshadows all. There is greed for wealth, for rank, for position, for worldly honours, for comfort, for popularity: yet it is not of these one would speak, because even they are, in comparison, harmless.

最可怕的是，貪婪會控制人們的心神，且其普遍的程度，讓大眾漸漸視之為理所當然；即使如此，也無法減輕它所招致的罪行－操控別人的慾望或影響人的個性，因為這些都是篡奪造物者權力的行為。

The worst of all is the greed to possess another individual. True, this is so common amongst us that it has come to be looked upon as almost right and proper : yet that does not mitigate the evil: for, to desire possession or influence over another individual or personality, is to usurp the power of our Creator.

各位，你們多少人能清楚地指出身旁親友中有沒被貪婪支配的？有多少人是不受他人束縛或影響的？又有多少人能夠每年、每月、每日對自己說：「我堅定地不被別人影響，只遵從靈魂深處所傳達的指令？」

How many folk can you number amongst your friends or relations who are free? How many are there who are not bound or influenced or controlled by some other human being? How many are there who could say, that day by day, month by month, and year by year, 'I obey only the dictates of my Soul, unmoved by the influence of other people?'

我們每個人都是自由的靈魂，我們的一舉一動都是為了回應上天而做的。

And yet, everyone of us is a free Soul, answerable only to God for our actions, aye, even our very thoughts.

或許在我們的生命旅程中，最大的課題便是「自由」；從各種際遇、環境、他人，甚至是從自己身上獲得自由；也唯有我們自由的那一刻，才有能力完完全全地去服務所有的同胞。

Possibly the greatest lesson of life is to learn freedom. Freedom from circumstance, environment, other personalities, and most of all from ourselves: because until we are free we are unable fully to give and to serve our brother-men.

千萬不要忘記，不管是遭逢疾病、困難，或是因周遭的朋友以及各種關係而煩惱，或是被迫活在想控制和支配我們的人們當中，他們干擾和阻礙了我們的計畫，這都是自己造成的，因為我們內心深處還存在著妨礙自由的痕跡、或是缺乏了大聲宣告自主權的勇氣。

Remember that whether we suffer disease or hardship: whether we are surrounded by relations or friends who may annoy us: whether we have to live amongst those who rule and dictate to us, who interfere with our plans and hamper our progress, it is of our own making: it is because there is still within us a trace left to bar the freedom of someone: or the absence of courage to claim our own individuality, our birthright.

一旦我們把自由交還給每個人，不再想要束縛或阻礙他人、不再期望他人必須為自己付出，全心付出而不求回報；從那一刻起，我們就能解除身上的束縛和枷鎖，並且在生命中第一次真正體會到自由的美好，脫離所有人的束縛，樂意並喜悅地只為我們的高我服務。

The moment that we ourselves have given complete liberty to all around us: when we no longer desire to bind and limit: when we no longer expect anything from anyone: when our only thought is to give and give and never to take, that moment shall we find that we are free of all the world: our bonds will fall from us: our chains be broken: and for the first time in our lives shall we know the exquisite joy of perfect liberty. Freed from all human restraint, the willing and joyous servant of our Higher Self alone.

　　在人們尚未體認並糾正自己所犯下的錯誤之前，就已經形成了嚴重的疾病，這股支配的力量已在西方國家如火如荼地延續著。疾病的樣貌依我們強迫他人的程度及種類而有不同；只要我們依舊篡奪他人的自由意志，就注定了受苦的命運。

　　So greatly has the possessive power developed in the West that it is necessitating great disease before people will recognize the error and correct their ways: and according to the severity and type of or domination over another, so must we suffer as long as we continue to usurp a power which does not belong to man.

　　要知道，絕對的自由獨立是每個人與生俱來的權力；唯有給予別人自由，自己才能獲得自由，就如同要收割就必須先播種、種因必得果。

　　Absolute freedom is our birthright, and this we can only obtain when we grant that liberty to every living Soul who may come into our lives. For truly we reap as we sow, and truly 'as we mete so it shall be measured out to us'.

　　如果我們阻撓了另一個生命，不論是年輕的或年老的，這項行為將會向我們反撲；如果限制了別人的行動，就會發現自己的身體同時也被僵硬的疾病所苦；如果我們還造成別人的苦痛，就必須要有心理準備，在尚未彌補該錯誤以前，自己也將承受同樣的痛苦。每一個疾病的發生，就代表著我們必須反省自身的行為，以求錯誤即時改正。

　　Exactly as we thwart another life, be it young or old, so must that re-act upon ourselves. If we limit their activities, we may find our bodies limited with stiffness: if, in addition, we cause them pain and suffering, we must be prepared to bear the same, until we have made amends: and there is no disease, even however severe, that may not be needed to check our actions and alter our ways.

至於那些受到別人迫害的人，請鼓起勇氣！因為當你被教導要追求自由之後，你就已經向上提升了，而你所承受的那些苦痛，正是在教導你如何糾正自身的錯誤；只要你瞭解並改正錯誤，所有困擾就會消失。

To those of you who suffer at the hands of another, take courage; for it means that you have reached that stage of advancement when you are being taught to gain your freedom: and the very pain and suffering which you are bearing is teaching you how to correct your own fault, and as soon as you have realized the fault and put that right, your troubles are over.

林筱岑：

　　這邊還是延續前面所講的自由，不要去阻撓他人的生命。

陳慧玲：

　　我覺得要給別人自由比較容易，要給自己自由比較不容易。

李穎哲：

　　可是我覺得給自己自由很難，是因為自己沒有給別人自由，如巴赫醫師說的「要獲得自由必須先給別人自由」，他的意思就是說很多事情不是單一方面就會發生的，其實是雙方促成的，這就是所謂的「一個銅板打不響」。

　　所以過度關心他人福祉的族群，我覺得需要關係的雙方都同時服用花精，例如說你一直覺得某個人很菊苣，可是要思考一下，為什麼你會讓他散發出菊苣的負面情緒，可能你身上也有某種特質引發對方的菊苣，有可能是你

矢車菊特質，或者你也有菊苣特質讓雙方互相依賴糾纏，所以我覺得有時候在處理個案的情況時，不能只考慮單方面的問題。像之前曾經有菊苣的母親帶小朋友來看氣喘或過敏性鼻炎，卻在小孩子身上檢測出菊苣和紅栗花的能量，那時我給自己的解釋是小朋友可能對母親也很擔心，現在則認為，一個問題通常是雙方互動影響所產生的。

像今天有一對金童玉女的情侶來看診，他們最近在鬧分手，因為男生一直很菊苣，希望女朋友待在他的身邊，可是女生個性比較喜歡與朋友相處，所以就鬧的很不開心。如此分析下來，雖然有菊苣情緒的是男方，但由於兩人同處於一段關係之中，所以我建議女生也使用菊苣花精。

而實現這個教導的方法就是，經常要實踐美善與柔和的精神，不是用行為、言語或是思想去傷害別人。因為每個人都在為各自的救贖而努力著，都在為了讓自己的靈魂更趨完美而學習著；唯有透過親身實踐，獲得屬於自己的經驗，克服重重難關，尋得自己的道路。我們可以做的就是不要忘了以自身的知識與經驗去引導年輕人。他們願意傾聽，就循循善誘；如果沒有意願，就耐心等待他們自己學習，直到他們願意認錯，屆時就會來尋求協助。

The way to set about to do this work is to practise exquisite gentleness: never by thought or word or deed to hurt another. Remember that all people are working out their own salvation; are going through life to learn those lessons for the perfection of their own Soul; and that they must do it for themselves: that they must gain their own experiences: learn the pitfalls of the world, and, of their own effort, find the pathway which leads to the mountain top. The most that we can do is, when we have a little more knowledge and experience than a younger brother, very gently to guide them. If they will listen, well and good: if not, we must patiently wait until they have had further experience to teach them their fault, and then they may come to us again.

我們必須努力保持和善、寧靜和願意助人的心，就像一陣微風或一道煦陽一樣，當有人需要時給予幫助，絕不強迫他人認同自己的信念。

We should strive to be so gentle, so quiet, so patiently helpful that we move among our fellow men more as a breath of air or a ray of sunshine: ever ready to help them when they ask: but never forcing them to our own views.

第二個我所要闡述的就是，盲目崇拜將阻礙我們獲得健康的情況。盲目崇拜在今日社會也相當普遍，同時它也是醫師治病時所遭遇到的最大難題之一。耶穌曾經說過：「你們不能同時信奉主又信奉瑪門（財富與貪婪的邪惡神祇）。」而對瑪門的信奉正是當前最麻煩的絆腳石之一。

And I want now to tell you of another great hindrance to health, which is very, very common today, and one of the greatest obstacles that physicians encounter in their endeavour to heal. An obstacle which is a form of idolatry. Christ said 'Ye cannot serve God and mammon,' and yet the service of mammon is one of our greatest stumbling blocks.

魏愛娟：

　　我覺得以下兩句話，可以當成我往後花精教學的座右銘：「他們願意傾聽，就循循善誘；如果沒有意願，就耐心等待他們自己學習。」

李穎哲：

　　我覺得治療師常常會落入馬鞭草或甜栗的情緒中，因為我們會覺得「跟你說要如何如何，怎麼你都不聽」。

吳謝興：

　　像我們去外地教課，來聽課的大部分都已經是治療師，可是他們也都遇到了這層關卡。

李穎哲：

　　另外，巴赫醫師在這邊提到的「我們現在很多人都在盲目崇拜」，我記得巴赫醫師的另一篇手稿也提到，許多人正陷入了靈性的貪婪，就是說我們常希望自己不斷提升，或希望自己越來越有靈性，因此一直學東西、參加靈性成長工作坊，因而落入了貪婪的陷阱。但看到這裡我又不禁覺得自己的領悟不是很正確，後來我突破了這點，覺得還是可以去接觸一些新東西，是應該要抓住重點，就是要確定自己的方向，學習其他新的東西則是為了加強這個方向主軸。

陳慧玲：

　　我以前也有想過這個問題，後來決定依循自己心裡的渴望，就像進了一間屋子，屋子裡有很多窗戶；窗戶是關於

> 屋子這主題可以互通有無的，所以可以經由這些窗戶來把其他長處結合到這個屋子裡。像我之前看了一本書，裡面說一開始大家對於靈性的學習都有一股狂熱，因為每個人都需要接往自己的內在，因此變成了一種貪婪，跟這裡講的一模一樣，所以需要去確認那是真心渴望的、還是只是想要與眾不同。
>
> 林筱岑：
>
> 　　我覺得去學習，有一個很重要的目標就是要變的比較柔軟，不會因為說今天接受了某個系統，就覺得其他東西不好，因此變的僵化而故步自封。

　　從前有個莊嚴而聖潔的天使現身於聖約翰面前，讓聖約翰不禁生起了傾慕與崇拜之心。而天使對他說：「千萬行不得，因為我是你的兄弟、你的僕人，你要崇拜的應是上帝。」可在今天，成千上萬的人們不信奉上帝、不信奉聖潔的天使，卻崇拜另一個人類同胞；我向你們保證，人們所必須要克服的最大難題之一就是病患的盲目崇拜。

　　There was an angel once, a glorious, magnificent angel, that appeared to St John, and St John fell in adoration and worshipped. But the angel said to him, 'See thou do it not, I am thy fellow servant and of thy brethren. Worship God.' And yet today, tens of thousands of us worship not God, not even a mighty angel, but a fellow human being. I can assure you that one of the greatest difficulties which has to be overcome is a sufferer's worship of another mortal.

像這樣的措辭是多麼地普遍：「我必須先問問我父親，我必須先問問我姊妹或我丈夫。」這真是可悲啊！一個獨立的個體在尋求神性進化與發展的同時，竟然需要隨時停下來去向另一位同樣是生命的旅者徵詢認可；難道他以為創造生命的是這些旅者而不是造物主？

How common is the expression: 'I must ask my father, my sister, my husband.' What a tragedy. To think that a human Soul, developing his Divine evolution, should stop to ask permission of a fellow traveller. To whom does he imagine that he owes his origin, his being, his life - to a fellow-traveller or to his Creator?

我們必須瞭解，自己的所作所為和想法都只需對上帝負責。此外，允許被他人干擾、遵守他人的命令，過度考慮他人的渴望，都是盲目崇拜的行為。而盲目崇拜所造成的後果是很嚴重的，它會將我們禁錮，就像被關在牢籠一樣，侷限了我們的生命；即便我們唯一需要回應的是賜予我們生命與認知的造物主，只要我們仍聽令於他人，前述現象就會一直存在。

We must understand that we are answerable for our actions, and for our thoughts to God, and to God alone. And that to be influenced, to obey the wishes, or consider the desires of another mortal is idolatry indeed. Its penalty is severe, it binds us with chains, it places us in prisons, it confines our very life; and so it should, and so we justly deserve, if we listen to the dictates of a human being, when our whole self should know but one command - that of our Creator, Who gave us our life and our understanding.

一個人如果把妻子、小孩、父親或朋友視為比自己的人生使命還重要，那是盲目的崇拜者；而他們所崇拜的就是瑪門而不是上帝。

Be certain that the individual who considers above his duty his wife, his child, his father, or his friend, is an idolator, serving mammon and not God.

記住耶穌曾經說過：「誰是我母親？誰是我兄弟？」暗喻了即使是這般渺小和微不足道的我們，都是來這個世界為同胞服務的；即便生命只是短暫的一刻，也不能因為他人的命令而違反了靈魂的指引。要遵循自己靈魂的指引，做自己命運的主人（即意味讓自己只受內在神性的指引，不去理會外在的阻礙），永遠依照上帝的法則行事，並且只對上帝負責。

Remember the words of Christ, 'Who is My mother, and who are My brethren,' which imply that even all of us, small and insignificant as we may be, are here to serve our brother-men, humanity, the world at large, and never, for the briefest moment, to be under the dictates and commands of another human individual against those motives which we know to be our Soul's commands.

最後，還有一件事要特別提醒你們，要記住耶穌曾教導過信徒的一句箴言：「不要與眾惡作對。」因為疾病或錯誤不是靠強硬對抗來解決的，相反地，是要用與之對應的美德去取代，就好像不能用更深沈的黑暗趕走黑暗，而是要用光去照耀；以愛化解仇恨；用同情憐憫化解殘酷；以健康取代疾病。

Be captains of your Souls, be masters of your fate (which means let your selves be ruled and guided entirely, without let or hindrance from person or circumstance, by the Divinity within you), ever living in accordance with the laws of, and answerable only to the God Who gave you your life. And yet, one more point to bring before your notice. Ever remember the injunction which Christ gave to His disciples, 'Resist not evil.' Sickness and wrong are not to be conquered by direct fighting, but by replacing them by good. Darkness is removed by light, not by greater darkness: hate by love: cruelty by sympathy and pity: and disease by health.

我們此生的目的就是要從自身的錯誤中學習，努力發展相對的美德，讓錯誤就像白雪消融於陽光之下。與其和你的擔憂爭戰，在疾病中一味掙扎，與自己的各種缺點做拉鋸戰，還不如忘卻它們，專心發展你所欠缺的美德。

Our whole object is to realise our faults, and endeavour so to develop the opposing virtue that the fault will disappear from us like snow melts in the sunshine. Don't fight your worries: don't struggle with your disease: don't grapple with your infirmities: rather forget them in concentrating on the development of the virtue you require.

所以現在總結一下，我們可以明白未來同類療法在治療疾病時所扮演的重要角色。

And so now, in summing up, we can see the mighty part that homoeopathy is going to play in the conquest of disease in the future.

並瞭解疾病的本質是「相似治療相似」，疾病是自己造成的，是為了糾正我們的錯誤且讓自己更完美而存在的；只要願意虛心學習並即時修正錯誤，就能夠避免疾病的產生。這些真理都是哈尼曼偉大研究的延續；沿著這條道路走下去，將對疾病與健康有更深一層的認識，然後慢慢地從他的研究往神聖療癒的榮光邁進。

Now that we have come to the understanding that disease itself is 'like curing like': that it is of our own making: for our correction and for our ultimate good: and that we can avoid it, if we will but learn the lessons needed, and correct our faults before the severer lesson of suffering is necessary. This is the natural continuation of Hahnemann's great work; the consequence of that line of thought which was disclosed to him, leading us a step further towards perfect understanding of disease and health, and is the stage to bridge the gap between where he left us and the dawn of that day when humanity will have reached that state of advancement when it can receive direct the glory of Divine Healing.

爾後，這些通曉疾病本質的醫師，將能從大自然中挑選出神聖的植物，來幫助病患打通身體與靈魂之間交流的管道，發展美德並除去錯誤，帶給人們心靈上真正的健康。

The understanding physician, selecting well his remedies from the beneficent plants in nature, those Divinely enriched and blessed, will be enabled to assist his patients to open up those channels which allow greater communion between Soul and body, and thus the development of the virtues needed to wipe away the faults. This brings to mankind the hope of real health combined with mental and spiritual advance.

而病患則必須準備好面對疾病的真相，瞭解疾病是完全肇因於病患自身的錯誤，就像罪惡的代價即是死亡。即使病患可從醫生那裡獲得指引和協助，但他們仍必須親自改正錯誤，過著更美好有益的生活。

For the patients, it will be necessary that they are prepared to face the truth, that disease is entirely and only due to faults within themselves, just as the wages of sin is death. They will have to have the desire to correct those faults, to live a better and more useful life, and to realise that healing depends on their own effort, though they may go to the physician for guidance and assistance in their trouble.

真正的健康無法以金錢買到，就如同教育不是靠繳學費就能獲得知識的，而是要靠自己的意願去學習。

Health can be no more obtained by payment of gold than a child can purchase his education: no sum of money can teach the pupil to write, he must learn of himself, guided by an experienced teacher. And so it is with health.

在此，有兩個聖經戒律必須遵守：愛上帝和愛你的鄰居！讓我們成為自由而獨立的個體，順服於自己內在的神性，然後進一步將自由送給我們的同胞，讓大家都從各種束縛中解放。

There are the two great commandments: 'Love God and thy neighbour'. Let us develop our individuality that we may obtain complete freedom to serve the Divinity within ourselves, and that Divinity alone: and give unto all others their absolute freedom, and serve them as much as lies within our power, according to the dictates of our Souls, ever remembering that as our own liberty increases, so grows our freedom and ability to serve our fellow men.

從而真切地瞭解疾病的面貌乃是自身錯誤所造成。真正的療癒將著重在協助病患重獲身心靈的和諧，且唯有病患本身可以成就這件事，而醫生所能做的就是從旁給予指引和協助。

Thus we have to face the fact that disease is entirely of our own making and that the only cure is to correct our faults. All true healing aims at assisting the patient to put his Soul and mind and body in harmony. This can only be done by himself, though advice and help by an expert brother may greatly assist him.

自從哈尼曼過世之後，各種非自我療癒的技巧蘊育而生，這些都是唯物方式；這種靠他人力量取得的療方，缺少病患自身的省思與自救，只能讓病患獲得症狀抒解，卻傷害了內在靈魂本質，病患無法習得他所欠缺的部分，因而讓錯誤延續。

As Hahnemann laid down, all healing which is not from within, is harmful, and apparent cure of the body obtained through materialistic methods, obtained only through the action of others, without self-help, may certainly bring physical relief, but harm to our Higher Natures, for the lesson has remained unlearnt, and the fault has not been eradicated.

這些用金錢和錯誤的方法所煉造出來的療方違反自然而且膚淺，它們僅能壓抑住病症而非徹底根除疾病，這是很可怕的一件事。

It is terrible today to think of the amount of artificial and superficial cures obtained through money and wrong methods in medicine; wrong methods because they merely suppress symptoms, give apparent relief, without removing the cause.

真正的療癒一定是來自我們的內在，藉由認知並糾正自身的錯誤，重新獲得內在寧靜。造物者為了協助我們，而在原野中創造某些花草植物，使其蘊含神聖力量，幫助我們一步步進化，朝完美的道路邁進。

Healing must come from within ourselves, by acknowledging and correcting our faults, and harmonising our being with the Divine Plan. And as the Creator, in His mercy, has placed certain Divinely enriched herbs to assist us to our victory, let us seek out these and use them to the best of our ability, to help us climb the mountain of our evolution, until the day when we shall reach the summit of perfection.

實際上真正的療癒比哈尼曼所領悟到的「相似治療相似」道理的層次還要高；真正的療癒是用愛與美德去克服我們的錯誤，並非卸除病患自身應負的責任，而是給予協助，讓他們去克服自己的錯誤。

Hahnemann had realised the truth of 'like curing like', which is in reality disease curing wrong action: that true healing is one stage higher than this: love and all its attributes driving out wrong. That in correct healing nothing must be used which relieves the patient of his own responsibility: but such means only must be adopted which help him to overcome his faults.

就我們現在所知，有些同類療法的療方可以提升我們的心靈感應，促進靈肉合一，讓效果更顯著，而達到更大的和諧。

That we now know that certain remedies in the homoeopathic pharmacopoeia have the power to elevate our vibrations, thus bringing more union between our mortal and Spiritual self, and effecting the cure by greater harmony thus produced.

最後，我們的工作就是要更進一步地讓這些療方更精純，並且加入新療方，使其變成有益且能向上提升。

And finally, that it is our work to purify the pharmacopoeia, and to add to it new remedies until it contains only those which are beneficent and uplifting.

Part Ⅲ 　　　　　　　　　　　　 讓自己自由

Free Thyself

【導讀】

自由的幸福人

吳謝興

　　《自我療癒》（Heal Thyself）一書是巴赫醫師在 1930 年時所撰寫的（1931 年出版），完成之後的兩年間，巴赫醫師在花精的使用及人生的經歷上，都有了更多的心得與體會，他認為人之所以會生病的重要原因之一是「缺乏自主性」，因此兩年後，他又寫了《讓自己自由》（Free Thyself）這本書。在看過這本書之後，你或許會發現，雖然《讓自己自由》所陳述的道理在《自我療癒》裡已經有所涵蓋，但《讓自己自由》這本書，像是把《自我療癒》內最重要的精華給提選出來，並且在「如何使自己自由」、「如何釋放自己」這些主題上作更深入的探討。

　　總有許多人覺得自己不快樂、不幸福，終日為人辛苦、為人忙，生活中充滿無奈的忙、茫、盲！煩躁、緊張而又無趣，永遠都找不到讓自己快樂的事，而每天也累的無法去省思和發現快樂，到底原因何在？到底是為了什麼？於是有人開始怨天尤人，開始埋怨父母、家庭、國家，甚至開始討厭自己、討厭人生，也放棄去建立人生中愛的互動，慢慢地，生命中的熱力和追尋消失了，變成一個別人和自己都討厭的人。

　　巴赫醫師透過對人性的觀察，以及自己親身的體驗，發現以上的種種問題，很多都來自於我們的心無法自由發展，無法做真正的自己。所幸巴赫醫師發現的 38 種花精，就像是上天派來凡塵的天使或菩薩一樣，慈悲而又耐心地教導指引我們找到自己，察覺和釋放我們僵固封閉的心靈，然後慢慢地打開溫暖誠摯的心，讓心自由自在地思考，無憂無懼地感受生活。

　　閱讀巴赫醫師的這本著作，或許可以替我們打開一扇通往自由、幸福人生的大門；透過愛的花精協助，建立正向思考的能力，情緒日見平穩，好的習慣也慢慢養成，大家將會發現，你不再是壓力、批評、壞心情下的囚奴，而是一個自由自在，活在當下的幸福人！

【導讀者簡介】吳謝興先生（1966~2011），曾任 IFEC 國際花精研究推廣中心負責人及專任講師。

讓自己自由
Free Thyself

· ·

引 言

儘管文字無法完全體現真理，且本書作者也不願以說教方式來
傳達真理，但他仍然試圖以簡單清楚的文字，來與我們分享生
命的目的、困境背後的意義，以及重獲健康的方法；而事實上
，是要讓我們明白，人人皆可成為自己的良醫。

Introduction

It is impossible to put truth into words. The author of this book has
no desire to preach, indeed he very greatly dislikes that method of
conveying knowledge. He has tried, in the following pages, to show
as clearly and simply as possible the purpose of our lives, the uses of
the difficulties that beset us, and the means by which we can regain
our health; and, in fact, how each of us may become our own doctor.

第 *1* 章
Chapter One

生命，是一則簡單的故事

It is as simple as this, the Story of Life

　　從前，有個小女孩想畫一間漂亮的小屋送給媽媽當生日禮物。在她幼小心靈中，屋子的模樣大到輪廓小至每個細節，都已經成形了，只差沒畫出來而已。

　　A small child has decided to paint the picture of a house in time for her mother's birthday. In her little mind the house is already painted; she knows what it is to be like down to the very smallest detail, there remains only to put it on paper.

　　於是她打開畫箱、拿出畫筆與畫布，帶著純然熱情與愉悅的心情開始作畫。她毫不分心、全神貫注地繪製著，希望這幅畫能趕在媽媽生日前完成。

　　Out comes the paint-box, the brush and the paint-rag, and full of enthusiasm and happiness she sets to work. Her whole attention and interest is centred on what she is doing - nothing can distract her from the work in hand.

　　最後，她心目中的藍圖終於呈現出來了！畫中的每扇窗、每扇門都那麼恰如其份地出現在適當的位置，而且每個筆觸都代表著她對母親的愛，所以稱得上是一幅傑作！即使屋子看起來像是凌亂的乾草堆，它依舊是完美無暇的成功作品，因為這位小畫家已經盡心盡力將她的生命灌注在這幅畫中。

The picture is finished in time for the birthday. To the very best of her ability she has put her idea of a house into form. It is a work of art because it is all her very own, every stroke done out of love for her mother, every window, every door painted in with the conviction that it is meant to be there. Even if it looks like a haystack, it is the most perfect house that has ever been painted: it is a success because the little artist has put her whole heart and soul, her whole being into the doing of it.

透過這個故事我們看到的是，所謂的健康、快樂與成功，必須是一種發自內心的付出，因為那是用愛、自由與真我的付出。

This is health, this is success and happiness and true service. Serving through love in perfect freedom in our own way.

我們最初來到這世上時，就已經知道應該畫下什麼樣的圖，也已然規劃出自己的生命道路，剩下的就只是親自將它付諸實現。就像傾注愉悅和熱情於畫作上一樣，無論我們來到這世上選擇了什麼樣的環境，都能將我們的心念和目標努力地呈現在自己的生命中。

So we come down into this world, knowing what picture we have to paint, having already mapped out of our path through life, and all that remains for us to do is to put it into material form. We pass along full of joy and interest, concentrating all our attention upon the perfecting of that picture, and to the very best of our ability translating our own thoughts and aims into the physical life of whatever environment we have chosen.

因此，假如我們懂得聆聽內心的聲音，並且貫徹始終，就沒有所謂的失敗，我們的生命已經是極大的成功了，而且健康快樂。

Then, if we follow from start to finish our very own ideals, our very own desires with all the strength we possess, there is no failure, our life has been a tremendous success, a healthy and a happy one.

　　然而，如果我們屈服於生命中的不如意，它就會破壞這份健康、快樂與成功的和諧，使我們偏離了人生的道路。

　　The same little story of the child-painter will illustrate how, if we allow them, the difficulties of life may interfere with this success and happiness and health, and deter us from our purpose.

　　以此故事為例，假如小女孩在專心作畫的過程中，有人告訴她：「窗戶應該畫在這邊…門應該在那邊…這裡最好再畫一條通往花園的小徑…」小女孩很可能因為這些外在聲音而失去了作畫的興趣；或者她會繼續畫下去，但是畫出來的卻是別人心中的藍圖。困惑、不快樂、煩躁等情緒可能讓她開始討厭這幅畫，甚至將它撕毀。

　　The child is busily and happily painting when someone comes along and says, "Why not put a window here, and a door there; and of course the garden path should go this way." The result in the child will be complete loss of interest in the work; she may go on, but is now only putting someone else's ideas on paper: she may become cross, irritated, unhappy, afraid to refuse these suggestions; begin to hate the picture and perhaps tear it up: in fact, according to the type of child so will be the reaction.

　　最後雖然畫出我們所認為的屋子，但卻是一件不完美的失敗作品。因為呈現出來的不是她自己的構思，而是別人的；更糟的是，她可能因此來不及在媽媽生日前把它畫好！

　　The final picture may be a recognisable house, but it is an imperfect one and a failure because it is the interpretation of another's thoughts, not the child's. It is of no use as a birthday present because it may not be done in time, and the mother may have to wait another whole year for her gift.

　　這種因外在力量的干預而產生的反應，可以說就是一種疾病，一種暫時性的失敗和苦痛，所以我們必須學習不讓外在的干擾在心中種下懷疑、害怕和冷漠的種子，因而偏離了自己要走的路。

　　This is disease, the reaction to interference. This is temporary failure and unhappiness: and this occurs when we allow others to interfere with our purpose in life, and implant in our minds doubt, or fear, or indifference.

李穎哲：

　　我有個個案想與大家分享：有一位被西醫診斷為患有過動症 (ADHD) 的小孩，他給我的第一印象是他非常聰點，眼睛炯炯有神，與人講話時像個小大人似的，卻又不失小孩天真無邪的一面，和一般被診斷為 ADHD 的小孩很不相同。根據媽媽的敘述，當他與大人或其他年紀比他大的青少年相處時非常乖巧，但是當他在學校上課時卻經常坐不住，並且會打其他同年齡的孩童；當我問他最喜歡上哪一門課時，他說是畫畫課。他在上畫畫課的時候表現的最專注，心情最穩定快樂，可是當規定畫畫的主題必須是自畫像或是自己父母親時，他就開始坐不住、和其他同學起衝突…

　　所以當我讀到巴赫醫師這段文字的時候，就聯想到這個個案。其實很多人從小就被規定必須做這個做那個，如果一個小孩在畫畫時不按照「規定」而喜歡全憑想像自由發揮隨興作畫，就會被視為是不守規矩的行為；另外，關於這個個案的另一個現象是，當他在閱讀某些有興趣的書籍時，他也會表現出非常專注的樣子。所以從閱讀與作畫這兩點來看，其實不甚符合過動兒的表現特質，現在有越來越多人被診斷為過動兒，就我看來可能有不少是誤判。

　　另外，我覺得學校的通才教育方式也有問題，因為強迫每個小朋友都要按照傳統的教育價值觀，反而會產生相當多的問題。就以上這個案例來說，每當星期四上課時間變成整天，雖然他早上情緒還相當穩定，不過到了下午，就開始變得躁動易怒，還喜歡打其他小朋友，可以想見他在傳統教育方式下學習是一件痛苦的事。所以我覺得，除了花精

對他的幫助之外，或許他母親可以對他嘗試不同的教育方式，因為限制他自由的外在環境仍然存在著。

林鈺傑：

　　就此個案而言，家長或學校的教育方式是否也是造成問題的主要原因之一？

陳惠玲：

　　我覺得是耶！因為他所表現出的行為不單純只是過動而已，家長與老師都給他相對的壓力，所以他累積了很多情緒，不一定是他本身的問題，而是外在環境的壓力造成了他的情緒表現。這個個案跟一個我班上遇到的情形相似，我通常會跟母親溝通，說明她的孩子不是過動，而是太聰明了，並且給他一些可以讓他專注的書籍，像是昆蟲圖鑑、封神榜…等等；我覺得這樣的小孩也很可憐，他其實是需要老師瞭解他，環境給他的束縛感會造成他一些誇張的行為，進而使其他同學排斥他，所以老師可以教導其他同學接納他。

李穎哲：

　　以前的時代好像很少聽說有過動和注意力不集中的現象？

陳惠玲：

　　有種說法是，以前的孩子都在田野間奔跑，所以可以很直接地接收到天地的能量，因而排解了自身的一些壓力，可是現在的小朋友都關在水泥屋裡，無法消耗過多的精力，與大自然嚴重失聯，所以會變得比較躁動。

　吳謝興：

　　另外也有一個可能是，有不少過動兒生長在富裕的家庭中，所以進學校之前就已經補了很多習，以致於進學校之後，發現學校教的課程太簡單，老早就學過了，因而完全不感興趣；再者就是剛剛提到的，似乎在都市裡的小孩比較容易被診斷出有 ADHD，有些個案搬到鄉下跟爺爺奶奶住之後就痊癒了。

陳惠玲：

　　「我們最初來到這世上時，就已經知道應該畫下什麼樣的圖，也已然規劃出自己的生命道路，剩下的就只是親自付諸實現而已。」我想問各位，當你們來到這世上的時候，從小就知道自己的道路該怎麼走嗎？

陳家莉：

　　我到現在都還是不知道！以前念的是商學院，現在繞了一大圈成了中醫師，自己常常會想這是怎麼一回事…？會成為中醫師是很偶然的。有一次走在街上，拿到一張關於學士後中醫系的傳單，那時我從美國唸完大學回到台灣，找了很多工作但都做不久，本來考慮要回美國繼續念碩士，但後來

放棄了要考的 GMAT，卻在第三年考上學士後中醫系，一路念到畢業成為中醫師…，所以我剛才念到這段文字時覺得很困惑，因為我對於自己的人生道路一直都很不清楚。

李穎哲：

　　巴赫醫師在某篇文章中提到，幼鳥被父母養育長大之後，就懂得如何飛翔覓食、就懂得如何去尋找自己的天空，因為這是一種生物本能；其實人也是一樣，如果小孩能夠不要成長在一個充滿約束和制式化的社會、不要被時時刻刻告知怎麼做才是成功的，那麼他們就能夠找到自己的人生道路。

陳家莉：

　　近幾年常常聽到一個廣告詞 —「不要讓你的孩子輸在起跑點上」我覺得這個廣告詞真的害死人，現在的小孩很早就被父母逼著要向前衝。

陳惠玲：

　　小孩子會承受到父母親緊張的情緒，像我們班上的小朋友，有些一不小心犯了錯就會緊張得大哭；當這些小朋友的媽媽來到學校時，會不停地跟我說她對小孩的擔憂，並細數小孩的所有缺點…

陳家莉：

　　像我的中醫老師曾經說過，第一個小孩照書養，第二個小孩照豬養，可是通常第二個小孩會養得比第一個小孩來的

好，因為當父母太緊張而把所有注意力都放在小孩身上時，反而造成他不能有任何犯錯的空間，那種緊繃的情緒容易讓孩子的行為產生偏差。

陳惠玲：

　　我再仔細看了一遍以上的文章，覺得這裡談的「生命道路」好像不是指職業，而是一種人生更大的方向。

林鈺傑：

　　所以說假如我從小想要走的人生方向是服務人群，那麼不論我長大後從事什麼職業，都可以在這個職業中實現這個目標。

吳謝興：

　　像有些人如果喜歡大自然，長大後可能會選擇去研究昆蟲或植物，那是他的方向；但是假如他被父母強迫讀商或讀法律，那就沒有辦法去實現他的人生方向了…。昨天我看了網站上兒童花精那則主題裡的一部短片，主題是 Children see, Children do，拍的很好，其實小孩的一言一行常常都是被父母影響的，所以當小孩看見父母親亂丟垃圾，他就學著亂丟垃圾；當小孩在學校對同學暴力相向，常常也是因為家中父母親經常拳打腳踢。

陳惠玲：

　　可是我也要幫家長講講話，來自同個家庭的兄弟姊妹，彼此之間的個性氣質有時可能相去甚遠。有時小孩子

犯錯，父母都會很惶恐地道歉，說是自己沒有教好，我就會安慰他們說沒有關係，因為其實小孩子都有自己先天的氣質，有的時候不是父母的錯，所以要平衡一下，免得變成父母比小孩還要緊張。

吳謝興：

沒錯！小朋友有自己先天的特質，即使父母親壞事作盡，他還是能保有自己的善念，他有天分可從周邊老師同學身上學到好的特質；但如果今天這個小朋友是屬於海綿型的特質，他就很有可能從父母親身上學到一切，包含壞的；不過可以從逆境中脫穎而出的畢竟是少數…。在面相學中有個理論是「一命、二運、三風水、四積陰德、五讀書」，意思是說，當一個小孩命不好，或出生在一個不好的家庭中，但如果他的運好，碰到貴人或好老師，就會對他有好的影響，或者是好的風水如孟母三遷，選擇好的生活環境，說不定就可以由壞轉好；再者就是多做好事、看好書，其實看好書也會對小孩有潛移默化的效果。

李穎哲：

這就是林雲大師所說的「多元緣生論」，就是說當一件事情發生了，其實不單純只是某些佛家說的因果業障所造成；因果業障只是其中一個因素，還有許多其他因素集合起來才造就出一件事情的發生。

林鈺傑：

我覺得「假如我們懂得聆聽內心的聲音，並且貫徹始終，就沒有所謂的失敗」這段文字描寫的好像很難做到，

因為身邊總是有父母親或是誰會試圖去影響你的走向，
要如何做到「貫徹始終」？

李穎哲：

　　我覺得巴赫醫師的這段文字所要傳述的是一個真理，
或許大部分的人都無法做到，但從今天開始去嘗試，
不管做什麼事都能夠傾聽自己內在的聲音，那麼就會越來
越接近這個真理。

陳惠玲：

　　後來想想有很多的例子，像是一些音樂家或藝術家，
他們一開始可能也是做不喜歡的事情，但是當他們開始傾聽
內在的聲音、去實行自己喜歡的事物時，就變得很快樂、
很有成就，或許他們也是經過一段找尋的日子，找尋的過程
也是一種經驗、一種學習，生命的安排通常都不會是白費
的。

第 2 章
Chapter Two

健康，仰賴與自己的靈魂保持和諧

Health depends on being in harmony with our souls

我們必須要瞭解疾病與健康所代表的意義，因為那是非常重要的。

It is of primary importance that the true meaning of health and of disease should be clearly understood.

健康，並非是遙不可及的難事，而是自然又簡單的道理，甚至簡單到讓我們都忽略了它：健康，是我們與生俱來的權利，是身心靈完整契合的結果。

Health is our heritage, our right. It is the complete and full union between soul, mind and body; and this is no difficult far-away ideal to attain, but one so easy and natural that many of us have overlooked it.

世間萬物，即使最微不足道的事，都是具有靈性的，而且都蘊含著神聖的法則。

All earthly things are but the interpretation of things spiritual. The smallest most insignificant occurrence has a Divine purpose behind it.

就連我們每個人來到這世上，也都有神聖的任務要去實現，我們的身心就如同樂器一般，要把靈魂的指示實現成美妙的音符。如此和諧的狀態，便造就了最完美的健康與愉悅的人生。

We each have a Divine mission in this world, and our soul' s use our minds and bodies as instruments to do this work, so that when all three are working in unison the result is perfect health and perfect happiness.

神聖任務所代表的，並不是一味的犧牲奉獻，也不是從這個世界上退縮，更不是要拋棄自然與完美所帶來的快樂；相反地，是希望你能夠全然擁抱萬物及其所帶來的喜悅。換句話說，就是要我們投入熱情，不論是管理家務、務農、繪畫、戲劇，或是在一般商店中提供民眾服務。只要我們所選擇的工作是生命中最熱愛的，那這就是來自於自身靈魂最明確的指引，就是我們此生該投入的工作。而我們將在這工作中誠實地表現出自我，平凡地把真我所要傳達的訊息展現出來。

A Divine mission means no sacrifice, no retiring from the world, no rejecting of the joys of beauty and nature; on the contrary, it means a fuller and greater enjoyment of all things: it means doing the work that we love to do with all our heart and soul, whether it be house keeping, farming, painting, acting, or serving our fellow-men in shops or houses. And this work, whatever it may be, if we love it above all else, is the definite command of our soul, the work we have to do in this world, and in which alone we can be our true selves, interpreting in an ordinary materialistic way the message of that true self.

所以，我們可以透過一個人所表現出來的健康與快樂程度，來瞭解他是否無礙地把自己靈魂的訊息傳達出來。

We can judge, therefore, by our health and by our happiness, how well we are interpreting this message.

我們說，在一個完整而和諧的人的身上，所有靈性特質都得到了彰顯。所以我們來到這世上，為的就是希望可以一一將這些特質加以強化然後彰顯，儘可能地不被困境給動搖而偏離了這個目的。我們在這世上所選擇的工作以及外在的環境，都是為了給我們機會來考驗自己，讓我們趨於完整。其實，我們來到這世界之初，就是一個完整的個體，不僅具備彰顯此生任務的能力，也已經知道我們終將戰勝

所有考驗，因為，我們是至高無上造物主的子民。明白了這個道理之後，我們就可以把所有的困境和考驗當作是一次又一次的冒險，運用自身內在的神性度過考驗，讓生命充滿愉悅的光輝。

There are all the spiritual attributes in the perfect man; and we come into this world to manifest these one at a time, to perfect and strengthen them so that no experience, no difficulty can weaken or deflect us from the fulfilment of this purpose. We chose the earthly occupation, and the external circumstances that will give us the best opportunities of testing us to the full: we come with the full realisation of our particular work: we come with the unthinkable privilege of knowing that all our battles are won before they are fought, that victory is certain before ever the test arrives, because we know that we are the children of the Creator, and as such are Divine, unconquerable and invincible. With this knowledge life is a joy; hardships andexperiences can be looked upon as adventures, for we have but to realise our power, to be true to our Divinity, when these melt away like mist in the sunshine. God did indeed give His children dominion over all things.

只要懂得傾聽，我們的靈魂將會帶領我們的身心穿越重重的考驗，綻放出喜樂與健康的光彩，像個孩子一樣地無憂而自在。

Our souls will guide us, if we will only listen, in every circum stance, every difficulty; and the mind and body so directed will pass through life radiating happiness and perfect health, as free from all cares and responsibilities as the small trusting child.Page

李穎哲：

　　「健康，仰賴與自己的靈魂保持和諧」這句話雖然我們讀起來覺得理所當然，但對巴赫醫師當年來說，是一個很不得了的全新觀念。一直以來，醫生對於「健康」通常都會有個定義，但很少人講到要與自己的靈魂保持和諧，所以我覺得這個觀念是巴赫醫師很大的一個創見。

陳家莉：

　　換句話說，這句話在我們現在的討論場合中是沒有問題的，而且大家也都認為理所當然的；可是如果這是在醫院，那麼會有一堆人瘋掉，覺得這根本就是怪力亂神。

林鈺傑：

　　我覺得現在的醫學觀念，所謂的健康是指外在沒有任何擦傷、疤痕或缺陷，長的白白胖胖的就是健康，可是卻忽略了這裡所提到的「身體」以外「心靈」的健康。

李穎哲：

　　其實花精的效用就是在幫助我們的靈魂保持和諧，以前很多人會納悶花精的作用到底是什麼，其實就是這個作用，就算是拿能量、波動、經絡、脈輪等理論來加以解釋，都只能說明花精的部分作用面向，我個人認為花精的作用是什麼呢？總歸一句話，就是能夠讓我們的心智與靈魂保持和諧。

　　另外，我覺得這邊有一句話很重要，就是「平凡地把真我所要傳達的訊息展現出來」，裡面的「平凡地」很重要，因為我們有時在做一件事情的時候都會太過努力或刻意，

巴赫醫師要我們平凡地去展現而不要太過度，像馬鞭草、岩水特質的人常常會太刻意要去完成某項任務或達到某個完美的境界，反而表現得太超過。

陳慧玲：

　　我覺得「換句話說，就是要我們投入熱情」，這裡所提到的「熱情」對我來說意義很大。

李穎哲：

　　我想巴赫醫師認為，如果我們不管做什麼事情都失去熱情，就表示與靈魂失去平衡和諧。

陳慧玲：

　　是野玫瑰的負面情緒嗎？

李穎哲：

　　對！還有角樹現象也會如此。

林鈺傑：

　　這句話讓我想到一部電影「深夜加油站遇見蘇格拉底」，片中主角在加油站遇見一位老人，他問這位老人說：「既然你這麼厲害，為什麼只是在加油站裡做些微不足道的工作？」老人回答他：「這也是一種可以服務人群的工作啊！」

陳慧玲：

　　請問第一句話，「我們可以透過一個人所表現出來的健康與快樂程度，來瞭解他是否無礙地把自己靈魂的訊息傳達出來」是真的嗎？如果一個人很健康就代表他已充分地把靈魂的訊息傳達出來嗎？

李穎哲：

　　我覺得可以在小孩身上看到這種全然的健康，亦即與靈魂保持和諧的狀態；常看到他們在草地上無憂無慮地打球、玩耍，其實他們就是處在這種狀態，可是當他慢慢長大，開始接受來自四面八方的期望，就慢慢忘記自己，越來越達不到和諧的狀態。耶穌基督也曾說：「每個人都要恢復孩童般的天真無邪，才能夠進入天堂。」就是說我們需要慢慢地找回赤子之心，才能夠找回內在真正的平靜和喜樂。因為我們來到這世上，不斷地受到外界環境的影響以及傳統文化的限制，因而漸漸地失去了真我；然而在這過程中，我們也學著去掙脫束縛，倘若能夠回復我們的赤子之心，就能夠更容易與靈魂保持和諧，達到真正的健康。

　　另外，一些臨終關懷的個案研究，發現人在即將死亡的時候能把很多事情都放下、最接近赤子之心，可以說像天使一樣美麗，展現出真我來。其實我之前對於臨終關懷這個領域很有興趣，買了很多書來看，因為我覺得花精可以在臨終關懷發揮相當不錯的效用。

吳謝興：

　　能夠接到一些花精的臨終關懷個案都是很巧合的，家屬原先希望花精可以在個案身上創造出奇蹟，雖然不盡然能如他們所願，但他們還是很感謝花精所帶來的效果，因為花精讓臨終個案可以先回歸平靜、安詳，然後才離開人間。

第 3 章
Chapter Three

我們的靈魂是完美的，都是造物主的子民
所有靈魂引導我們去做的事，都是為了讓自己更好

Our souls are perfect, being children of the Creator,
and everything they tell us to do is for our good

　　健康，其實就是真我實現的結果：我們是造物主的子民，我們生來就是完美的！所以健康是我們出生即被賦予的禮物，不需要經過一番掙扎、奮鬥才能得到；相反地，我們只需要在此時此地把這份完美展現出來，就能得到健康。進一步解釋：健康，就是專注地聆聽我們靈魂的指示，像孩童般地全然信任，拒絕用知識（代表善與惡的知識）來推理、判斷及期待所造成的恐懼。同時，我們要小心避開傳統的制約和他人瑣碎的意見，才能不受影響地去服務眾生。

Health is, therefore, the true realisation of what we are: we are perfect: we are children of God. There is no striving to gain what we have already attained. We are merely here to manifest in material form the perfection with which we have been endowed from the beginning of all time. Health is listening solely to the commands of our souls; in being trustful as little children; in rejecting intellect (that tree of the knowledge of good and evil) with its reasonings, its 'fors' and 'againsts,' its anticipatory fears: ignoring convention, the trivial ideas and commands of other people, so that we can pass through life untouched, unharmed, free to serve our fellow-men.

　　健康，可以從一個人是否快樂來判斷；而一個人快樂與否，則取決於他與靈魂是否能夠和諧一致。要達到與自己的靈魂和諧一致，而得到真正的健康與快樂，其實不表示一定要獻身於造物者，成為僧侶或尼姑，或隱居離世；我們來到這個世上，是為了要服務眾生並享受其中的，也唯有發自內心的愛和喜悅，才能發揮我們的影響力，真正

造福這個世界；假如我們的行為是發自錯誤的責任感，並帶著惱怒與不耐煩的心情，那麼這些努力將無法真正助人，而不過是浪費時間罷了！

We can judge our health by our happiness, and by our happiness we can know that we are obeying the dictates of our souls. It is not necessary to be a monk, a nun, or hide away from the world; the world is for us to enjoy and to serve, and it is only by serving out of love and happiness that we can truly be of use, and do our best work. A thing done from a sense of duty with, perhaps, a feeling of irritation and impatience is of no account at all, it is merely precious time wasted when there might be a brother in real need of our help.

真理是不需要被分析、不需要爭論，更不需要用言詞去包裝的，它就存在你我和萬物之中。只有那些次要和複雜的知識需要不斷地被驗證；生命中真正重要的事情一定是簡單易懂的，對每個人來說都是再自然不過的，它就是它，不需要多加解釋。這就和健康的道理相通，一旦我們與靈性和諧一致，就會感到歡喜；越是與靈性緊密結合，歡喜的程度就越熱烈。試想你我曾遇見過的，不管是婚禮上新娘子所散發出的光彩，或是喜悅地望著初生嬰兒的母親，還是剛完成一幅鉅作的畫家所表現出來的狂喜，這些例子都是與靈性緊密相連的表現！

Truth has no need to be analysed, argued about,- or wrapped up in many words. It is realised in a flash, it is part of you. It is only about the unessential complicated things of life that we need so much convincing, and that have led to the development of the intellect. The things that count are simple, they are the ones that make you say, "why, that is true, I seem to have known that always," and so is the realisation of the happiness that comes to us when we are in harmony with our spiritual self, and the closer the union the more intense the joy. Think of the radiance one sometimes sees in a bride on her wedding mom; the rapture of a mother with a new-born babe; the ecstasy of an artist completing a masterpiece: such are the moments where there is spiritual union.

想想看！假如一生都能夠沈浸在這股喜悅中，這將是多麼美好的一件事啊！而相對的，我們也可能因為繁雜的生活方式而失去自我。

Think how wonderful life would be if we lived it all in such joy: and so it is possible when we lose ourselves in our life's work.

李穎哲：

　　「健康是我們出生即被賦予的」，這個觀念顛覆了一般人對健康的價值觀，而且對醫者而言，聽到這句話簡直快要跳腳！但是如果靜下心來仔細想想，就可以理解巴赫醫師所要傳達的訊息。從這段話中還可以抓到一些花精特色的描述，例如「不被他人的意見左右，傾聽靈魂的指示」是紫金蓮 (Cerato)。

黃韋睿：

　　巴赫醫師是否意味著他並不鼓勵「離群索居」的行為？

吳惠容：

　　我想應該不是！巴赫醫師想要傳達的是，不管你選擇出世或入世，只要這個決定是你內心靈魂的指示，那就是好的！

李穎哲：

　　從這段話可以了解一些花精的特色，例如「隱居離世」、「用發自內心的愛與喜悅去服務眾生」是水菫 (Water Violet)的正向人格發展的表徵。

林鈺傑：

　　關於「真理是不需要去分析驗證的」，有些人在使用花精的時候，會不斷地想用能量去解釋它，卻變的一味地強調能量高低強弱的問題。

李穎哲：

　　關於「真理是不需要去分析驗證的」這句話說的很好，如同巴赫醫師所描述的這些畫面「婚禮上新娘子所散發出的光彩」、「喜悅地望著初生嬰兒的母親」這些都是非常自然而然的反應，是發自內心的真實喜悅，難道還需要用能量測定去分析，這個喜悅是因為眼睛看到事物，然後刺激了腦內某某神經傳導物質的分泌，然後又經過了如何的神經傳導，終於在你的內心充滿了喜悅？

第 4 章
Chapter Four

假如我們遵循自己的本性、想法與渴望
就能擁有喜樂與健康

If we follow our own instincts, our own wishes, our
own thoughts, our own desires, we should never
know anything but joy and health

聆聽我們靈魂的聲音並保持單純，是簡單而明瞭的，而且是萬物初創時所要傳達的主旨。

Neither is it a difficult far-away attainment to hear the voice of our own soul; it has all been made so simple for us if we will but acknowledge it. Simplicity is the keynote of all Creation.

我們靈魂的聲音 (亦即來自上帝的聲音)，已經儘可能用最簡單的方式，透過所謂的直覺、靈感，還有日常生活所透露出來的念頭、慾望以及喜好來給予我們方向。因為大部分的人無法直接與自己的高我溝通，所以它 (高我) 才透過靈感、慾望和喜好等各種肉體層面的認知方式來給我們指示。我們的靈魂瞭解每個人的個性和需求，所以不管是小大事、不管是否想要喝杯茶，或需要完全改變生活習慣，對於我們而言，這些指示都是最適合的，應該加以遵循。我們的靈魂也知道，唯有「滿足」才能真正地療癒那些所謂的錯誤和罪惡的情事，或者必須等到某種相反的力量出現，否則這些錯誤無法真正根除，而僅是簡單地被藏匿起來而已；就如同一個喜歡吃果醬的人，唯有一股腦地猛吃果醬，他才會開始厭煩。

Our soul (the still small voice, God 's own voice) speaks to us through our intuition, our instincts, through our desires, ideals, our ordinary likes and dislikes; in whichever way it is easiest for us individually to hear. How else can He speak to us? Our true instincts, desires, likes or dislikes are given us so that we can interpret the spiritual commands of our soul by means of our limited physical perceptions, for it is not possible for many of us yet to be in direct communion with our Higher Self. These commands are meant to be followed implicitly, because the soul alone knows what experiences are necessary for that particular personality. Whatever the command may be, trivial or important, the desire for another cup of tea, or a complete change of the whole of one's life's habits, it should be willingly obeyed. The soul knows that satisfaction is the one real-cure for all that we, in this world, consider as sin and wrong, for until the whole being revolts against a certain act, that fault is not eradicated but simply dormant, just as it is much better and quicker to go on sticking one's fingers into the jam-pot until one is so sick that jam has no further attraction.

千萬不要把我們內心真正的渴望和需求，和「別人寄予我們的厚望」、「良心」、「對錯的價值觀」給搞混了，也不要去在意其他人會怎樣解讀我們的一舉一動，我們的靈魂會導引我們走上對的道路，我們的名譽也會被它看護著；唯一可以稱得上罪過的是不願意遵從神性的指引，違抗造物主以及同胞的行為。來自我們內心真正的渴望和需求，都是為我們好的，可以帶給我們健康和諧的身心。

Our true desires, the wishes of our true selves, are not to be confused with the wishes and desires of other people so often implan ted in our minds, or of conscience, which is another word for the same thing. We must pay no heed to the world's interpretation of our actions. Our own soul alone is responsible for our good, our reputa tion is in His keeping; we can rest assured that there is only one sin, that of not obeying the dictates of our own Divinity. That is the sin against God and our neighbour. These wishes, intuitions, desires are never selfish; they concern ourselves alone and are always right for us, and bring us health in body and mind.

吳謝興：

我對於最後那一句「吃果醬」的比喻不是很瞭解…？

黃韋睿：

我在翻譯的時候，對於這段比喻也很摸不著頭緒，原以為所謂的「滿足才能真正療癒那些錯誤和罪惡的情事」是在說明，如果我們能夠與自己的靈魂和諧一致，那麼不管做什麼都將會充滿熱情地投入其中，所以會得到很豐富的滿足感，而處於感到滿足的狀態下，就不會動了行惡的念頭；可是反過來看「吃果醬」的比喻，難道是說要做壞事就一股腦兒地拼命使壞，直到厭倦了為止？

吳謝興：

我懂了！應該說當我們處於與靈魂不和諧一致的狀態下，會想要透過很多世俗慾望（吃喝嫖賭）來滿足自己，希望這樣做可以療癒自己的空虛，然而這樣的作法就如同吃果醬一樣，誤把這些慾望當作解決的辦法而不斷猛吃，直到有一天身心俱疲，才明白這是一條錯誤的道路，然後才會回頭去找正確的道路；就如同巴赫醫師在《自我療癒》（Heal Thyself）裡所強調的，真正的療癒和真正的滿足是必須去聽從內心靈魂的聲音，呼應到前一章所提到的那個喜悅，就是真正療癒過程所會發生的。

陳慧玲：

之前讀書會也提到關於不斷追求物質生活上的享受，例如喜歡看電視的人就拼命看，一直在進行著他所謂的享樂，可是靈魂卻無法滿足，就像這邊「果醬」的比喻一樣。

林鈺傑：

　　「吃果醬」這個行為其實是 OK 的，但是問題是出在「猛吃」，因為這就代表這個人有很嚴重的不滿足感。

陳家莉：

　　這裡我有個問題，「我們內心真正的渴望和需求，都是為我們好的，可以帶給我們健康和諧的身心」，讀到這裡，我腦中閃過了一個念頭，就是中國哲學幾千年來不斷在辯論的「人性本惡」以及「人性本善」問題，假設是荀子說的對（人性本惡），那麼這個論點放到這裡感覺好像怪怪的；如果是儒家所言為真，感覺上對照到這裡的敘述就比較合理；甚至有另外一個說法是－「人性不惡不善」…其實從小我就對這個議題感到困惑，作了很多研究和思考，直到現在仍然沒有一個正確答案，只是覺得要把人性本善說的如此肯定，我會保留一些態度。

李穎哲：

　　我比較認同「人性不善不惡」的這個看法，應該說內在的靈魂引導我們去做一件事情的時候，並沒有所謂的善惡，只要聆聽我們內在的聲音，做的時候感到喜悅就是對的；可是很多人會在意自己做的事情到底是對還錯，這樣的反應其實就是沒能與內在靈魂達到和諧。所以我認為巴赫醫師並未特別闡述人性本惡或本善，他倒是認為當你違背神性的指引或造物者的定律時，才是真正的錯誤；他覺得這個宇宙存在著神性的定律，也就是愛的定律，若你去破壞這個定律的話，就代表你在破壞整體，你的靈魂不會引導你去破壞

這個愛的定律；這樣說起來，或許孟子或荀子的人性本善和本惡其實都只是看到事情的某個面向而已。

林鈺傑：

今天稍早剛好有位媽媽來中心購買花精，她說她正值青春期的女兒臉上長了痘痘，所以很在意同學的眼光，甚至排斥穿有卡通圖案的衛生衣，因為同學會笑，這段情境我覺得呼應到巴赫醫師所說的「不要去在意別人如何解讀我們的一舉一動，讓靈魂指引我們走上對的道路。」

陳慧玲：

如果一個人很在意別人如何解讀自己的一舉一動，這情緒是否該使用龍芽草 (Agrimony)？

李穎哲：

我以前也會覺得要使用龍芽草，因為龍芽草性格的人很愛面子，可是現在這樣討論下來我會覺得應該需要紫金蓮 (Cerato)；另外，如果她被別人批評之後覺得自行慚穢的話，可以考慮使用野生酸頻果 (Crab Apple)、落葉松 (Larch) 或松 (Pine)。

林鈺傑：

現在使用紫金蓮的機率好像很高…

吳謝興：

因為現在是紫金蓮的年代啊！廣告、媒體那麼氾濫，都在宣揚著我們該活在什麼標準之下。

李穎哲：

　　前一陣子我在巴里島的飯店游泳池看到一個很有趣的畫面，有個人一整天就是在重複地抹著防曬油，然後躺在海灘椅上曬太陽，當滿身大汗的受不了時就到游泳池裡清涼一下，然後繼續回到岸邊抹防曬油曬太陽；真是辛苦，因為他很執著地追求古銅色的膚色。

吳惠容：

　　我讀到這裡，看到「靈魂」、「高我」和「不要去在意別人的看法」，我會覺得這是不是跟西方的基督教／天主教文化有關，因為他們的信徒天天都會禱告，而禱告基本上就是一種跟內在聯繫的方法，透過禱告可以去思考和面對自己的內心，這是我讀到這裡很自然會聯想到的。

陳慧玲：

　　其實巴赫醫師所書寫的這些文字，很多時候看起來像在傳福音……

陳家莉：

　　我覺得這是因為宗教已經在他成長的環境過程中成為他思想的一部分了。

李穎哲：

　　雖然巴赫醫師是屬於基督／天主教系統的宗教，但其實他所傳遞的這些道理，拿去和佛教教義比較後會發現，很多地方其實是相通的，只是在語言和用字上可能有些出入。

疾病是因為我們拒絕靈魂的指引而在肉體產生的結果。因為我們忘記神性就存在我們之中，搗住耳朵拒絕聆聽來自靈魂的聲音，我們把自己的意願強加在別人身上，或者讓別人的建議、想法來左右我們；這些都是造成疾病的原因。

Disease is the result in the physical body of the resistance of the personality to the guidance of the soul. It is when we turn a deaf ear to the 'still small voice', and forget the Divinity within us; when we try to force our wishes upon others, or allow their suggestions, thoughts, and commands to influence us.

當我們越是能夠不被他人的意見所左右，我們的靈魂就越能夠指引我們去執行此生的任務。

The more we become free from outside influences, from other personalities, the more our soul can use us to do His work.

企圖支配、控制他人的意志是自私的行為，然而，整個世界企圖說服我們「跟隨自己內心的渴望才是自私的行為」，那是因為世界想要奴役我們。所以唯有領悟到這點，掙脫束縛，我們才能真正為人類帶來善果；就像大文豪莎士比亞所書：「對自己誠實，永遠聽從它的聲音，日日夜夜，那麼你就不會再對任何人虛偽了。」

It is only when we attempt to control and rule someone else that we are selfish. But the world tries to tell us that it is selfishness to follow our own desires. That is because the world wishes to enslave us, for truly it is only when we can realise and be unhampered our real selves that we can be used for the good of mankind. It is the great truth of Shakespeare, 'To thine own self be true, and it must follow, as the night the day, thou canst not then be false to any man.'

像蜜蜂一樣自由地挑選喜愛的花朵去採集花粉，卻同時也藉由這個動作為植物完成授粉而造福了它。

The bee, by its very choice of a particular flower for its honey, is the means used to bring it the pollen necessary for the future life of its young plants.

李穎哲：

　　我覺得這段話，「我們忘記神性就存在我們之中，摀住耳朵拒絕聆聽來自靈魂的聲音」是在講述紫金蓮 (Cerato) 的表徵，而胡桃 (Walnut) 也稍微被帶了出來，因為處在胡桃狀態的人，很容易被別人影響而改變自己決定。

林鈺傑：

　　另外，這裡也提到不要把自己的意願強加在別人身上，這部分應該是馬鞭草 (Vervain)。

李穎哲：

　　對，沒錯！不過像葡萄藤 (Vine)、菊苣 (Chicory)、岩水 (Rock Water)、山毛櫸 (Beech)，這群屬於過度關心別人福祉的人也都會有如此的態度。

黃韋睿：

　　最後那段話的意涵，我覺得蜜蜂去採花蜜，雖然目的是為了自己，但無意間也造福了那株植物，幫它作了授粉的動作，所以如果我們能聽從自己靈魂的聲音去做某件事，因為

懂得和我們的靈魂保持和諧，所以在進行這件工作的同時，也可以與他人的互動維持和諧，而這種和諧，間接地也就造福了他人。

吳惠容：

這個論點我認同，蜜蜂其實是出於自己的意願而選擇了某一株花，但這樣的行為卻造福了這株花，花粉因而得以傳遞。

李穎哲：

所以說無心插柳柳成蔭，有的時候如果我們想要控制別人，是一種奴役別人的行為；可是當我們只是單純地為自己挑一株花、採個蜜，卻出乎意料地幫這株植物授粉。

第 5 章
Chapter Five

一旦容許他人的意見左右我們
我們將會失去與靈魂的連結
招致內心的不和諧與疾病
別人的聲音，可能會使我們偏離了人生的道路

It is allowing the interference of other people
that stops our listening to the dictates of our soul,
and that brings disharmony and disease.
The moment the thought of another person enters our minds,
it deflects us from our true course

在我們初生之時，造物主就賜予我們完整的個性；祂給予我們任務，而且是只有我們才能夠完成的任務。他也給予每個人一條人生道路，一條不容許任何干擾的道路，而且不單只是不容許任何的干預介入；更重要的是，我們絕不可以干預他人，如此，才能達到真正的健康、真正的奉獻和自我實現。

God gave us each our birthright, an individuality of our very own: He gave us each our own particular work to do, which only we can do: He gave us each our own particular path to follow with which nothing must interfere. Let us see to it that not only do we allow no interference, but, and even more important, that we in no way whatsoever interfere with any other single human being. In this lies true health, true service, and the fulfilment of our purpose on earth.

來自外界的干擾常常有，這也是神性安排的一部分，而且這些干擾的存在是必要的，讓我們得以學習如何面對和處理。事實上，我們還可以視其為有益於我們的挑戰，讓我們變得更堅強，更瞭解神性的存在和自己的完整無懼。相反地，如果因為一時怯懦而讓別人干擾了我們，他們就會壯大，然後進一步阻礙我們。這些干擾之所以能夠阻礙我們，完全是端視我們的是否要讓干擾來讓我們偏離人生道路；是否讓這些干擾顯現為疾病，然後限制和傷害我們的肉身。然而，換個角度來看，有時這些干擾反而能讓我們的生命目的更加清晰和確定；別忘了，我們是造物主的子民。

Interferences occur in every life, they are part of the Divine Plan, they are necessary so that we can learn to stand up to them: in fact, we can look upon them as really useful opponents, merely there to help us gain in strength, and realise our Divinity and our invincibility. And we can also know that it is only when we allow them to affect us that they gain in importance and tend to check our progress. It rests entirely with us how quickly we progress: whether we allow interfer ence in our Divine mission; whether we accept the manifestation of interference (called disease) and let it limit and injure our bodies; or whether, we, as children of God, use these to establish us the more firmly in our purpose.

這些干擾、考驗越是艱難,就越顯得此生任務的可貴。如南丁格爾,即便是遇到敵軍傷兵,仍慈悲地付出醫療照顧;如伽利略堅定相信地球是圓的,即使全世界都不願意信他;如醜小鴨小時候雖然受盡家人的藐視與嘲笑,最後還是蛻成美麗的天鵝。

The more the apparent difficulties in our path the more we may be certain that our mission is worth while. Florence Nightingale reached her ideal in the face of a nation's opposition: Galileo believed the world was round in spite of the entire world's disbelief, and the ugly duckling became the swan although his whole family scorned him.

每個人都有屬於自己的任務,同時也只有我們才有能力可以將它完美地實現。不論如何,我們都沒有權力去干預別人的生命;一旦我們干預別人,或別人干預我們,內心就會開始出現衝突與不和諧。

We have no right whatever to interfere with the life of any one of God 's children. Each of us has our own job, in the doing of which only we have the power and knowledge to bring it to perfection. It is only when we forget this fact, and try and force our work on others, or let them interfere with ours that friction and disharmony occur in our being.

不和諧與疾病，只不過是我們肉身反應出靈魂裡的衝突，就像臉部表情傳達情緒一般，快樂就笑、生氣就皺眉。因此，可以從顯現在我們肉身的疾病，去瞭解背後真正的原因到底是恐懼、優柔寡斷還是懷疑。

This disharmony, disease, makes itself manifest in the body for the body merely serves to reflect the workings of the soul; just as the face reflects happiness by smiles, or temper by frowns. And so in bigger things; the body will reflect the true causes of disease (which are such as fear, indecision, doubt, etc.) in the disarrangement of its systems and tissues.

因此，疾病是干擾的結果，不管是干擾別人或被別人干擾。

Disease, therefore, is the result of interference: interfering with someone else or allowing ourselves to be interfered with.

陳家莉：

　　這讓我想到很多人常到廟裡擲筊，那些人深信擲筊的結果是表示上天的旨意，這樣的行為該怎麼解釋呢？我有朋友當初選填志願的時候，就是用擲筊去決定的，還有個朋友對於現在交往的對象一有遲疑就去擲筊⋯

李穎哲：

　　我覺得有些時候拿不定主意，想要藉由擲筊、花精卡、塔羅牌等工具來協助是無妨的，但是若每件事情都必須仰賴能量測定，或者是求神問卜的話，恐怕就需要服用紫金蓮 (Cerato) 了。

第 6 章
Chapter Six

保持真我、活出自己
成為自己生命的舵主，駛往美好的未來

All we have to do is to preserve our personality,
to live our own life, to be captain of our own ship,
and all will be well

　　每個人身上都存在許多美好特質，而我們也不斷地在學習，使自己的每個面向逐漸趨於完美；此外，更有降生於世的大師們來到我們面前教導克服困境的簡要之道，那其實一點也不難，只要瞭解並且培養以下美德：

There are great qualities in which all men are gradually perfecting themselves, possibly concentrating upon one or two at a time. They are those which have been manifested in the earthly lives of all the Great Masters who have, from time to time, come into the world to teach us, and help us to see the easy and simple way of overcoming all our difficulties. These are such as:

愛　　　Love

憐憫　　Sympathy

和平　　Peace

堅定　　Steadfastness

溫柔　　Gentleness

力量　　Strength

領悟　　Understanding

容忍　　Tolerance

智慧　　Wisdom

寬恕　　Forgiveness

勇氣　　Courage

喜悅　　Joy

　　藉由持續培養以上美德，並且摒棄私我的功績，就能夠一步一步讓世界變得更美好；不管是富裕或貧窮、高或矮，每個人在神聖的安排下都是平等的、都被賦予相同的恩典，只要明瞭我們是造物者的完美子民，就能成為拯救世界的人。

And it is by perfecting these qualities in ourselves that each one of us is raising the whole world a step near to its final unthinkably glorious goal. We realise then that we are seeking no selfish gain of personal merit, but that every single human being, rich or poor, high or low, is of the same importance in the Divine Plan, and is given the same mighty privilege of being a saviour of the world simply by knowing that he is a perfect child of the Creator.

　　既然有這些美德可以讓我們學習走向完美，就一定會出現相對的阻礙與干擾來強化我們的決心；這些阻礙與干擾，也就是造成疾病的真正原因：

As there are these qualities, these steps to perfection, so there are hindrances, or interferences which serve to strengthen us in our determination to stand firm. These are the real causes of disease, and are of such as:

限制	Restraint
恐懼	Fear
焦躁不安	Restlessness
猶豫不決	Indecision
漠不關心	Indifference
軟弱	Weakness
懷疑	Doubt

過於熱忱	Over-Enthusiasm
無知	Ignorance
沒耐性	Impatiens
驚恐	Terror
悲傷	Grief

　　如果我們容許這些干擾的阻礙，它們就會以疾病的型態反映、出現在我們的肉體。如果不瞭解這一點，就會把這個不協調的狀況歸咎於病菌、感冒、發燒等身體症狀，然後為這些症狀取各種名字（如：關節炎、癌症、氣喘），把問題侷限在肉體層面上。

These, if we allow them, will reflect themselves in the body causing what we call disease. Not understanding the real causes we have attributed disharmony to external influences, germs, cold, heat, and have given names to the results, arthritis, cancer, asthma, etc.: thinking that disease begins in the physical body.

　　很明確地，這個世界上的人類有不同的群體，每個群體都在發揮它的功能，把他們所學習到的展現在這個世界上。而群體中的每個人都有屬於他獨特的個性、獨特的任務和執行任務的方法。所以一旦我們沒保持這種獨特性，就可能招致不調和而生病。

There are then definite groups of mankind, each group performing its own function, that is, manifesting in the material world the particular lesson he has learnt. Each individual in these groups has a definite personality of his own, a definite work to do, and a definite individual way of doing that work. These are also causes of disharm ony, which unless we hold to our definite personality and our work, may react upon the body in the form of disease.

　　真正的健康是從快樂得到的；而快樂，可從許多細微之事中輕易獲得，例如：做自己喜歡的事以及和喜歡的人在一起。其實快樂不需要費盡全力去爭取，它就存在我們身邊，隨時隨地皆可接受。以「工作」為例，每個人都應該找出適合自己的工作並且樂在其中。但是有許多人壓抑內心真正的渴望，做自己不喜歡和不合適的工作；可能因為父母親的期許，放棄自己想成為木匠的願望，而成為律師、軍官或生意人；女兒可能因為母親的期望所以嫁入好人家，而使世上少了一位南丁格爾。這種因為他人的期許而允諾的，其實是錯誤的責任感，不但對這個世界成就不了貢獻，可能還會造成損害。就這樣，心中充滿不快樂的感覺，直到人生已耗去大半，才開始想要改變。

Real health is happiness, and a happiness so easy of attainment because it is a happiness in small things; doing the things that we really do love to do, being with the people that we truly like. There is no strain, no effort, no striving for the unattainable, health is there for us to accept any time we like. It is to find out and do the work that we are really suited for. So many suppress their real desires and become square pegs in round holes: through the wishes of a parent a son may become a solicitor, a soldier, a business man, when his true desire is to become a carpenter: or through the ambitions of a mother to see her daughter well married, the world may lose another Florence Nightingale. This sense of duty is then a false sense of duty, and a disservice to the world; it results in unhappiness and, probably, the greater part of a lifetime wasted before the mistake can be rectified.

　　耶穌基督曾說過：「我必須投身於天父的事務啊！」此話代表著他所必須遵從的不是父母的指引，而是來自神性的指引。

There was a Master once Who said, "Know ye not that I must be about My Father's business?" meaning that He must obey His Divinity and not His earthly parents.

　　所以，讓我們找出熱情所在，並且予以投入吧！讓它成為我們的一部分，像呼吸一樣自然、像蜜蜂採蜜、樹葉會在秋天落葉而在春天發芽一樣，成為自然的一部分。如果我們研究大自然就會發現，鳥、樹、花等每個生命都有其獨特的角色，透過這個角色讓整個宇宙完整、豐碩；哪怕只是一隻小蟲，每天幫助土壤更純淨，有了純淨的土地讓綠色植物得以成長，就能供應所有動物生存；等到動物死去，牠們的肉體則回歸大地而成為養分。如此生生不息的萬物，是美麗而有益的存在。

　　Let us find the one thing in life that attracts us most and do it. Let that one thing be so part of us that it is as natural as breathing; as natural as it is for the bee to collect honey, and the tree to shed its old leaves in the autumn and bring forth new ones in the spring. If we study nature we find that every creature, bird, tree and flower has its definite part to play, its own definite and peculiar work through which it aids and enriches the entire Universe. The very worm, going about its daily job, helps to drain and purify the earth: the earth provides for the nutriment of all green things; and, in turn, vegetation sustains mankind and every living creature, returning in due course to enrich the soil. Their life is one of beauty and usefulness, their work is so natural to them that it is their life.

　　當我們找到自己興趣所在時，那將是屬於並適合我們的，也將是輕鬆自在而愉悅的，我們不可能感到厭倦，它是我們習性的一部分！它能夠激發出我們的能力與天賦，以及最真的特質，讓我們好像回到家中一樣地快樂；也唯有快樂，才能讓我們有所發揮，把事情做得完美。

　　And our own work, when we find it, so belongs to us, so fits us, that it is effortless, it is easy, it is a joy: we never tire of it, it is our hobby. It brings out in us our true personality, all the talents and capabilities waiting within each one of us to be manifested: in it we are happy and at home; and it is only when we are happy (which is obeying the commands of our soul) that we can do our best work.

　　如果我們已經找到了此生的工作，那該是多美好的一件事！有些人生來便知道自己要做什麼，所以就能朝著目標前進；有些人雖然小時候知道，但受到周遭人的意見或勸阻因而改變了心意。不過，我們還是可以試著尋找那最初的理想，或許不是那麼容易，但在這尋找的過程中，我們的靈魂會耐心相伴，讓我們感到欣慰。只要是源自正確的慾望和動機，不管最後結果如何，都將是真正的勝利。

We may have already found our right work, then what fun life is! Some from childhood have the knowledge of what they are meant to do, and keep to it throughout their lives: and some know in child hood, but are deterred by contra-suggestions and circumstances, and the discouragement of others. Yet we can all get back to our ideals, and even though we cannot realise them immediately we can go on seeking to do so, then the very seeking will bring us comfort, for our souls are very patient with us. The right desire, the right motive, no matter what the result, is the thing that counts, the real success.

　　所以，如果你捨棄當律師而想成為農夫，捨棄當公車司機而想成為理髮師、或者捨棄當蔬果商而想成為廚師，那麼就放手去實現吧。往後你將會感到快樂而滿足，帶著熱情工作，而成為傑出的農夫、理髮師或廚師，成就你之前無法成就的一切。

So if you would rather be a farmer than a lawyer; if you would rather be a barber than a bus-driver, or a cook than a greengrocer, change your occupation, be what you want to be: and then you will be happy and well, then you will work with zest, and then you will be doing finer work as a farmer, a barber, a cook, than you could ever achieve in the occupation that never belonged to you.

　　那麼，你將願意全然地服從你內在神性所給予的指引。

And then you will be obeying the dictates of your Spiritual self.

李穎哲：

　　之前我在花蓮上課的時候，有位同學說他很認同巴赫醫師大部分的觀念，但只有一點他不能接受的是，他覺得巴赫醫師說每個人都有「錯誤」，好像某些宗教說每個人都是有「罪」的；但是我今天看這段文字，並不覺得巴赫醫師的意思是這樣，因為這裡說「每個人身上都存在許多美好特質……」，所以意思應該是說，我們每個人出生來到這世上就已具備有某些美好的特質，只是我們在後續不斷學習當中要讓這些特質更加完美，所以，我不認為巴赫醫師的意思是「每個人都有錯誤」，其實錯誤是因為我們把這些美好的特質給遺忘了，或者無法讓它更完美地發揮出來，所以產生了負面情緒，而負面情緒導致錯誤，然後才有疾病的展現。因此我覺得巴赫醫師要告訴我們的是，當我們來到這世上，是要讓以上的這些特質更加完美，而這些特質探究到最後，其實就是對應到十二個基本人格所要培養的相對美德。

　　另外，「藉由持續培養以上的美德，並且摒棄私我的功績，就能夠一步一步讓世界變得更美好……」，這段文字其實透露出了為什麼巴赫醫師很強調「自我療癒」，因為只要從我們的「小我」開始做起，一旦小我越臻完美，透過宇宙整體的一致性，世界也會跟著變得更加完美，因此很多時候只要改變自己的一小部分，世界也就會跟著改變，所以說小乘佛教真的不好嗎？其實先獨善其身從自己做起，似乎對整個世界也會有很大的幫助。

黃韋睿：

　　呼應到第四章提到的蜜蜂採花蜜的例子…

陳慧玲：

　　我很同意李醫師所說的，這讓我想到上星期自我療癒讀書會跟大家分享，小時候我的偶像是怎麼從史懷哲變成金城武的，後來吳老師幫我抽花卡說我是溝酸漿，因為我悲天憫人；但後來我想想覺得不是悲天憫人，而是婦人之仁加上眼高手低，我現在覺得這輩子最有可能成為的是「路人甲」，可是這樣也不錯，因為路人甲在行走時可以把路上的石頭搬開來，不讓後面的人跌倒或受傷，這也是一件很完美的事情。如果這一生可以做這樣的事情也不錯，所以不一定要成為拯救世界的人，可是如果自己已經認知到這一生的責任是什麼的話，那周圍的人應該也可以變的比較光亮一點。另外，巴赫醫師說的「讓自己的每個面向逐漸趨於完美」，我覺得這意思是說我們本來就很完美，只是要讓這個特質彰顯出來。

李穎哲：

　　這邊可以觀察到一件有趣的事情，巴赫醫師前一本書取名為「自我療癒」，可是在我們自我療癒之前，最深層的內在是要先「讓自己自由」；自己自由了之後，才有辦法提什麼叫做自我療癒，就像本章的標題「保持真我、活出自己，成為自己生命的舵主，駛往美好的未來」所要嘗試道出的是，只要你可以保持在這樣的狀態之下，就能夠進入所謂的自我療癒。

林筱岑：

　　「保持真我」的意思是不是指接受我們本來的樣子？

李穎哲：

文中 "preserve our personality" 就是要我們去保持我們原來的個性。

陳慧玲：

上文中提到「……有降生於世的大師們來到我們面前教導克服困境的簡要之道，那其實一點也不難……」，但是我覺得好難。

吳謝興：

這裡其實很簡單，但是我當年學花精的時候覺得這是最困難的部分，因為剛初學時以為花精是一種治療藝術，只要找出某情緒對應的花精是什麼就好，但後來讀到這邊發現巴赫醫師開始傳教，其實我覺得這個是花精療法的精神所在，因為巴赫醫師認為我們來到這世上的功課可以簡化成這十二項特質，我覺得就好像十二把上天堂的鑰匙一樣。我以前對於這十二項特質的實行方法是用「對抗式」的方法，可是對抗的過程其實很痛苦，因為必須硬把自己的個性扭曲，像馬鞭草、鳳仙花等等的特質，我很努力地吃花精，然後想要扭轉自己的個性去符合其花精的正向特質，可是覺得好痛苦，因為一直用理智去強迫自己不能這樣不能那樣，後來讀到這裡才瞭解，其實巴赫醫師不是要我們這樣，不是說馬鞭草個性的人不能夠很馬鞭草，其實可以，但是要維持在平衡的狀態，成為正向的馬鞭草。

這十二個人格特質的用字其實是巴赫醫師最後給花精的精華字彙，很值得深思。所以在知道自己的特質之後，就知道要吃什麼花精、自己的功課是什麼；這些精華字彙當初在研讀的時候覺得很有趣，覺得好像在領悟禪理一樣，思考著為什麼巴赫醫師要選擇這些字彙，例如「領悟」代表的是龍膽草人格的特質，其實不容易一看就明白，所以那時候光是討論這些字彙就討論了很久，而如果這些東西懂了，花精的使用就沒問題了。

李穎哲：

我自己使用花精的經驗覺得最難的就是這個部分，也就是花精療法的中心思想。很多醫生剛開始使用花精的時候都覺得很神奇，尤其是很多實習醫生來跟診時，發現有的病人喉嚨痛或頭痛，貼敷花精之後竟然就不痛了！實在是很神奇了！哪有這種神奇妙藥？其實醫生運用花精最難的是跳脫把花精當成「藥」的想法，或許剛開始會覺得它是藥，但後來會領悟它其實不僅僅只是藥而已。

巴赫醫師認為醫療人員的最終目標，是要能夠引導病人走向自我療癒之路，可是現在很多治療師在使用花精時沒辦法瞭解到這一點，都還是把花精當成藥，所以當病人用了這38種花精而覺得沒有效果時，就會想辦法去找出更厲害的花精；慢慢地，花精就從38種變成一百多種、一千多種，因為大家都在找更神奇的花精去把某個情緒或症狀給解決掉，可是大家忘記了巴赫醫師的教誨：「醫療人員必須引導病人走上自我療癒的道路，而不是一直在替病人找尋療方。」所以很多花精派別會互相攻訐說：「我明明覺得現在人只用這38種花精根本不夠，為什麼你們覺得夠？」

然而巴赫中心的回應是：「因為這是巴赫醫師說的，我們一定要遵照他的指示，不能改變！」，我覺得只要你對花精療法深入領會，就會知道最後療癒的決定權在病人身上，治療師只要引導病人讓他們自己去療癒自己就夠了。

所以如果可以做到這一點，這十二把鑰匙就足夠了，很多現在新的花精系統沒有巴赫醫師所謂的這十二把鑰匙，乍看之下會覺得這些新的系統很厲害，可以處理巴赫醫師沒提到的問題，但是最終還是得回到這十二項人格特質所代表的問題上。

陳家莉：

我覺得現在的病人都不願意為自己的生命負責，來看病都一副「我來掛你的號，你就必須給我解藥，然後我回去繼續過我的生活」，即便告訴他，他的生活方式就是問題的來源，他也不願意去改變；所以如果照巴赫醫師所說的，醫生到最後就會變成有點像傳教士，把病人丟過來的包袱還回去，然後告訴他某些問題必須自己學著去解決。

李穎哲：

之前我開始嘗試把這些包袱還回去給病人，可是幾次之後，如果發現病人仍然不願意改變的時候，就會陷入一種甜栗的狀態，對人性很失望，而我現在慢慢跳脫這個想法，覺得如果病人一直不改變，那我還是很樂意繼續給他藥吃，然後把賺來的看診費用在花精的推廣工作上使更多人受惠，就讓他們繼續依賴我，直到他們自己醒了為止，所以還是要繼續依照巴赫醫師所說的去做，等待病人醒來的那一刻給他

指引。剛接觸花精的時候可能只是把它當作一個技巧去學習，但就像許多學問一樣，到最後還是得往靈修的方向去走，我認為巴赫醫師的花精特別強調自我的修行（自我療癒）。

李穎哲：

　　我覺得巴赫醫師在看這些負面情緒時有一種與眾不同的看法，他覺得這些負面情緒其實是我們在學習這些美德時所產生的一些干擾，它們是用來強化我們決心的一種方式，所以苦難和生活中的阻礙都可以讓我們的靈魂進化與提升；若沒有這些苦難和阻礙，生命就無法去學習完美，每個人常常都會碰到困難、阻礙、生病，就是為了讓我們的靈魂去學習完美。

　　巴赫醫師並不把我們日常生活中遇到的苦難當成是宿命或業障，來到人世間本來就是以學習為目的的；學習本來就會苦悶，所以巴赫醫師的主張跟某些宗教的觀點不太一樣，他在看待人世間的這些苦難與困難時，有他自己特別的看法。一些新時代心靈成長的大師們，通常也主張要去面對自己內心的黑暗面；黑暗也是一種力量，我們可以利用自己的黑暗面來督促自己學習和成長。

黃韋睿：

　　可是聽說有一些新時代的觀念都會避開黑暗面而不去談論？

林筱岑：

　　就我所知，新時代的觀念其實還蠻強調要面對自己內心深層的恐懼。如果可以做到的話，其實是對自己一個很大的突破，所以我覺得他們並不避諱去面對黑暗面。

陳慧玲：

　　新時代的心靈成長會避諱談黑暗面的東西嗎？

李穎哲：

　　我聽到和看到的大部分都是主張要去接受黑暗面。

陳慧玲：

　　嗯，然後去擁抱它，給它光和愛，大部分好像是這樣。

李穎哲：

　　可能他們是用另外一種方式去面對，是用光和愛；話說回來，其實巴赫醫師的花精到最後也是一種光和愛，只是他用不同的語言去描述罷了。

魏愛娟：

　　剛剛我們在討論的就是這一章的第一段所描述的，我覺得不管是新時代、靈氣、花精等等的，我們人類擁有很多美好的特質，而且我們一直在往美好的部分前進，所以才會有很多大師以世俗的肉身來這裡教導我們，只是用的是不同的語言或方式，哪個人適合哪一種法門就用哪一種。

李穎哲：

　　嗯，這一段所提到的「這個世界上的人類有不同的群體，每個群體都在發揮它的功能，把他們所學習到的展現在這個世界上」，所以各宗教在他們的族群裡是用不同的語言在傳述，但探究到最後會發現其實大家都是一樣的。那為什麼後來會有這麼多派別之分？因為後來的教主在這個部分沒有看透徹，代表了他們在「葡萄藤」這一關還有待考驗。

陳慧玲：

　　所以新時代的大師們或許也沒有想要這樣分，而是後來的人才這樣區別，就像宗教派別一樣。

李穎哲：

　　我覺得巴赫醫師在舉例「你想當什麼」的時候，很有趣的都不是律師、醫生，而是農夫、蔬果商、理髮師等等屬於中下階層的職業，我想在巴赫醫師的那個年代，從事這些工作是被瞧不起的。所以這一段一直在強調說我們天生就知道要從事什麼工作，只要順著自己的神性指引、並且做的很快樂就 OK 了。

吳謝興：

　　這一段雖然寫的很簡單，但我的感想還很多，我補充說明一下跟佛教有關的一個想法，是本章前面所述的「摒棄私我的功績」。這個敘述其實與金剛經講的相互呼應，像有些人認為念經幾萬次就能成佛或上天堂，其實佛陀從未這樣說過，都是後人的誤解，而且金剛經裡有特別提到說，當我

們作了善事，就必須要把它完全忘記；只要你一直惦記著自己做了什麼善事，你的功德就完全歸零。譬如你今天去當慈濟媽媽，幫忙炒了很多米粉，但一直覺得自己很棒、成就了很多功德；一旦動了這樣的念頭，這些功德就完全歸零了。所以巴赫醫師在這裡說的「摒棄私我的功績」其實是有深遠的含意的。

另外一點是巴赫醫師提到：「快樂，可從許多細微之事中輕易獲得。」我覺得現代人之所以不快樂，部分原因是廣告看太多了，認為要得到快樂必須擁有雜誌上所刊登的名車或名包，但這種快樂是假象，因為商品會不斷推陳出新。像我很愛吃，以前到法國都特地去找米其林星級的餐廳，但後來發現這些人家認為的美味其實對我來說並不好吃，反而一些路邊轉角不起眼的餐廳卻最讓人驚喜，這些體驗讓我感受到「快樂，可從許多細微之事中輕易獲得」。

還有，聖經裡記述耶穌基督曾說祂的父母親不是祂真正的父母，他是神所創造的，是神的兒子；其實這是要強調說我們應該要遵循神性的指引。台灣因為這幾年經濟不景氣，反而出現一個有趣的現象，就是某些人覺得在都市裡混不下去了，所以決定回到鄉下，如同巴赫醫師這裡所說的「捨棄律師而去當農夫」，而當這些人回到家鄉做自己時，才赫然發現這是他們一輩子所要追求的。

第 7 章
Chapter Seven

只要實現了我們內在的神性
那麼其餘的就能從容面對

Once we realise our own Divinity the rest is easy

　　在世界創造之初，上帝即賜予了人類統轄萬物的權力。身為造物主的子民，發生在我們身上的不和諧一定有其原因，就如同莎士比亞所說的：「錯不在於命運，而在我們自己。」只要能瞭解這一點，我們的內心就會充滿感激與希望！所以讓我們把這些不調和、恐懼和猶豫不決通通拋開，讓心靈和身體重獲祥和。

In the beginning God gave man dominion over all things. Man, the child of the Creator, has a deeper reason for his disharmony than the draught from an open window. "Our fault lies not in our stars, but in ourselves," and how full of gratitude and hope can we be when we realise that the cure also lies within ourselves! Remove the disharmony, the fear, the terror, or the indecision, and we regain harmony between soul and mind, and the body is once more perfect in all its parts.

　　不管這個不和諧最後造成什麼樣的疾病，很肯定地，其相對應的療方就存在於我們能力所及之處，因為我們的靈魂絕不可能要求任何超過我們能力範圍的事。

Whatever the disease, the result of this disharmony, we may be quite sure that the cure is well within our powers of accomplishment, for our souls never ask of us more than we can very easily do.

　　每個人心中都有愛，不管是愛同胞、愛動物、愛大自然或是愛美好的事物，所以每個人都是治療者；每個人都曾經經歷過苦難，於是每個人也都富有同理心，能為苦難中的他人付出愛。所以每個人除了擁有治癒自己的力量之外，還有幫助他人自我療癒的力量，而這個過程唯一需要的就是「愛」與「憐憫」。

Everyone of us is a healer, because everyone of us at heart has a love for something, for our fellow-men, for animals, for nature, for beauty in some form, and we every one of us wish to protect and help it to increase. Everyone of us also has sympathy with those in distress, and naturally so, because we have all been in distress ourselves at some time in our lives. So that not only can we heal ourselves, but we have the great privilege of being able to help others to heal themselves, and the only qualifications necessary are love and sympathy.

　　身為造物主的子民，我們的內在就擁有完美的特質，我們來到這世界上，就是為了彰顯這份完美所代表的神性，平安地穿越困難和險阻，讓不可能成為可能。

We, as children of the Creator, have within us all perfection, and we come into this world merely that we may realise our Divinity; so that all tests and all experiences will leave us untouched, for through that Divine Power all things are possible to us.

李穎哲：

　　這裡有一句話我覺得蠻有意思的：「不管這個不和諧最後造成什麼樣的疾病，很肯定地，其相對應的療方就存在於我們能力所及之處。」也就是說，巴赫醫師認為要治療疾病很簡單，就是把自己內在的神性實現，把不協調之處調整回來，就能治療疾病，而巴赫醫師所提出來的 38 種花精就是其中一種方式。現在我們一般人尋找療癒的方法都是直接找某某名醫或治療師來幫我們治療疾病，可是按照巴赫醫師所說，療方其實就在我們每個人身上，靠自己就能夠找出來，不需要依賴治療師，所以這一章到了最後他說，自我療癒很重要的力量就是愛與憐憫，只要先把愛找出來，療癒自己之後，再透過同理心的發揮去愛別人，這些愛的流動就是療癒的一種方式。

黃韋睿：

　　我覺得人有經歷過一些磨難、考驗之後，對很多事情會多出很多的包容與同情，所以這些磨難和考驗其實是好的。

第 *8* 章
Chapter Eight

這些擁有治癒力的花草
能夠給我們力量，保持我們的本性

The healing herbs are those which have been given
the power to help us preserve our personality

　　就像我們被賜予食物一樣，這些來自原野的美麗花草，也是上帝賜予我們的療癒之物，有如上帝延伸到這個世界的雙手，幫助我們渡過生命中的黑暗期，趕走恐懼與痛苦的烏雲，重新找回我們神性的光輝。這些花草如下：

Just as God in His mercy has given us food to eat, so has He placed amongst the herbs of the fields beautiful plants to heal us when we are sick. These are there to extend a helping hand to man in those dark hours of forgetfulness when he loses sight of his Divinity, and allows the cloud of fear or pain to obscure his vision. Such herbs are:

菊苣　　　　CHICORY (*Chichorium intybus*)

溝酸漿　　　MIMULUS (*Mimulus luteus*)

龍芽草　　　AGRIMONY (*Agrimonia eupatoria*)

線球草　　　SCLERANTHUS (*Scleranthus annuus*)

鐵線蓮　　　CLEMATIS (*Clematis vitalba*)

矢車菊　　　CENTAURY (*Erythroea centaurium*)

龍膽草　　　GENTIAN (*Gentiana amarella*)

馬鞭草　　　VERVAIN (*Verbena officinalis*)

紫金蓮　　　CERATO (*Ceratostigma willmottiana*)

鳳仙花　　　IMPATIENS (*Impatiens royalei*)

岩玫瑰　　　ROCK ROSE (*Helianthemum vulgare*)

水菫　　　　WATER VIOLET (*Hottonia palustris*)

　　每一種花草皆對應至一項特質，並且用來協助我們持續強化這個正向特性，避免負向發展。以下針對每種花草及其對應之正向與負向特質作出整理：

Each herb corresponds with one of the qualities, and its purpose is to strengthen that quality so that the personality may rise above the fault that is the particular stumbling block. The following table will indicate the quality, the fault, and the remedy which aids the personality to dispel that fault.

負向特質（缺點） Failing		花草（療方） Herb	正向特質（美德） Virtue	
限制	Restraint	菊苣 Chicory	愛	Love
恐懼	Fear	溝酸漿 Mimulus	同情	Sympathy
焦躁不安	Restlessness	龍芽草 Agrimony	和平	Peace
猶豫不決	Indecision	線球草 Scleranthus	堅定	Steadfastness
漠不關心	Indifference	鐵線蓮 Clematis	溫柔	Gentleness
軟弱	Weakness	矢車菊 Centaury	力量	Strength
懷疑	Doubt	龍膽草 Gentian	領悟	Understanding
過度熱忱	Over-enthusiasm	馬鞭草 Vervain	寬容	Tolerance
無知	Ignorance	紫金蓮 Cerato	智慧	Wisdom
沒耐性	Impatience	鳳仙花 Impatiens	寬恕	Forgiveness
驚恐	Terror	岩玫瑰 Rock Rose	勇氣	Courage
悲傷	Grief	水堇 Water Violet	喜悅	Joy

這些花草具有的療癒能力是明確的，不會因為服用者的信念或給予者的身分而有所不同；就好像安眠藥一樣，不管是由護士或醫生拿給病人服下，都能讓他們安穩地睡去。

The remedies are endowed with a definite healing power quite apart from faith, neither does their action depend upon the one who administers them, just as a sedative sends a patient to sleep whether given by the nurse or the doctor.

> 魏愛娟：
>
> 　　最後這一段話似乎值得商榷，因為臨床上給予花精的人不同，確實效果會有不同，端看治療師的修為，以及對於個案自我療癒的引導方式是否正確。
>
> 李穎哲：
>
> 　　花精其實受到心理作用或其他作用的影響很少，不過在給花精的時候要有愛與憐憫心是很重要的；如果一個治療師一心想賺錢，他在給花精的時候缺少了愛與憐憫心，我覺得效果就會打折扣。讀這本書可以發現，巴赫醫師在每一章都把最重要的精神精簡化成一句話寫在開頭，很多人害怕吃了花精會改變自己的本性，其實在這裡巴赫醫師就說了，花精會保持我們的本性，除此之外，還會把每個人獨有的特點給展現出來。
>
> 魏愛娟：
>
> 　　我對花精有一個想法，花精是來自神性大愛，不管你怎麼用，在它之中就是蘊含了這個大愛；可是最近很多人只是

在討論花精一定要怎麼用、能量高低等等的問題，如果用這一章的文字去解釋，其實都是沒有意義的。

李穎哲：

這些植物其實都是被賜福的，所以這些花精不管怎麼用都會有效，因此是否會受到干擾並不重要；干擾當然會有，譬如有些人很堅持花精使用劑量的問題，可是所謂的花精療法不單只是劑量或能量的問題，還有很多東西我們沒有辦法探討到。像是被治療者的意願也很重要，如果他對花精充滿懷疑，花精能產生的效果可能就有限，所以可以說花精本身所蘊含的愛，再加上被治療者有想要改變自己而變得更好的信念，以及治療者的愛和憐憫，這三者加在一起所產生的加乘效應，便是花精是否有效的主要關鍵，而不是去執著在劑量上的拿捏。

魏愛娟：

是否必須要考量某些狀況，譬如說服用花精的人沒有被告知關於花精的資訊，反而他會更明顯感受到花精的效用？相反地，有些人在吃花精前就對它有所瞭解，所以會帶著預期要有什麼變化的心理，而當花精沒在他身上產生預期變化時，他就會認為花精沒有用。

李穎哲：

是的，沒錯！預期的心理經常會干擾對花精療效的判定。我在使用花精的臨床經驗中，遇到不少人根本不清楚什麼是花精，結果在貼敷花精之後，他們的症狀就消失了，這些人是完全不預期花精能有什麼效用的人，反而花精在

他們身上的效果很好；還有某些七八十歲的老先生老太太，你若跟他們說自我療癒的道理通常都聽不懂，但是花精在他們身上卻普遍都有不錯的效果。可是如果是一些已經事先在網路上找過花精資訊的人來使用，他們的效果通常都是普普而已。像我以前剛學花精的時候，聽說花精有多麼神奇的功效，心中充滿著相當的期待，結果自己服用後卻感覺不到；現在想想，應該是自己先帶著預期的心理去服用花精，所以當「預期反應」沒有出現時，就以為花精沒有效用。

魏愛娟：

　　我一開始使用花精時也有這樣的狀況。第一次服用岩玫瑰時，對花精沒什麼認識，那時當下很強烈地感覺到了情緒的變化，可是後來再使用時就不自覺地帶著這樣的預期心理去服用，反而就沒什麼感覺了。

　　另外，最近我去翻譯一些巴赫中心的醫案，發現有很多醫案的治療成效都非常神奇，可是在我們周遭，卻很難發現有效果如此顯著的案例。

李穎哲：

　　其實我曾遇到過這樣的案例，可是比例上是很少的。我猜想巴赫中心的醫案應該也有不少是效果不那麼明顯，只是沒有提出來罷了。如果治療師認為花精的療效本來就該這麼神奇，那麼他們可能會覺得很沮喪，因為多數個案的反應其實不會這麼明顯。我個人的經驗發現，大多數的人都是在服用花精一段時間之後，才開始感覺到改變，反而是用在有明顯病症的人身上，會有比較明顯的效果。

魏愛娟：

　　之前我公公住進加護病房，總共進出了兩次，第二次的時候我就幫他貼敷花精，沒想到病情很快好轉，然後離開加護病房，一直到現在。

陳慧玲：

　　其實我第一次使用花精時就有很明顯的感受，那是一種「愛」的能量耶！不過我現在有個障礙，就是我雖然很想把花精給出去，可是很擔心對方會感受不到花精所帶給我的感受。像我有個山毛櫸同事，前陣子因為要參加演講比賽非常緊張，所以調了花精給她使用，可是她使用後覺得沒什麼感覺，還說：「我本來就沒有很緊張」…，因此有些敏感的人在使用花精時可以感受到效果，可是有的人就沒有辦法覺察到自己情緒的改變，反而會覺得那是自己本來就能做到的，是心理作用，跟花精無關。所以現在我給出花精時會很擔心沒效果。

李穎哲：

　　你覺得你會「擔心」是哪一種花精情緒？

陳慧玲：

　　我覺得是馬鞭草，因為我很想讓別人知道花精是很有用的東西，想要他們也認同花精。

李穎哲：

　　那如果對方用了花精之後跟你說：「我覺得沒什麼感覺耶」，那你會有什麼感受？

陳慧玲：

　　我會覺得沒關係啊，因為每個人的感受不一樣嘛，不過可能心裡還是會覺得有點受傷。

李穎哲：

　　你覺得「有點受傷」的情緒是何種花精的負面情緒？

陳慧玲：

　　嗯，菊苣！可是我之前沒有想過菊苣，因為我以為菊苣的情緒通常是對家人的？

李穎哲：

　　不一定，只要當你付出的時候希望得到一些回饋，這種情緒就屬於菊苣。

第 9 章
Chapter Nine

疾病的本質

The real nature of disease

　　以真正的療癒而言，疾病並非是必然的結果，疾病只是反應出我們靈魂與心智交戰所造成的不和諧。所以可以說疾病只是因為這種心理狀態而出現的身體症狀，而且同樣的心理狀態可能在不同人身上會產生不同的反應；不過，只要懂得找出這個源頭，加以化解，身體上的症狀就會消失。

　　In true healing the nature and the name of the physical disease is of no consequence whatever. Disease of the body itself is nothing by the result of the disharmony between soul and mind. It is only a symptom of the cause, and as the same cause will manifest itself differently in nearly every individual, seek to remove this cause, and the after results, whatever they may be, will disappear automatically.

　　我們可以用「自殺」這個現象為例進一步去瞭解，發現在所有自殺者當中，不是所有人都採取溺斃的方式，有些人選擇從高處墜下，有些人選擇服毒；但其實他們背後真正的動機都是絕望的情緒，如果單純奪走他們手中的毒藥，只是阻止了當下的慘劇，過不了多久，可能又會故態復萌；其實只要幫助他們走過絕望，重新找到活著的意義，就可以治癒他們想自殺的行為了。再以恐懼這個「情緒」為例，每個人對恐懼的反應都不一樣，有的人會臉色發白，有的人臉部漲紅，有的人歇斯底里，有人則說不出話來；當我們嘗試對他解釋恐懼為何物，並且告訴他其實他擁有面對困難的能力，所以不需要害怕，那麼他將不會再對任何事情感到恐懼；所以如果家中有小孩害怕牆上

的黑影，那就點一隻蠟燭，讓他知道黑影其實是光所產生的，他可以藉由移動光源來改變黑影的型態，如此一來，就不會再害怕黑影了。

We can understand this more clearly by taking as an example the suicide. All suicides do not drown themselves. Some throw them selves from a height, some take poison, but behind it all is despair: help them to overcome their despair and find someone or something to live for, and they are cured permanently: simply taking away the poison will only save them for the time being, they may later make another attempt. Fear also reacts upon people in quite different ways: some will turn pale, some will flush, some become hysterical and some speechless. Explain the fear to them, show them that they are big enough to overcome and face anything, then nothing can frighten them again. The child will not mind the shadows on the wall if he is given the candle and shown how to make them dance up and down.

長久以來，我們都怪罪病菌、天氣或食物是讓我們致病的原因，但同時卻不難發現仍有許多人能在感冒流行期間保持健康，甚至為那颼颼的冷風感到愉悅；還有人可以在深夜中大啖起士和黑咖啡，卻不會生病。所以其實只要保持心情愉快和內心祥和，就不會因為大自然的任何小變動而生病；大自然的一切都是為了讓我們喜悅而存在的。相反地，如果我們允許懷疑、消沈、猶豫或恐懼佔據我們的心，那麼我們就會變得對大自然的任何小變化都很敏感。

We have so long blamed the germ, the weather, the food we eat as the causes of disease; but many of us are immune in an influenza epidemic; many love the exhilaration of a cold wind, and many can eat cheese and drink black coffee late at night with no ill effects. Nothing in nature can hurt us when we are happy and in harmony, on the contrary all nature is there for our use and our enjoyment. It is only when we allow doubt and depression, indecision or fear to creep in that we are sensitive to outside influences.

由此可知，造成疾病的原因是病人的心理狀態，而非生理症狀。

It is, therefore, the real cause behind the disease, which is of the utmost importance; the mental state of the patient himself, not the condition of his body.

任何疾病，不論多嚴重、多久，生活上的變化，不論是固執的成見或是錯誤的責任感所造成，都可以透過讓病者重拾歡樂和生命的目標而獲得療癒。不僅如此，療癒過程中還會出現許多美好的改變，例如：

Any disease, however serious, however long-standing, will be cured by restoring to the patient happiness, and desire to carry on with his work in life. Very often it is only some slight alteration in his mode of life, some little fixed idea that is making him intolerant of others, some mistaken sense of responsibility that keeps him in slavery when he might be doing such good work. There are seven beautiful stages in the healing of disease, these are:

祥和	Peace
希望	Hope
喜悅	Joy
信念	Faith
確信	Certainty
智慧	Wisdom
愛	Love

李穎哲：

這一章的最後一段話說「療癒過程中還會出現許多美好的改變」，我覺得花精確實可以帶來許多美好的改變。雖然現在很多治療師會把花精治療期分成幾個階段，譬如第一個階段是症狀緩解階段，第二個階段是自我成長階段，第三個階段是反抗期，最後是靈性提升；台灣花精的陳祈明老師也提出了花精治療的七個階段，這些是不同的治療師所賦予的各自闡述。

我個人比較喜歡巴赫醫師所講的，在花精治療的過程中會有祥和、希望等等的改變。我曾經有過一個癌症末期的病人，剛開始使用花精時他不太想談論個人的問題，後來從他太太那邊知道，他最希望媽媽能去探望他，因為他一直認為媽媽比較疼弟弟。

經過一段時間的諮詢以及脖子反應區的檢測發現，他已經對醫師的治療感到絕望，所以我給了他「荊豆」；還有他的病情很嚴重，已經讓周遭的人都覺得沒有希望，因此使用「岩玫瑰」；還有另一個花精是楊柳，因為他認為沒有把病治好，都是因為醫生治療方向不對，覺得現在已經沒有任何人願意幫助他了，這三個花精是我第一次所給他的處方。

另外，也配給他一瓶菊苣的單方花精裝在噴瓶中，讓他老婆把菊苣花精噴在他的病床周圍，我的用意是希望他可以感受到媽媽隨時都陪伴在他的身邊；另外一個原因是，我曾經跟許老師談過關於人在臨終時會有很多的焦慮不安，因為身體即將要分解成四大元素（地、水、火、風）回歸到大地

之母（其實回歸大地是可以重新感受大地母親的愛的），所以菊苣花精在這個時候就很重要了，可以幫助一個即將死亡的人，安心地把自己交給大自然。

結果隔了一個禮拜後再看到這個病人時，他變的很祥和，一直感謝我和他太太對他的照顧，也謝謝他媽媽生下了他，過了兩個禮拜，這個病人就去世了。從這個個案中我們可以發現到花精所扮演的角色，不是在把這個病人救活，而是帶給他的希望、平靜和安祥，還有最重要的就是「愛」與「感恩」。所以很多時候，花精帶來的不是能不能讓病人存活下來，而是巴赫醫師所講的這些美好的改變。

第 *10* 章
Chapter Ten

要獲得自由，就必須給予自由

To gain freedom, give freedom

　　人類的終極目標就是要進化至完美，而為了要成就這一點，人們就必須在各式各樣的經驗歷程中學習對抗誘惑和挑戰，並且保持真我；如此一來，就可從生命的苦難中被釋放出來，從真知中累積愛、智慧、勇氣、寬容與瞭解，進而成為自己的主人。

　　The ultimate goal of all mankind is perfection, and to gain this state man must learn to pass through all experiences unaffected; he must encounter all interferences and temptations without being deflected from his course: then he is free of all life's difficulties, hardships and sufferings: he has stored up in his soul the perfect love, wisdom, courage, tolerance and understanding that is the result of knowing and seeing everything, for the perfect master is he who has been through every branch of his trade.

　　如果我們瞭解「釋放自己，才能真正獲得自由」這個道理，就可以把生命視作是一趟喜樂的冒險；要獲得自由，就必須給予自由；所以當我們願意放下每個接觸到的人以及身旁的每樣事物時，我們自己也就獲得了自由。換句話說，就是不要支配或干預他人的生命，因為欲束縛他人者，必讓自己陷於束縛之中。就像某個被自己財產束縛的年輕人一樣，最後可能無法接受上天的禮物。

　　We can make this journey a short joyful adventure if we realise that freedom from bondage is only gained by giving freedom; we are set free if we set others free, for it is only by example we can teach. When we have given freedom to every human being with whom we are in contact; when we have given freedom to every creature, everything around us, then we are free ourselves: when we see that we do not, even in the minutest detail, attempt to dominate, control, or influence the life of another, we shall find that interference has passed out of our own lives, because it is those we bind who bind us. There was a certain young man who was so bound to his possessions that he could not accept a Divine gift.

　　要釋放別人加諸在自己身上的束縛其實很容易。首先，你必須釋放掉你給對方的束縛，然後溫柔地、充滿愛地拒絕對方的束縛。像英國歷史上有名的戰神納爾遜子爵，在 1801 年的哥本哈根戰役中，用瞎了的右眼對著望遠鏡頭，宣稱沒看見上層從遠方發出的軍令訊號，堅定地拒絕這些外來的束縛，以過人的膽識和決心持續進攻，最後終獲勝利。面對我們生命中的對手時，不需要帶著強迫、憎恨和刻薄的態度，因為他們其實是貴人，讓我們的生命更精彩，應該用感謝的心情與他們和平共處。

And we can free ourselves from the domination of others so easily, firstly by giving them absolute freedom, and secondly, by very gently, very lovingly, refusing to be dominated by them. Lord Nelson was very wise in placing his blind eye to the telescope on one occasion. No force, no resentment, no hatred, and no unkindness. Our opponents are our friends, they make the game worthwhile, and we shall all shake hands at the end of the match.

　　同樣地，我們也不應該要求他人按照我們的期望去做。對他們而言，自己心中所想的才是屬於他們的良方，即使彼此之間的觀念可能大相逕庭，但最後的結果都一樣良善。而且我們可以發現，當我們希望他人的所做所為能夠一一落在我們期望的範圍內時，我們就成了讓他們失望的來源。

We must not expect others to do what we want, their ideas are the right ideas for them, and though their pathway may lead in a different direction from ours, the goal at the end of the journey is the same for us all. We do find that it is when we want others to 'fall in with our wishes' that we fall out with them.

我們每個人就像是一艘艘的貨船，各自身負責任要把貨物運往不同國家，有人前往非洲，有人要前往加拿大，有人則要前往澳洲，然後回到同一個港口。於此，一艘應該前往澳洲的船又何必跟隨其他前往加拿大的船呢？這只會讓時間延誤罷了。

We are like cargo-ships bound for the different countries of the world, some for Africa, some for Canada, some for Australia, then returning to the same home port. Why follow another ship to Canada when our destination is Australia? It means such a delay.

此外，我們必須注意，生活中任何小事物都可能會成為我們心中的束縛，當我們擁有了那些非常想望的事物時，我們也被它所擁有。即使是一棟房子、一座花園或一件家具，我們都應該懂得給予它們自由。這世界上所謂的財產或所有物，都只是短暫的存在，我們都明白這些東西終將會消失，所以有些人內心就升起了焦慮與擔憂。要瞭解，這些東西的存在是為了供人欣賞和使用而存在的，不要反倒變成綑綁住我們的枷鎖。

Again, we perhaps do not realise what small things may bind us, the very things that we wish to hold are the things that are holding us: it may be a house, a garden, a piece of furniture; even they have their right to freedom. Worldly possessions, after all are transient, they give rise to anxiety and worry because inwardly we know of their inevitable and ultimate loss. They are there to be enjoyed and admired and used to their full capacity, but not to gain so much importance that they become chains to bind us.

如果我們可以讓周遭的人、事、物都以其最自由的型態存在，就會發現我們在物質上及心靈上都變得更富裕；因為愛，讓我們自由，也因為愛，讓我們的心更靠近。

If we set everybody and everything around us at liberty, we find that in return we are richer in love and possessions than ever we were before, for the love that gives freedom is the great love that binds the closer.

魏愛娟：

　　要獲得自由就要先給別人自由，我記得第一次我要來參加花精課程時，因為我先生有疑慮，我不想造成衝突，所以就暫時放棄了，但是最近這一次他的反應就不一樣了，因為他讓我來參加課程的這幾天，他反而比較自在。

李穎哲：

　　我覺得這一段文字也很有意思，也是巴赫醫師的創見，我們通常在使用花精時都只著重在被治療者這一邊，但是通常一個銅板是打不響的。例如為什麼你會受到菊苣情緒的影響，其實是因為你自己也身在菊苣的情緒當中，所以會發現當一個陷入菊苣情緒的關係，若某一方不願意吃花精、而另一方吃了，結果沒有吃的那一方竟然也產生了作用，這就是因為雙方都緊密地牽綁在一起，你去約束了別人，別人也會以相同的力量來束縛你，因此巴赫醫師認為「要獲得自由，就先給予自由」。我們在使用花精時可以利用這個道理，將花精效果發揮到極致，亦即可以考慮讓一段關係中的雙方共同接受花精的調理，有這項考量的花精有：過度關心別人的花精（如：菊苣、葡萄藤、馬鞭草、山毛櫸），此外還有冬青、紅栗花。

魏愛娟：

　　我覺得真的是這樣耶！在三、四個月前，我去印了菊苣的照片貼在家裡，是為了給我公公看的，因為他還不能接受吃花精，所以李醫師建議可以讓他看圖片，結果我今天要出門的時候望著菊苣的照片，突然覺得這好像是貼給我自己看的。

李穎哲：

　　嗯，所以「要獲得自由，就先給予自由」這句話實在很有意思。大家想想馬鞭草性格的人，如果他們一直將自己的觀念灌輸給別人，一旦別人不能接受，自己就很難過，所以我覺得馬鞭草或者整個過度關心他人的族群都需要學習給別人自由，例如你用馬鞭草（或葡萄藤、山毛櫸）的態度對待別人，可能別人也一樣會用馬鞭草（或葡萄藤、山毛櫸）的態度回應你，所以這個族群很有趣，會有互相束縛的現象，或者當你一直在抱怨某同事或家人很菊苣啦、山毛櫸啦，有可能你自己也在同樣的情緒當中，因為外在世界的表象，通常是自己內心世界的展現。

陳慧玲：

　　對呀！新時代的東西也是這樣講，說當你在別人身上看到的其實是自己狀態的投射，像我就是這樣。我有一個山毛櫸的同事，她會一直跑來我的教室數落我，說教室哪邊哪邊很亂，後來我生氣了，竟然也變成跟她一樣跑去她的教室數落東數落西，可是我平常根本一點都不山毛櫸啊！因為我只想當路人甲，下了班趕快回家，所以真的是會有互相牽扯的狀況耶！

吳謝興：

　　戰神納爾遜子爵這個典故我知道，那個時候英軍跟西班牙打仗快要打輸了，所以英國上級就下令要撤退以保留英國艦隊的命脈，上級的命令是透過旗號傳達的，可是納爾遜相信他可以打贏，所以就故意宣稱沒看見旗號，堅持繼續進攻，因而擊敗了西班牙的無敵艦隊，成就了英國一代的豐功偉業。

魏愛娟：

　　我那時剛買 Heal Thyself 這本書的時候，覺得看不下去，所以就先從 Free Thyself 開始看，尤其是前面的幾句話我在捷運上看的時候覺得很感動，會想哭！

陳慧玲：

　　對呀！第一章的那個小女孩作畫的例子真的很感人。

第 11 章
Chapter Eleven

療癒

Healing

　　自古以來人類就知道，造物主因為愛，而賜予各式穀食水果來滋養我們，同時也賜予我們生長於田野中的花草，以供治療之用。所以研究星辰的占星學家和研究植物的藥草學家，一直以來便致力於找尋適合的花草，幫助我們保持健康與快樂。

　　From time immemorial humanity has recognised that our Creator in His love for us has placed herbs in the field for our healing, just as He has provided the corn and the fruit for our sustenance. Astrologers, those who have studied the stars, and herbalists, those who have studied the plants, have ever been seeking those remedies which will help us to keep our health and joy.

　　要找到能夠幫助我們的花草，就必須先找到需要我們努力奮鬥的人生目標，並且瞭解這條道路上將出現的難關。這些所謂的難關就是我們個性上的缺點，然而，無須擔憂，因為這些缺點的存在意味著我們將能克服，並達到更高的層次；缺點是在鼓勵我們往更高處爬。這些花草就像聖餐一般，是來自造物主神聖的恩典，所以讓我們找到屬於自己的戰役和該擊敗的對手，然後帶著感恩的心讓這些花草協助我們。

　　To find the herb that will help us we must find the object of our life, what we are striving to do, and also understand the difficulties in our path. The difficulties we call faults or failings, but let us not mind these faults and failings, because they are the very proof to us that we are attaining bigger things: our faults should be our encouragements, because they mean that we are aiming high. Let us find for ourselves which of the battles we are particularly fighting, which adversary we are especially trying to overcome, and then take with gratitude and thankfulness that plant which has been sent to help us to victory. We should accept these beautiful herbs of the fields as a sacrament, as our Creator 's Divine gift to aid us in our troubles.

　　真正的療癒是不從疾病本身下手的，而從病者的心理狀態，也就是疾病乃不遵照靈魂指示所造成的結果。這種靈性上的不和諧而導致的生理疾病可能有幾百種樣貌（因為我們的身體是內心的顯現），但這一點也不重要！只要把我們的心調回正確的狀態，疾病就會馬上被治癒，如同耶穌基督說的：「對一個瘸子說你的罪被赦免了，或者說你起來行走，哪樣比較容易呢？」

In true healing there is no thought whatever of the disease: it is the mental state, the mental difficulty alone, to be considered: it is where we are going wrong in the Divine Plan that matters. This disharmony with our Spiritual Self may produce a hundred different failings in our bodies (for our bodies after all merely reproduce the condition of our minds), but what matters that? If we put our mind right the body will soon be healed. It is as Christ said to us, ˝Is it easier to say, thy sins be forgiven thee or take up thy bed and walk?˝

　　所以容我再次強調，身體的疾病症狀不是重點，而是心理狀態。不要理會讓我們感到痛楚的身體疾病，試著思考自己落入了哪一種負向情緒。

So again let us clearly understand that our physical illness is of no consequence whatsoever: it is the state of our minds, and that, and that alone, which is of importance. Therefore, ignoring entirely the illness from which we are suffering, we need consider only to which of the following types we belong.

如何選擇花精一點都不難，想看看你從別人身上感受到最讓你欣賞的美德是什麼，或者從別人身上看到最令你討厭的特質是什麼；甚至那些自己最想根除的缺點，也就是我們最討厭在別人身上看到的，所以可以藉由這些方式察覺自己應該改進的地方。

Should any difficulty be found in selecting your own remedy, it will help to ask yourself which of the virtues you most admire in other people; or which of the failings is, in others, your pet aversion, for any fault of which we may still have left a trace and are especially attempting to eradicate, that is the one we most hate to see in other people. It is the way we are encouraged to wipe it out in ourselves.

每個人都可以是治療者，因為我們都擁有愛與憐憫的天性，可以協助他人獲得健康。只要找出病者身上最明顯的矛盾，給予鼓勵、希望，以及對治的花藥，幫助他克服這個問題，然後就能啟動他自身的療癒系統，把剩餘的問題給一起解決了。

We are all healers, and with love and sympathy in our natures we are also able to help anyone who really desires health. Seek for the outstanding mental conflict in the patient, give him the remedy that will assist him to overcome that particular fault, and all the encouragement and hope you can, then the healing virtue within him will of itself do all the rest.

李穎哲：

　　我覺得本章的文筆相當優美。自古以來，人類就知道造物主因為愛而賜予我們很多食物；同樣地，他也因為愛而賜給我們很多療癒良方，因此我們可以知道，巴赫醫師的花精原來就是愛的化身，而和其他治療方式不一樣的地方就是－所有的花精都是愛！很多傳統的治療方法都是用對抗的方式，巴赫醫師認為，用對抗的方式只能讓症狀暫時緩解，其實要真正的療癒還是需要用愛，去協助我們達到真正的療癒。

　　另外，我覺得巴赫醫師的花精是有理論基礎的，而不是隨便用感應方式找到的治病療方，所以他才在這邊寫說「要找到能夠幫助我們的花草，就必須先找到需要我們努力奮鬥的人生目標，並且瞭解這條道路上將出現的難關」，瞭解問題之後再去尋找療癒的花草，然後製作成花精，否則這種尋找只是漫無目的而已。

　　此外，對人生沒有深入瞭解就去尋找花草製成花精，會落得與其他治療方式一樣，會不知道這個治療方式是要協助服用者走向什麼方向，或是花精多到大家都不知所措，不僅不容易學習，而且也沒有系統性；且不知道人類的問題癥結在哪裡，變成散槍打鳥，抓不到主要的問題點，只是往外尋求枝微末節的問題去解決。

　　我覺得巴赫醫師領悟到這一點，他的花精不僅有系統性，而且他也瞭解人類最根本的情緒問題。像他在這一段後面寫的「這些所謂的難關就是我們個性上的缺點」，所以他才會認為，最重要的是從個性上的缺點去找尋適合的花精。

吳謝興：

　　我們讀到後來知道巴赫醫師說不要去對抗，要用愛去滋長愛，可是這裡用到「擊敗對手」等字眼，有點兒奇怪…

陳慧玲：

　　我覺得這可能只是一種象徵性的說法。

李穎哲：

　　這裡所說的「該擊敗的對手」應該指的是我們自身個性上的缺點，而且後面他提到「……然後帶著感恩的心，讓這些花草協助我們」。

魏愛娟：

　　我覺得是因為他後面要引申如何從十二個花精中去找到自己對應的缺點，所以巴赫醫師才會說「找到屬於自己的戰役」，就是找出自己個性上的缺點，另外，在 Heal Thyself 中也有類似的說法。

陳慧玲：

　　我覺得這一段的重點不是在於「對抗」上，而是要我們用美德把這些缺點趕走。

魏愛娟：

　　對！而且要帶著感恩的心。

陳慧玲：

　　這樣我比較能對那些基督教或天主教的朋友們產生同理心。他們在吃飯前有禱告的習慣，我也能夠跟著他們一起靜下來感謝造物主賜給我這一餐。

李穎哲：

　　我一直覺得他們禱告的習慣蠻好的，像證嚴法師她也一直提醒我們要感恩，所以其實基督教和天主教徒的餐前祈禱就是一種感恩的心態，而且這種儀式可以先把你的心思抓回來才開始吃飯，不像我們現在很多人都很急，一邊講手機一邊吃飯，祈禱這個儀式很好，能讓大家都回到家中用餐，由一家之主帶領著祈禱，這也是一種學習家庭觀念的方式；我一直很喜歡西方聖誕節的傳統，因為到現在他們的聖誕節都還是很有過節氣氛，讓人覺得回家團聚有幸福的感覺，可是中國人的年節氣氛好像變淡了，以前那種過年一定要回家的感覺好像越來越消失了。

陳慧玲：

　　我覺得雖然證嚴法師告訴我們要感恩，但這道理的重要性對於那些生活無憂無慮的人來說可能有點兒難暸解，所以巴赫醫師在這邊才會先提「要暸解難關」、「克服缺點」，然後才知道這些花草就像聖餐一樣，讓我們帶著感恩的心。

李穎哲：

「帶著感恩的心讓這些花草協助我們」這句話很有意思，如果我們每次服用花精時都是帶著感恩的心，那麼效果一定會不一樣，可是我們常常在服用花精的時候，這個心是不在的，反而多加了一些懷疑心。

陳慧玲：

耶穌基督說的：「對一個癱子說你的罪被赦免了，或者說你起來行走，哪樣比較容易呢？」

吳謝興：

這句聖經的話是不是說：叫癱子走路比較困難，而相較之下，告訴他罪被赦免了，他反而就能夠走路了！

李穎哲：

耶穌基督在治療人們的時候都會告訴他們：「你的罪被赦免了」，讓病人懂得悔改，所以他的病就痊癒了。可是如果一個人沒有經過這個過程，而直接要用花精來治療某個疾病，效果不會太好。譬如說今天你用花精來治療頭痛，假如你一直往頭痛這個症狀去思考花精，效果通常不會太好；可是如果先去內省自己有什麼缺點或錯誤，然後認為我必須改正，再去選取適合的花精協助，疾病就能很快獲得痊癒。

所以我覺得這一段話主要是在傳達花精最重要的精神是要從不和諧的核心去處理，而不是從疾病本身；而不和諧所引發的疾病可能有幾百種可能，譬如鐵線蓮狀態可能會引起眼睛的問題、頭昏的問題、過敏性鼻炎或胃痛，可是一般普遍的習慣是思考胃痛要用什麼花精、失眠要用什麼花精。像我開始學花精的時候也是這樣，可是後來發現最重要的是要以失衡的情緒為主，這就是使用花精療法必須重視的──情緒辯證法則。

陳慧玲：

我覺得當一個人被告知「你的罪被赦免了」，就算他的疾病沒辦法立即痊癒，可是他的心理狀態已經調回到正確狀態，此時會有如釋重負的感覺；或許已經勝過生理疾病上的痛楚，因此對以前那種罪惡感很重的社會來說，這比生理疾病被治癒更讓他感到欣慰。

李穎哲：

所以說我們必須對健康和痊癒重新下一個定義，因為通常當採用某種自然療法來調理某些疾病的時候，我們常常會說「這個花精或某某療法不是很厲害嗎？為什麼我的病沒辦法痊癒？」經過我對病人狀況的臨床觀察，我覺得「療癒」不完全是指他的身體症狀或殘缺完全恢復，而是他變得快樂了，或者是人生觀改變了，生活從此變得充實美滿。

李穎哲：

你從別人身上看到「最討厭的特質」其實就是你「內在的反射」，所以就可以從這一點去找到自己的問題。而你最

「崇拜的偶像」就是代表你最「欠缺的美德」，從這一點可以找到自己想要的特質，或找到自己的負面情緒。

吳謝興：

　　英國花精訓練的工作坊，也都會讓大家玩這個遊戲，像是「你最喜歡哪個偉人？為什麼？」

魏愛娟：

　　我覺得最令人震撼的是「你最討厭別人身上的缺點，也就是你自己的缺點」，通常你這樣告訴別人時，他們都不能接受。

陳慧玲：

　　以下這段文字我感受很深—「甚至那些自己最想根除的缺點，也就是我們最討厭在別人身上看到的，所以可以藉由這些方式察覺自己應該改進的地方」。當我看到別人讓我難以忍受的缺點時，我很難去同理心或包容他們，我覺得這個是我要學習的功課。

魏愛娟：

　　有的時候是在「認清」的那一剎那會覺得情何以堪，通常會有一個掙扎的過程，因為原來自己也是那樣。

第 *12* 章
Chapter twelve

花精

The Remedies

Chicory | 菊苣
Chichorium intybus

愛　　　　　　　（Love）
約束、侷限　　　（Restraint）

　　你是否是屬於渴望為世界付出的人？總是渴望張開雙臂，祝福身邊的每一個人，總是希望幫助、安慰、同情別人；然卻因某種原因、情狀或人為因素而阻礙了你？你是否發現你不但沒為他人付出，反而被某些人所束縛了，因此你想全心全意付出的機會受限了？你是否已經到了想知道「為什麼所有人都依靠你，卻沒有人想特別親近你」的地步？

　　Are you one of those who long to serve the world: who long to open out both arms and bless all around you; who wish to help and comfort and sympathise, and yet for some reason circumstances or people stop you? Do you find that instead of serving many you are held in the grip of but a few, so that your opportunity of giving as fully as you wish is limited: are you getting to that stage when you wish to realise that it is, "when all men count with you, but none too much?"

而田野中美麗的藍色菊苣將協助你獲得自由；每個人都需要自由，才能夠為世界付出。

Then that beautiful blue Chicory of the cornfields will help you to your freedom, the freedom so necessary to us all before we can serve the world.

李穎哲：

　　我覺得這一章是巴赫醫師對每一個人格特質花精的詮釋，從這裡去探討，可以對花精有更深一層的認知。

陳慧玲：

　　我覺得巴赫醫師真的是太神了！他說：「每個人都需要自由，才能夠為世界付出」，菊苣的負向人格是限制，當一個情感受限時，將無法付出無條件的愛…好崇拜喔！

李穎哲：

　　這一段話其實就是在講 Free Thyself，也就是說當你付出愛的時候，假如沒有想要別人回報，那你就是自由的、不受限制的；相反的，如果你付出時希望得到對方的回報，你就被自己給束縛住了，就無法全心地去付出全部的愛。巴赫醫師在一開始的時候講的很好，其實菊苣的人是很有愛的、也很希望去付出，只是他在付出的時候，倘若心中出現想要回報的念頭時，他就會變的不夠自由，他的付出就會受限。

Mimulus ｜ 溝酸漿
Mimulus guttatus

同情　　（sympathy）
恐懼　　（Fear）

　　你是否是個畏懼的人：害怕人群或環境：雖然勇敢面對現實，但因畏懼而失去了生活的快樂；害怕那些永遠不會發生的事情；害怕那些事實上沒有能力控制你的人；害怕明天可能發生的事；害怕生病或失去朋友；害怕世俗的限制，害怕的事成千上萬？

　　Are you one of those who are afraid; afraid of people or of circumstances: who go bravely on and yet your life is robbed of joy through fear; fear of those things that never happen; fear of people who really have no power over you; fear of tomorrow and what it may bring; fear of being ill or of losing friends; fear of convention; fear of a hundred things?

　　你是否希望捍衛自己的自由，但卻沒有勇氣掙脫束縛；果真如此，清澈溪旁的溝酸漿能讓你自由地愛自己的生活，並教導你對別人抱持著最富溫柔的同理心。

Do you wish to make a stand for your freedom, and yet have not the courage to break away from your bonds; if so Mimulus, found growing on the sides of the crystal streams, will set you free to love your life, and teach you to have the tenderest sympathy for others.

陳慧玲：

　　我不太明白為什麼溝酸漿的正向與負向特質有點兒連不起來？是說去同情那些同樣被恐懼折磨的人嗎？

魏愛娟：

　　同理心嘛！就是說如果去認清你所害怕的事情，就不會再害怕了。

李穎哲：

　　所以說溝酸漿的人如果克服了恐懼，他就會成為一個很好的傾聽者或治療師，其實我覺得同理心很重要，當你的同理心一出去，就如同溝酸漿的能量出去了，對方就可以感受到這個溫暖，就有勇氣可以去面對，甚至就跨越了這個恐懼。

Agrimony ｜ 龍芽草
Agrimonia eupatoria

寧靜祥和　　（Peace）
慌張不安　　（Restlessness）

　　你是否是屬於那種會去忍受苦痛的人？你的心靈總是慌張不安，靜不下來，雖然能勇敢面對外在環境，卻總在別人面前掩飾自己的苦悶；經常大笑、微笑或開玩笑，即使遭受困難了，也總是在幫助周圍的人保持心情愉快，但自己卻強忍痛苦。你是否要藉由酒精藥物才能幫你面對考驗？你是否覺得必須要有一些刺激才能保持清醒？

　　Are you one of those who suffer torments; who soul is restless: who can find no peace, and yet bravely face the world and hide your torture from your fellow-men: who laugh and smile and jest, and help those around you to keep a cheery heart whilst you are suffering. Do you seek to soothe your sorrows by taking wine and drugs to help you face your trials: do you feel that you must have some stimulant in life to keep you going?

　　果真如此，生長在道路旁和草地上，而花穗像教堂尖塔、種子像鈴鐺一樣美麗的龍芽草，將帶給你平安，傳達寧靜祥和的領悟。龍芽草可讓你平靜地面對考驗和困難，沒有任何事物能煩擾你。

If so, that beautiful plant Agrimony, growing along the sides of our lanes and in our meadows, with its church-like spire, and its seeds like bells, will bring you peace, the peace that 'passeth understanding.' The lesson of this plant is to enable you to hold peace in the presence of all trials and difficulties until no one has the power to cause you irritation.

李穎哲：

　　我最近看了一本書，作者認為來作心理諮商的人，通常都需要使用龍芽草，因為能讓個案有病識感且勇於面對自己的問題。

Scleranthus ｜ 線球草
Scleranthus annus

堅定　　　　　（Steadfastness）
猶豫不決　　　（Indecision）

　　你是否是屬於很難作決定的人？需要表達意見時總是很矛盾，以致於難以作出正確決定；猶豫擋在你面前，阻礙了你的進步？是否一開始認為某件事情是正確的，但過會兒又認為別件事情才是正確的？

　　Are you one of those who find it difficult to make decisions; to form opinions when conflicting thoughts enter your mind so that it is hard to decide on the right course: when indecision dogs your path and delays your progress: does first one thing seem right and then another?

　　果真如此，你需要在艱難的環境中學會果斷地行動；作出正確的選擇並堅持下去；田野中綠色的線球草，將可幫助你抵達終點。

　　If so you are learning prompt action under trying circumstances; to form correct opinions and be steadfast in following them; and the little green Scleranthus of the cornfields will help you to this end.

吳謝興：

　　我的星盤是屬於蹺蹺板型的，個性很矛盾，所以容易有線球草的特質，常常覺得兩樣選擇都差不多好或差不多不好，所以很難決定。不過跟紫金蓮很不一樣的是，線球草的人的猶豫不決只會暗自在心中困擾著，而紫金蓮的人則是會一直問別人意見；更有趣的是，有些人會兩種狀況合併在一起。

Clematis ｜ 鐵線蓮
Clematis vitalba

溫和柔順　　（Gentleness）
漠不關心　　（Indifference）

　　你是否發現自己是個對生活沒有太大興趣的人？早晨醒來總是
不想面對新的一天，現實生活太困難、太艱辛且缺乏樂趣；是否也
覺得沒有任何事情值得我們努力改善，如果能繼續在睡夢中那該有
多好？你是否總是眼神矇矓，好似活在夢中，而且認為夢想總比現實
更美好？或者你總喜歡想著一些虛幻不實的人？如果你覺得如此，
你要學習的正是「堅持下去」。當你不去多想，而只告訴自己「堅持
下去」，那麼勝利將完完全全屬於你。

　　Are you one of those who find that life has not much interest: who wake
almost wishing there were not another day to face: that life is so difficult, so
hard, and has so little joy: that nothing really seems worth while, and how
good it would be just to go to sleep: that it is scarcely worth the effort to
try and get well? Have your eyes that far-away look as though you live in

dreams and find the dreams so much more beautiful than life itself: or are your thoughts, perhaps, more often with someone who has passed out of this life? If you feel this way you are learning "to hold on when there is nothing in you except the will which says to you - hold on!" and it is a very great victory to win through.

　　這種美麗的植物叫做鐵線蓮，喜歡生長在有堊土的籬笆裡，就是我們常說的「遊人樂」。種子如羽狀，總是希望被吹向遠方重新開始，它將協助你回到現實並面對生活，找到自己的工作並帶給你快樂。

That beautiful plant which adorns our hedges where there is chalk, the Clematis, better known as Traveller's Joy, and whose feathery seeds are. always longing to be blown away and start again, will help you so much to come back and face life and find your work, and bring you joy.

陳慧玲：

　　我還沒使用花精以前很適合用鐵線蓮，因為還是學生的時候，我每天都要睡上十幾個小時，一直在昏睡…所以這裡寫說「如果能繼續在睡夢中那該有多好」寫的很貼切。

黃韋睿：

　　那你以前睡很久，通常醒來是精神很好還是反而會覺得累？

陳慧玲：

　　不一定耶，有時候會覺得累，有的時候會覺得睡飽了。不過我大概知道我那時的情況是在逃避現實。

李穎哲：

　　現在在診所使用鐵線蓮的頻率很高，已經躍居楊柳之上了。巴赫醫師在這裡說鐵線蓮的人對生活沒有太大興趣；反觀現在的社會，我們每天要面對的挑戰實在太多，所以就會出現寧可進入一種昏沈的狀態。

陳慧玲：

　　如果睡了很久還是會覺得累，是不是橄欖？

李穎哲：

　　不一定，有些可能是鐵線蓮，其實鐵線蓮、角樹、橄欖都有可能，屬於對現實沒有興趣的花精族群也都有可能。另外，我覺得巴赫醫師在這邊寫說「堅持下去，不要多想；只要堅持下去，那麼勝利將完完全全屬於你」，所以鐵線蓮花精除了把服用者帶回到現實世界來，更讓我們可以堅持下去；這一點我會把它連結到「遊人樂」，因為像吉普賽人終年旅行，在旅途中無聊時會把鐵線蓮的莖剪下來當菸抽，他們抽了這個菸之後就能夠堅持下去，學習人生的各種課題。

Centaury | 矢車菊
Centaurium umbellatum

力量　　（Strength）
軟弱　　（Weekness）

你是否是屬於那種會被人家利用的人？因為你有顆善良的心，永遠都不願拒絕別人。你是否常常委曲求全而不去做你認為對的事，只因不想與別人爭辯？你的動機是好的，但卻一直被動地遭人利用，而不主動地選擇自己的作為，就好像門前的腳踏墊一樣，你還有一段很長的人生道路要走；只有當你體認到必須更加主動地把握自己的生命，才能真正偉大地付出。

Are you one of those people whom everybody uses, because in the kindness of your heart you do not like to refuse them anything: do you just give in for the sake of peace rather than do what you know is right, because you do not wish to struggle: whose motive is good, but who are being passively used instead of actively choosing your own work. Those of you who are door-mats are a very long way along the road to being of great service once you can realise that you must be a little more positive in your life.

生長在草原上的矢車菊，將幫你找回真正的自我，成為一個積極主動的行動者，而不是被動的代行者。

Centaury, that grows in our pastures, will help you to find your real self, so that you may become an active, positive worker instead of a passive agent.

魏愛娟：

　　原來我跟矢車菊也有關…我常常覺得自己很像牛，像我同事會跟我說：你應該去教音樂，或是去做什麼。他們講一樣，我就去做一樣。

吳謝興：

　　這是紫金蓮吧？

李穎哲：

　　巴赫醫師這邊所說的矢車菊特性是太善良了，所以容易被利用、壓榨，而紫金蓮則是容易受影響。

吳謝興：

　　最重要的是矢車菊特性的人常處於被動，被別人要求；但如果能化被動為主動，自己積極主動地去付出，就能成為正向的矢車菊。

Gentian ｜ 龍膽草
Gentian amarella

領悟　（Understanding）
懷疑　（Doubt）

　　你是否是個理想遠大、期待萬事順利進行，而一旦抱負沒有很快實現就會感到沮喪的人？成功在望時會感到欣喜，而當困難阻撓時卻又容易沮喪？

　　Are you one of those with high ideals, with hopes of doing good; who find yourself discouraged when your ambitions are not quickly realised? When success is in your path are you elated, but when difficulties occur easily depressed?

　　果真如此，丘陵地上的小小龍膽草，將協助你即使在烏雲遮蔽的天空下，也能保有堅定的目標，以及更快樂、更有希望的前景。它將時時刻刻鼓勵你，並讓你領悟到無論結果如何，只要盡了全力，就不算失敗。

If so, the little Gentian of our hilly pastures will help you to keep your firmness of purpose, and a happier and more hopeful outlook even when the sky is over-cast. It will bring you encouragement at all times, and the understanding that there is no failure when you are doing your utmost, whatever the apparent result.

魏愛娟：

　　我突然有個疑惑，我們一般人會思考自己處於什麼負向的情緒狀態，然後決定該使用哪種花藥。可是我今天看到一個部落格，他強調如果你想要成為什麼樣正向特質的人，你就去吃相對應的花藥，這樣的方法是好的嗎？

李穎哲：

　　我覺得不好，這樣好像是為了想達到某些目的才去使用花精，而不是先自我反省目前的缺點，承認自己所犯的缺失之後，然後再用花精來讓自己身心達到平衡，這樣會陷入一種貪婪的狀況。此外，不斷地想要讓自己變的很完美，其中可能也有「岩水」的情緒狀態。巴赫醫師曾說過，我們每個人自身已經完美地存在了，不需要特意去塑造自己成為如何完美的人；反之，如果一直覺得自己不夠好，就會出現「松樹」的負向情緒。所以這個方法，跟巴赫醫師所倡導的花精療法精神是不一樣的。

魏愛娟：

　　所以如果使用這種方法，可能不會得到他所期望要有的效果，因為並沒有完全瞭解自己目前的狀態！

陳慧玲：

　　我還有個問題，就是關於龍膽草的正向特質是「領悟」。我記得之前上課的時候，筆記上寫的是「信仰」，那麼領悟和信仰是一樣的嗎？

陳慧玲：

　　龍膽草的人到底要領悟什麼呢？巴赫醫師認為：「無論結果如何，只要盡力了就不算失敗」，而龍膽草負向特質的人就是失去了這個信仰，我們可以這樣去解釋。此外，我個人對龍膽草花精的領會是，所謂的失去信仰，可能是指我們的內在已經失去了如孩童般純真無邪的狀態，所以我們內心所投射出去的世界，將是灰暗、悲觀、失敗的；天底下哪有美好的事物？然而對孩童來說，其實世界上的事物沒有好與壞之分，做事也沒有成功與失敗之分，只要盡力去做就好了。龍膽草負向特質的人容易猶豫不決、躊躇不前，是因為他心裡有太多遲疑，失去了內在的信仰。

Vervain | 馬鞭草
Verbena officinalis

寬容 （Tolerance）
過度熱心 （Over-enthusiasm）

　　你是否是屬於充滿熱情、渴望做大事，並希望立刻完成所有事情的人？你是否發現很難耐心地完成規劃的事，因為總想一開始就出現結果？你是否發現因為自己過於熱心，以致對別人太嚴苛；希望他們依你的觀點看待事物，試圖逼迫他們同意你的想法；當他們不聽從時，就會感到不耐煩？

　　Are you one of those burning with enthusiasm: longing to do big things, and wishing all done in a moment of time? Do you find it difficult patiently to work out your scheme because you want the result as soon as you start? Do you find your very enthusiasm making you strict with others; wishing them to see things as you see them; trying to force them to your own opinions, and being impatient when they do not follow?

　　果真如此，你的內心有一種想成為領導者或指導者的願望。樹籬邊的淡紫色馬鞭草，將幫助你獲得所需的美德、對你同伴善良，並寬容別人的想法。它將幫助你了解生活中偉大的事物，也可以在沒有壓力和不緊張的氣氛下，溫和而平靜地達成。

If so, you have within you the power of being a leader and a teacher of men. Vervain, the little mauve flower of the hedge-banks, will help you to the qualities you need, kindness for your brothers, and toler ance for the opinions of others: it will help you to realise that the big things of life are done gently and quietly without strain or stress.

李穎哲：

　　我以前是負向的馬鞭草，可是我的負向不會去逼迫別人相信我的信仰，而是當別人不同意我的想法時會不耐煩或沮喪；而且我以前還有個狀況，就是我在實行某些原則方法之後，會想要很快看到成果。

陳慧玲：

　　這不是鳳仙花嗎？

吳謝興：

　　鳳仙花是動作很快，想要趕快去做，但不一定會想要很快有成果。

Cerato ｜ 紫金蓮
Ceratostigma willmottiana

智慧、般若　　（Wisdom）

無知　　　　　（Ignorance）

　　你是否覺得自己擁有智慧，能夠成為一個哲人或引導者？你是否感覺到內在力量，當別人遭遇困難時能給予建議，撫慰他們的悲傷，在有任何麻煩時總願意幫助他們；卻因缺乏自信，而無法完成這些任務？也許是因為聽了太多的意見，並且太在意社會的世俗標準？你是否了解這正是因為你缺乏自信，以及對自己智慧和智識的認知不夠，才讓你太過專注於別人的意見？

Are you one of those who feel that you have wisdom; that you could be a philosopher and a guide to your fellow-men? Do you feel the power within you to advise them in their difficulties, to soothe their sorrows, and at all times to be a help to them in their troubles; and yet, through lack of confidence in yourself, you are unable to accomplish this, possibly because you are listening too much to the voice of others and paying too great attention to the conventions of the world? Do you realise that it is only this lack of confidence in yourself, this ignorance of your own wisdom and knowledge, that tempts you to listen too intently to the advice of others?

而紫金蓮將幫你找到個性和自我，並且不被外在所影響，使你能夠依你擁有的天賦智慧來服務人群。

Then Cerato will help you to find your individuality, your per sonality, and, freed from outside influences, enable you to use the great gift of wisdom that you possess for the good of mankind.

李穎哲：

　　我最近紫金蓮花精用的很多，因為常有病人會說：「我覺得我的狀況是…，不知道是不是…？」，現在報章媒體的資訊太多，讓大家對資訊消化不良，可能也是其中的原因之一。昨天有個病人跟我說：最近他在準備考試，晚上睡不著，頭漲漲的不舒服，一般人聽這樣的敘述都會聯想到白栗花，但我使用的是紫金蓮，因為我覺得他在準備考試的期間收集了太多資訊而無法吸收。在使用紫金蓮之後，他表示眼前好像變亮了，頭也不漲了。所以紫金蓮特質的人雖然很會蒐集資料和做筆記，但在吸收融合上反而有問題。

　　根據我自己的觀察，我覺得紫金蓮的使用越來越頻繁，因為資訊和選擇越來越多，例如成長課程多如雨後春筍，所以造成很多人一個課程學完沒多久又接著想學別的，不僅停不下來，也不知道自己該繼續學些什麼好。最近我問吳謝興老師：「我應該繼續進修什麼好呢？」，他回答我：「你可以去用紫金蓮」。

Impatiens ｜ **鳳仙花**
Impatiens glandulifera

寬恕 （Forgiveness）
不耐煩 （Impatient）

　　你是否知道自己天性深處還留有一絲冷酷的痕跡，當被欺負或傷害時，你發現自己很難不帶有仇恨？你是否仍有想讓別人順從你思惟模式的慾望？你是否不耐煩，而且是這種性急讓你不得不冷酷？你的天性是否帶著審問者的痕跡？

　　Are you one of those who know that deep down in your nature there is still a trace of cruelty; when buffeted and harassed you find it difficult not to have a little malice? Have you still left within you the desire to use force to bring another to your way of thinking: are you impatient and does that impatience sometimes make you cruel: have you left in your nature any trace of the inquisitor?

　　果真如此，你需要努力去獲得細緻的溫柔和寬恕。生長在威爾斯小河畔美麗的淡紫色鳳仙花，將帶著祝福幫助你向前進。

If so, you are striving for exquisite gentleness and forgiveness, and that beautiful mauve flower, Impatiens, which grows along the sides of some of the Welsh streams, will, with its blessing, help you along the road.

吳謝興：

　　我讀了這一段之後有個問題，因為這描述聽起來跟冬青也很接近，要如何區分？

李穎哲：

　　這是因為巴赫醫師當年先找出來的是十二個療癒者花精，後來才慢慢發展出其他花精。所以，在還沒發現冬青花精時，「當被欺負或傷害時，你發現自己很難不帶有仇恨」所描述的冬青情緒，暫時被包含在鳳仙花裡，所以說如果你身邊剛好沒有冬青花精的時候，也可以使用鳳仙花去處理冬青的情緒。

黃韋睿：

　　往下看下一句，好像又是在描述葡萄藤的負向情緒…

李穎哲：

　　對，沒錯！而且再往下看，似乎又像在敘述菊苣或葡萄藤的狀態，這樣看起來，最後好像只有中間那句「你是否不耐煩，而且是這種性急讓你不得不冷酷？」，比較精準地在描述鳳仙花的特質。

陳慧玲：

　　我自己的鳳仙花性格是情緒來的快去的也快，譬如跟媽媽吵完架沒多久，又馬上可以跟媽媽親密地說她煮的東西好好吃，搞得我媽都有點兒不知如何是好。

李穎哲：

　　巴赫醫師最後抓到的一個關鍵字是「寬恕」，只要個案需要培養寬恕的美德，就可以給他鳳仙花的花精。

Rock Rose | 岩玫瑰
Helianthenum nummularium

勇氣 （Courage）
驚駭 （Terror）

　　你是否在遭遇可怕狀況時完全絕望？只怕自己可能再也承受不了更多了；為即將發生的事情驚慌不已，比如像是死亡、自殺、發狂、可怕的疾病或害怕面對物質世界的絕望等這類事情。

　　Are you one of those in absolute despair, in terror: who feel that you can bear nothing more; terrified as to what will happen: of death; of suicide; of insanity; of some awful disease: or fearful of facing the hopelessness of material circumstances?

　　果真如此，你需要學會勇敢地面對大挑戰，為自己的自由而戰。開滿丘陵的美麗黃色岩玫瑰，將帶給你贏得勝利的勇氣。

　　If so, you are learning to be brave against great odds, and fighting for your freedom, and the beautiful little yellow Rock Rose, which grows so abundantly on our hilly pastures, will give you the courage to win through.

李穎哲：

　　這邊大家看到「絕望」這個詞可能會覺得奇怪，這不是荊豆嗎？其實這是岩玫瑰合併荊豆的狀態。另外，我記得巴赫醫師曾經提到「看似無望的個案，可以給予岩玫瑰花精」。我自己對於這樣的個案，除了給他岩玫瑰之外，還會使用荊豆。

　　然後「發狂、自殺」等字眼比較像在描述櫻桃李，所以在櫻桃李花精發現之前，巴赫醫師就是用岩玫瑰花精去處理這樣的狀況。這邊寫說「對物質世界的恐懼」聽起來似乎是種明確的恐懼，大家可能會覺得用溝酸漿比較適合，但是我覺得如果是和「生存」比較相關的恐懼，可以使用岩玫瑰。

林鈺傑：

　　舉個「驚慌」的例子，像我在倒咖啡的時候，有的人會在咖啡快滿到杯緣時很緊張地說著「快滿了！快滿了！」這樣的反應算是岩玫瑰嗎？

李穎哲：

　　可以探討他背後的原因，如果他覺得「快滿了」不好，是因為滿了會造成各式各樣的缺點，可能是山毛櫸，但如果是因為覺得很恐慌的話，就是岩玫瑰。另外，那種恐慌感如果是害怕失控的感覺，那麼也可能合併了櫻桃李的狀態，我們還可以從個案說話的態度和語調來鑑別。

黃韋睿：

　　再延伸剛剛倒咖啡的例子，像我本身是很怕氣球的，因為我看到氣球就覺得它隨時會爆炸，感覺就像剛剛講的那種害怕失控的感覺…

李穎哲：

　　我覺得小睿的情況可能是溝酸漿或岩玫瑰，因為溝酸漿的人很怕吵和巨響，而氣球爆炸的聲音對他們來說很可怕。

吳謝興：

　　岩玫瑰的人倘若走過那段深遠恐懼的考驗之後，他就能夠感同深受，而成為一個很棒的療癒者。

李穎哲：

　　我觀察到岩玫瑰特質的人，當他們服用岩玫瑰花精後，會開始抗拒吃花精，因為處理的恐懼越來越深層；和龍芽草特質的人一樣，當情緒剝到核心的時候總是比較辛苦。

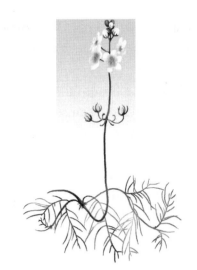

Water Violet ｜ 水堇
Hottonia palustris

快樂　　　（Joy）
悲傷　　　（Grief）

　　你是否是屬於那種勇敢但卻從不抱怨，努力服務同胞的偉大靈魂？默默承受痛苦，沒有退縮，從不讓悲傷打擾日常工作？你是否曾經歷過很大的打擊或悲傷的時刻，但卻很平靜地度過了？

　　Are you one of those great souls who bravely and without complaint, still endeavouring to serve your brother-men, bear suffering calmly and with resignation, not allowing your grief to interfere with your daily work? Have you had real losses, sad times, and yet go quietly on?

　　果真如此，自由地漂浮在最清澈溪流上的美麗水堇，將幫助你藉由悲傷讓自己更純淨，朝向更偉大的理想前進；因此即使在痛苦時，也能學著去服務同伴，學習獨然於世並獲得全然自由的真實快樂，如此才可完美地服務人類；在所有情境下，均能覺悟助人是高尚的

而不是一種犧牲。這種植物將幫助你領悟生活中許多冷酷和悲傷的事，對於你所憐憫的人們反倒是件好事。

If so, the beautiful Water Violet, which floats so freely on the surface of our clearest streams, will help you to understand that you are being purified through your grief, uplifted to a great ideal, so that you may learn to serve your fellow-men even in the hour of your affliction: that you are learning to stand absolutely alone in the world, gaining the intense joy of complete freedom, and therefore of perfect service to mankind. And when this is realised it is no longer sacrifice but the exquisite joy of helpfulness even under all conditions. Moreover that little plant will help you to the understanding that so much you think of in life as being cruel and sad, is truly for the good of those you pity.

李穎哲：

　　我覺得巴赫醫師所寫的這段描述，可以讓大家看到水堇的另外一面，也就是「悲傷」。因為他看到人世間殘酷的事實，可是他們沒有辦法放下身段去服務人們，無法和宇宙的大愛取得連結，愛的能量無法流動；而這邊所列的一些問題其實也就是在描述水堇的正向特質—「勇敢地面對」、「從不抱怨」、「服務同胞的偉大靈魂」、「默默地承受痛苦」、「不退縮」、「不讓悲傷打擾日常生活」，所以說水堇的人可以很勇敢地面對自己的苦難跟悲傷而獨自承受。

魏愛娟：

　　這段文字讀起來，好像有點兒岩水的特性？

李穎哲：

　　水堇的人雖然看到人世間的苦難，雖然他們覺得苦惱與悲傷，但也不會捨棄喜歡孤獨隱居的天性去協助他人，除非他們願意放下身段去協助他人，否則悲傷無法消除。因此我覺得以上的描述不像岩水的狀態，因為水堇特質的人其實已經覺得自己很好了，不會像岩水的人對自己不斷嚴格要求，希望成為大家的榜樣和學習的對象。

我們都能鼓起勇氣，保持一顆無畏的心，因為上天安排我們來到這世上，都是基於一個偉大的目的。

We can all take courage and keep a stout heart, for He Who placed us in this world, did so for a great purpose.

祂希望我們知道，我們是祂的孩子，並且明白自身的神性；希望我們是完美的，希望我們擁有健康和快樂。祂也要我們知道，透過祂的愛能夠記住，唯有忘卻自身的遭遇和不快樂，才能完成所有的事物；祂希望我們每個人的生活是快樂而健康的，並且樂於助人。就如同耶穌基督所說的：「我的負擔是輕鬆的，我的責任是不費力的」。

He wants us to know that we are His children, to know our own Divinity; to be perfect; to have health and to have happiness. He wants us to know that, through His Love, we can accomplish all things, remembering that it is only when we forget this that we suffer and are unhappy. He wants the life of each one of us to be one of joy and health, and loving service, for as Christ told us: "My yoke is easy, My burden is light."

這些花精可以從倫敦順勢療法師處取得，或者按照以下方法自行製作：

Stocks of these remedies can be obtained from the leading London Homoeopathic chemists, though they can be prepared as follows by anyone who cares to make their own.

準備一個薄玻璃碗，將裡頭盛滿乾淨的泉水或溪水，並於水面上鋪滿花朵，然後將之置於陽光下曝曬，等到花朵開始枯萎時，輕輕地把花朵挑掉，把剩下的水倒入玻璃瓶中，最後加入等量的白蘭地來做保鮮。

Take a thin glass bowl, fill with clear water from a stream or spring for preference, and float enough of the blooms of the plant to cover the surface. Allow this to stand in bright sunshine until the flowers begin to wilt. Very gently pick out the blooms, pour the water into bottles and add an equal quantity of brandy as a preservative.

這樣製作出來的原液只需一滴,即可使一瓶 8 盎司的水產生效用,而後就可從該瓶內取出想使用的劑量,直接滴到湯匙上服用。

One drop alone of this is sufficient to make potent an eight ounce bottle of water, from which doses may be taken by the tea-spoonful as required.

劑量服用的頻率應該視病患的情況而定,如果是急性,則可每個小時服用;如果是慢性,則一日服用三到四次即可,直到病患的苦痛得到緩解就可以停止服用了。

The doses should be taken as the patient feels necessary: hourly in acute cases; three or four times a day in chronic cases until relief occurs when they can be dispensed with.

最後,讓我們一起感謝上帝,
感謝他在原野中創造了這些具有療癒能力的花草,這是他的賜福。

And may we ever give thanks to God Who, in His Love for us, placed the herbs in the fields for our healing.